Progress To Some Devastation To Others

Lexington Kentucky's Historically Black Communities

Rico "Kyng Sankofa" Thompson

Sankofa Lexington 2023

2023

ISBN: 9798396640061

First Edition

Table of Contents

Introduction...1

Chapter 1: Warrentown, Maddoxtown, Jimtown & New Zion..7

Chapter 2: Bracktown..32

Chapter 3: Little Georgetown, Fort Springs & Frogtown...40

Chapter 4: Jonestown & Coletown......................54

Chapter 5: Cadentown...68

Chapter 6: Willa Lane...89

Chapter 7: Uttingertown, Columbus, Nihizertown, Centerville, & Pricetown.............102

Chapter 8: Branch Alley & West Water Street..111

Chapter 9: Brucetown...151

Chapter 10: Taylortown, Smithtown & Wolf's Row............175

Chapter 11: Yellmantown & Forest Hill............203

Chapter 12: Peach Orchard & Charlotte Courts Housing Project............235

Chapter 13: Pralltown............257

Chapter 14: Adamstown............275

Chapter 15: Davis Bottom & The South End....289

Chapter 16: Goodloetown............329

Chapter 17: Kinkeadtown............363

Chapter 18: Bluegrass Aspendale Housing Project............380

Introduction

The city of Lexington, was established in the year 1776. Kentucky formed from Fincastle County, Virginia that same year when the county split into three different counties, Washington, Montgomery and Kentucky. Four years later Kentucky County divided itself into three separate counties. These were Fayette, Jefferson, and Lincoln. Out of these three, six more counties formed before statehood. These six were: Nelson in 1784, Bourbon, Mercer and Madison in 1785, Mason and Woodford Counties in 1788. Four years later in 1792, Kentucky gained statehood, with a total of nine counties. Other counties would develop from these nine in later years. Kentucky, the state has a total of 120 counties. Lexington is the county seat of Fayette County and is the focus of this publication.

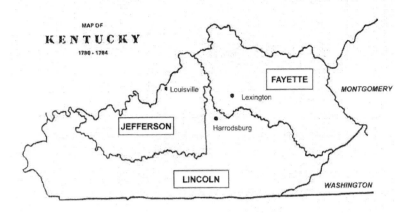

Illustration 1: Map of Kentucky and its original three counties. 1780 - 1784

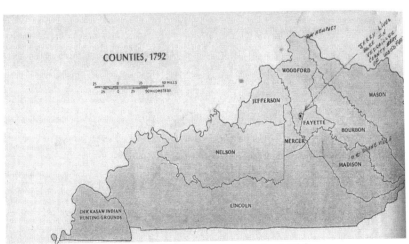

Illustration 2: Kentucky's nine counties in 1792

Introduction

The origin of the name "Kentucky," remains a bit of a mystery. It was believed that the term was of Native American origin and meant "dark and bloody ground," yet that has not been fully substantiated and unlikely the case. Originally, it was spelled "Kentucke." The last "e" was dropped in 1789 and replaced with the "y."

Those original settlers of Kentucky, Lexington, and Fayette County, did not travel here alone. Many of them brought their black enslaved servants along for the journey. These servants, as well as those who were imported during the slave trade, and those who were born upon "slave breeding," farms, are who made up the black populace of Lexington and it's county.

Black people made up about 10 percent of the "Kentucke" population in 1777. As the number of white settlers arrived, so did the number of blacks in the state. There were roughly 4,000 blacks in the state by the year 1784. This number was increased by 16 percent in 1790. There was about 11,830 who were enslaved and 114 that were free men. That number increased to 41,084 just ten years later. This number rapidly increased as the decades went on. In 1830, there was about 165,213 enslaved blacks and 4,917 freed blacks in the state. Five years prior to the ending of slavery, in 1860, the black population was at 236,167. This was about 20 percent of the population.[1]

The growing city of Lexington saw a rapid growth of blacks residing in the city as well. In 1800, there were about 4,313 blacks living in Lexington. Eighty eight of those were free. In 1850, there were about 11,475 black people in the city. The population had increased by 166 percent in fifty years. This number includes those en-

---

1. Lucas, Marion Brunson (2003). "Prologue". *A History of Blacks in Kentucky: From Slavery to Segregation, 1760-1891*. University Press of Kentucky. pp. xi–xxii

slaved, those freed, and the "mulatto" populations. In 1860, the county population black and white was about 12,585. This excludes those held in bondage. The number of enslaved was about 10,148.[2] This means that in 1860, nearly half the population was black, enslaved and freed.

Before the enslavement period ended, the enslaved populations often lived in cabins and shacks on the property of the slave owner. The freed ones lived throughout the city amongst the whites. Five years later, that enslaved population became a freed population and with that, the need for housing increased and each of the communities discussed in this book were established.

This book came about because I've searched for a text like this for quite a while and came up short. I began learning of various black communities in my own city that I had never heard of before. As I searched through books written about Lexington, I would only get small blurbs and short mentions, giving me clues to their existence but ultimately, I developed a desire to learn more. When I read the words of Toni Morrison "if a book you want to read doesn't exist, then you must write it," I decided that's exactly what I must do.

I chose to write this book starting first with the rural communities in Fayette County, followed by the ones within the city limits. The book begins with the rural north and moving counterclockwise, west, south, then east. This was done intentionally so that the last chapter, would be where it is. The city communities flow the same way, North, West, South, and East.

---

2. "Fayette County (KY) Enslaved, Free Blacks, and Free Mulattoes, 1850-1870," Notable Kentucky African Americans Database, accessed May 29, 2023, https://nkaa.uky.edu/nkaa/items/show/2333.

Introduction

One last thing, my first publication, Sankofa Lexington, written in 2020, is being reproduced within this text. It was only 86 pages and when I created that book, I honestly didn't know much about book writing and it contained numerous errors. It consisted of ten short chapters of black men and women from Lexington, who I felt deserved notoriety. Those individuals lived in these communities discussed in this book and I thought this is a great way to introduce new readers to that old book, while giving me an opportunity to expand the information and clean up the errors. Only two chapters, I could not find placement for anywhere in this book. Those were the chapters about Julia Britton Hooks and Shelby Davidson. The other eight are included in the chapters in which they apply. Those eight are Dr. Mary Britton, R.C.O. Benjamin, Isaac Scott Hathaway, Charlotte Dupuy, Luther Porter Jackson, Julia Amanda Perry, Aunt Charlotte, and the Reverend Frederick Braxton.

May the reader enjoy the information contained within and gain something from these pages. Thank you for reading. Let's begin.

Rural Communities North

"It is a call for black people in this country to unite, to recognize their heritage, to build a sense of community. It is a call for black people to define their own goals, to lead their own organizations."

- Stokely Carmichael

Chapter 1 – Warrentown, Maddoxtown, Jimtown, & New Zion

In this chapter, we will discuss three communities that existed in North Fayette County, outside the city of Lexington, and one just outside Fayette County. Three of them remain rural, while one is now a part of the city. These four communities are Warrentown, Maddoxtown, Jimtown and New Zion. We will begin with Warrentown, now apart of Lexington and work our way North.

Warrentown

Warrentown, got its name from the original white landowner, William Warren.[1] Another source suggests it

---

1. Slickaway: Warrentown. (1950, January 15). *Sunday Herald-Leader*, p.

was named after Ship Warren, which would be his son, F. Shipman Warren. At any rate, the community was established around 1890 on the Maysville Pike, now Old Paris Pike, near present day Constitution Park.

It was a small working class black settlement. Most of the men worked on horse farms and the women held the typical occupations as domestics and cooks.

There was a Methodist Church that dates back to around 1889. Information is scarce about its founding. After the 1940's, you don't see many mentions of the church in the newspapers, so it's likely that they consolidated into another Methodist Church, most notably at that time, Asbury.

Warrentown also had a schoolhouse. It was established in the early 1890's under the guidance of W.H. Johnson, who was principal for about ten years.[2] Mrs. E. Birdie Taylor would be it's next teacher for twelve years before she moved on to become supervisor of the Kentucky Colored Rural Schools, and having sixty-four counties under her charge.[3] This position she held until her death in 1933. The school would close its doors for good in 1936 after a continued decline in enrollment and the property was sold to Raleigh Milton, a black man, for $1800.[4]

139.

2. Colored Teachers, Close Successful Institute. (1901, September 22). *Lexington Leader*, p. 10.

3. Colored Notes. (1925, January 18). *The Lexington Herald*, p. 17.

4. School Property on Paris Pike Sold. (1942, October 23). *The Lexington Herald*, p. 21.

One final thing of note before we move on to the next section is that before the location for the Green-wood(Cove Haven) Cemetery was chosen on Whitney Avenue, the organization originally had plans to establish the cemetery in the vicinity of Warrentown. They were looking to acquire about 49 acres for this purpose. The residents however protested and the Whitney Ave. location was chosen.[5] More on this cemetery and organization in a later chapter.

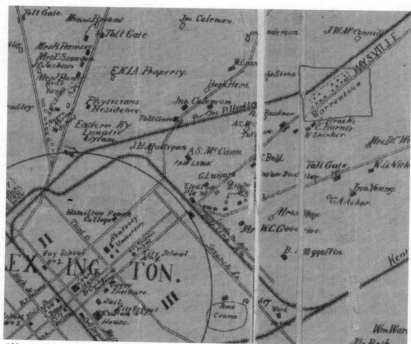

Illustration 1: 1891 Map of Fayette County, Kentucky, the rectangle shows the location of Warrentown.

---

5. Opposition: Likely to Confront Establishing of Proposed Colored Cemetery near Warrentown. (1906, November 20). *Lexington Leader*, p. 1.

Maddoxtown

Maddoxtown's origin date is estimated to be in the 1860's when Samuel Maddox subdivided his land and sold lots to African Americans. Located just off of Huffman Mill Pike, five miles north of Lexington, in Fayette County, this rural settlement was home to approximately 100 people by the early 1900's.

The community established the First Baptist Church of Maddoxtown in 1867 according to some sources. However, in a 1916 newspaper article, the church was celebrating their forty-second anniversary that year, placing the date in 1874. The church's website suggests that it's early history is mostly oral. Either no records were kept or they were destroyed at some point. It further states that they don't have much information about the first church that was built, it's size, or exact location.[6] Some rumors in Lexington in the early 1900's state that an eccentric negro preacher, known all over Lexington, by the name of Rev. Peter Vinegar, had a church in Maddoxtown.[7] Whether, its the first baptist church or some other is unknown. Nothing has been found to substantiate that.

It is stated that Peter Vinegar was the preacher of Main Street Baptist Church for nearly twenty years but members of the congregation split with the pastor due to his love of intoxicating whisky. He kept a flask in his

---

6. *Our History.* Maddoxtown Baptist Church. (n.d.). Retrieved January 27, 2023, from https://www.fbcm-lex.org/our-history

7. Coffin, T. P., & Cohen, H. (1974). A Dozen Legendary Figures: The Reverend Peter Vinegar. In *Folklore: From the Working Folk of America* (p. 378). essay, Anchor Books.

pocket and would drink during sermons without a care as to who saw or said something.[8] When one views the Main Street Baptist Church website, Peter Vinegar's name is not among the church pastors. Peter passed in 1905 and the list of pastors up until that time are: Pastor Frederick Braxton - 1st Pastor; 1854 to 1876 ; Pastor William Gray - 2nd Pastor; 1877 to 1883 ; Pastor Eugene Evans - 3rd Pastor; 1883 to 1884 ; Pastor George M. Moore - 4th Pastor; 1884 to 1896; Pastor Robert Mitchell - 5th Pastor; 1896 - 1898; Pastor E. A. Edwards - 6th Pastor; 1898 - 1901 ; Pastor Charles Douglas - 7th Pastor; 1901 - 1905 ; Pastor R. T. Frye - 8th Pastor; 1905 – 1909.[9]

Either he never preached at the church as was written, or due to the embarrassment that may have caused and the split, his name was left out of the records. Another source suggests that he was run away from the Maddoxtown Church for the same exact reason.[10] It's possible that the two churches were mixed up when that was reported. Maybe he was a member of Main Street for many years but not the preacher? Maybe he left and organized his own church in Maddoxtown? Or, if he didn't establish the church, he joined and soon became Pastor? I am merely speculating as the sources conflict. We do know that Rev. Braxton started the Main Street Baptist Church in 1854. It is said that Peter Vinegar came

8. Peter Vinegar: Enters The Realm Where De Streets Are Gold and De Lan' Is Filld Wid Milk and Honey. (1905, July 20). *Lexington Leader*, p. 3.

9. *Our History*. Main Street Baptist Church. (n.d.). Retrieved January 27, 2023, from https://www.mainstreetbaptistchurchlexky.org/about-us/our-history

10. Coffin, T. P., & Cohen, H. (1974). A Dozen Legendary Figures: The Reverend Peter Vinegar. In *Folklore: From the Working Folk of America* (p. 378). essay, Anchor Books.

to Lexington around the time of the civil war and affiliated himself with the black baptists. Main Street's own website suggests that the Maddoxtown Church branched off from the Main Street Church.

> "Several churches sprouted from the roots of Main Street Baptist Church: Lansomboro Baptist Church (now known as Greater Liberty Baptist Church), Mount Gilead Baptist Church, Houston Baptist Church, Bracktown Baptist Church, Maddoxtown Baptist Church, Fort Springs Baptist Church and Shiloh Baptist Church."[11]

We have to remember that the Maddoxtown Baptist church website states that they don't have the early church records, only oral history from it's oldest members, none of which I'm sure were alive at the time of the Rev. Peter Vinegar. Some other things of note that can connect Rev. Vinegar to Maddoxtown Church is an 1895 article that states:

> "Vinegar will hold a big meeting in Maddoxtown next week. Preaching every night."[12]

So with that, we can definitively connect Vinegar to Maddoxtown. Whether my other speculations are true or not, one can not say with certainty. And then there is

---

11. *Our History*. Main Street Baptist Church. (n.d.). Retrieved January 27, 2023, from https://www.mainstreetbaptistchurchlexky.org/about-us/our-history

12. First Sunday in July: Peter Vinegar Will Deliver Three Discourses in Gibson Woods. (1895, June 22). *The Leader*, p. 6.

this:

> "Rev. Mr. Campbell will dedicate the
> Maddoxtown Baptist Church today."[13]

This quote comes from an 1886 newspaper article and what makes it interesting is Peter Vinegar's real name is Alexander Campbell Vinegar. So, is Rev. Campbell the same person? I think we can make a strong argument that he is.

A few more things before we move forward, informants reported that Peter Vinegar would get drunk and start fights that sometimes involved the whole congregation. Please keep in mind that this is speculative at best but it's of note and you'll see why in just a moment. Here is what was written in one source:

> "According to this gentleman, Vinegar would get so drunk that he would start big fights; "there were at least forty fights a week." Pete is reported to have hit people on the head with his Bible, and to have "carried on" with the Elders' wives; the police would have to break up every gathering because Vinegar, being so drunk, would invariably start a brawl, involving the whole congregation. The informant asserted that "the fightin'est preacher that ever lived was ole Pete Vinegar!""[14]

Combine what was quoted with several reports of fighting, even shooting at the Maddoxtown church in

---

13. Congregational Notes. (1886, June 27). *The Courier Journal*, p. 11.

14. Coffin, T. P., & Cohen, H. (1974). A Dozen Legendary Figures: The Reverend Peter Vinegar. In *Folklore: From the Working Folk of America* (p. 379). essay, Anchor Books.

the 1890's, and it makes one wonder even further about the words above. Peter Vinegar's name was not mentioned in any of these articles but keep in mind, we know he was preaching in Maddoxtown in 1895 and the source stated the fights would involve many members of the church.

> "Tom Brown, Lucy Allen, and James Holland, all colored, were fined $50 and twenty days in jail each this morning by Judge G.W. Muir, for disturbing religious worship at a church in Maddoxtown suburb."[15]

> "Hazel Johnson and Will Davis are colored citizens of Maddoxtown, this county, and are poor marksmen. They had a church row, shot at each other, and both missed their mark"[16]

When one reads these things, and then reads the words someone said about Peter Vinegar being a fighting preacher, one can reason that this is his congregation even though he was not named. But one last time, this is all speculative. Also, this is in no way shape or form an attempt to slander the church and the beloved people of this community who value their service there, just simply finding interesting things from the past that went on in our communities, and reporting on them, the good, the bad, and the ugly.

Speaking of the ugly, one event that occurred in Maddoxtown made the headlines all across the country

---

15. Disturbing Church. (1888, May 7). *The Kentucky Leader*, p. 4.

16. City and Vicinity: Minor Happenings of the Bluegrass Metropolis. (1896, August 7). *The Daily Leader*, p. 5.

in 1884 and one man lost his life.

Klu Kluxing

On August 30, 1884, eight to ten white men raided the Maddoxtown section and opened fire randomly into several homes. After the shooting, the men retreated into a cornfield, only to return a short while later and open fire again. They retreated once more, and kept this up for several hours. It is reported that over 100 hundred bullets were fired and one man was hit and was mortally wounded.

About two in the morning, Henry Nichols was standing in his yard, when the unknown men returned, opened fire again, instantly killing Nichols.

Hours later, at about 4 A.M., three black men saw a few white men leaving the same cornfield in which the gang had fled to. These men, George Green, Elijah Cunningham, and Andrew Carr, recognized one of the white men. His name was Marcus McClain. The other two, they reportedly did not know.

The men stated that they did not know what prompted the attack but believed the motives were political because, this has happened a couple of other times in their community since the last election. The community was almost exclusively democrat.[17]

McClain was arrested and charged for the murder.

---

17. Cowardly Business: A Kentucky Town Attacked in the Night, One of its Inhabitants Mortally Wounded. (1884, September 1). *The Cincinnati Enquirer*, p. 1.

Maddoxtown School

Maddoxtown School dates back to around the communities inception. In the beginning, school was held in the church, but in the late 1800's, a small schoolhouse was erected and this served the community until the 1910's. Then a new schoolhouse was built. This is where the communities children were taught until the 1940's. There were not many children remaining in the town by that time, so the school was abandoned and the children left were bussed to Douglas High School in Lexington. The schoolhouse was sold in 1949 and converted into a home.

Illustration 2: The original Maddoxtown School

Will Harbut

We will conclude this section with a brief mention of the most known of all Maddoxtown residents, horse groomsman, Will Harbut. Harbut was the groom of the most famous race horse Man O' War and was said to be somewhat of a horse whisperer. People were in awe of his ability to communicate with the horse in English and the horse seemingly understanding his words. For more on Mr. Harbut, I recommend a book called Man O' War and Will Harbut by Ann S, Reilly. It tells the story of Harbut and Man O' War using his voice as if he is narrating the book.

Illustration 3: Will Harbut is buried in the Maddoxtown Cemetery that sits behind the church. I snapped this photo in 2017 on a visit to Maddoxtown.

Jimtown

The northernmost black settlement in Fayette County, would be Jimtown. Located off the Greenwich Pike, this community takes it's name from James Sidener, who in 1888, sold land to the newly freed people of African descent.

This community of approximately one hundred people had a school in its early days and two churches. One, the baptist church which organized the same year the community was founded, 1888, and the Methodist church. The Methodists would have their own church building built on land they acquired in 1908.[18] Prior to that, the two congregations shared the same church building and swapped Sundays for service.[19] Some families even belonged to both congregations.

There was about twenty-five homes in Jimtown by the 1960's and the community was without water up until 1968.[20] They would haul their water supply in from the city. At one time, a well was dug but the water became salty so it was abandoned and the residents returned to hauling in their water.

Jimtown did have one store but due to the law requiring stores that sell meat to have running water, they were forced to close.

---

18. Jimtown, To Have Colored Methodist Church in Which Lot Has Been Purchased. (1908, June 28). *Lexington Leader*, p. 15.

19. Unusual Customs Part of Settlements Rich Past. (1985, August 11). *Lexington Herald-Leader*, p. 1.

20. Cooper, B. (1968, October 24). Tiny Community Founded A Century Ago Gets Water. *The Park City Daily News*, p. 9.

New Zion

New Zion is a small rural community, just outside of the Fayette County line, in neighboring Scott County. Although this book is particularly about the black communities of Fayette County, Kentucky, due to it's proximity to Fayette and my ancestral connection, I could not exclude it from these pages.

Two formerly enslaved men are the founders of this rural community, Calvin Hamilton and Primus Keene. It was originally called Briar Hill, but the name was changed to New Zion sometime later.[21] Hamilton bought sixteen acres for $1345.68 and Keene purchased an additional seven acres for $827.[22]

Primus Keene married his wife Charlotte, August 3, 1887 in Scott County, Ky, however, the couple were living together in the 1870 Census. It's possible they were married during slavery, but slave weddings weren't official or documented. It was just a jump over the broom and they were declared married. With that said, it's likely they decided to make it official on that date in 1887. Three different birth years were listed for Keene on the 1870, 1880, and 1900 census. The 1870 census states he was born in 1833, while 1880 and 1900 lists his birth year about 1829 and 1810, respectively. The 1900 census also shows that he was widowed at that time, indicating

21. Andrew Patrick, "New Zion," *ExploreKYHistory*, accessed January 28, 2023, https://explorekyhistory.ky.gov/items/show/816.

22. Peryam, J. (2020, March 13). *New Zion Village celebrates 150 years with music, food, worship*. Georgetown News Graphic. Retrieved January 28, 2023, from https://www.news-graphic.com/news/new-zion-village-celebrates-150-years-with-music-food-worship/article_5927b0a8-aa37-11e8-a069-9b9e5a0a20fb.html

Charlotte had passed sometime prior. Keene himself passed away in 1908, and his property was left to his children Milford Keene and Jennie Keene.

Calvin Hamilton's 1870 census record suggests that his birth was around 1822 and his first wife's name was Harriet. He later remarried Margaret Speakes in 1887. He passed away in 1907.

My New Zion Ancestry

My father's paternal Grandmother lived in the New Zion community and her grandfather, Phil Jewett, was in an organization with the two founding fathers mentioned previously. Before we get to that organization and a little more about the community, please allow me to share what I've discovered about my own New Zion family.

My 3rd Great Grandfather Philip Jewett, sometimes spelled Juett, lived to be 98 years old. He was born in slavery in Montgomery County, Kentucky to Henry Jewett and Sarah Henderson around 1856. He came to Scott County, Kentucky in the 1870's and owned a farm just off of Crumbaugh Rd. That road is not in New Zion, but not that far away.

With his wife Nannie Jewett(Walker), who hails from Boyle County, they had several children: Robert, Mary, Fannie, Onnie, Philip Jr., Clarence, Sarah and Walter. Nannie, passed away in 1933.

Grandfather, who was known as "Uncle Phil," passed away tragically when his bed caught fire from a coal stove. He suffered third degree burns and died in the hospital on December 4, 1954, at the age of 98.

Burns Are Fatal To Former Slave

GEORGETOWN, Ky., Dec. 4— (Special) — Phillip (Uncle Phil) Juett, 96, was born a slave in Montgomery County and had lived in Scott County for about 65 years, died this morning of burns suffered Thursday night at his home on the Crumbaugh Pike when his bed was ignited by a coal stove.

He was taken to the John Graves Ford Memorial Hospital here suffering from third degree burns of his legs. He died in the hospital today.

Survivors include two sons, Onnie and Clarence Juett, both of Scott County; two daughters, Mrs. Sarah Cayson, Scott County, and Mrs. Mary Grace, Chicago, Ill.; 13 grandchildren and eight great-grandchildren.

Funeral services will be conducted at 2 p.m. Monday at the New Zion M. E. Church by the Rev. Robert Payne. Burial will be in the New Zion Cemetery. The body will be removed from the Gillespie Brothers Funeral Home here to the home of his son, Clarence Juett, on the Lexington-Newton Pike Sunday afternoon.

Illustration 4: Lexington Herald-Leader (05 Dec 1954,)

Phillip and Nannie Jewett's son, Onnie Jewett, is my 2nd Great Grandfather. Onnie was born February 9, 1884 in Scott County. He owned a farm in New Zion and according to newspaper accounts, there was a Health Camp for Colored Children that was annually held on the farm. This camp was presided over by educator Lucy Harth Smith and began in 1944.

> "Under-Privileged negro children of Lexington and Fayette County are now able to enjoy facilities of health camp recently established on the Onnie Jewett farm on the Newtown Pike through the efforts of the Blue Grass Association of Colored Women."[23]

Onnie was married to Scott County native Lucille Smith and the offspring that came forth from that union included my Great Grandmother Mary Lillian Jewett, who was born in 1907, as well as Lee Chester, David, James, Ruby, Paul, Laine, Alvin and Roger.

Onnie passed away on April 12, 1973 at the age of 89. On the obituary, his wife is listed as Margaret Jewett. Lucille passed away a few years prior in 1967. Whether they split and he remarried while she was alive or if it occurred after death, I can not say at this time. Both are buried in the New Zion Cemetery.

Mary Lillian Jewett met and married James W. Hayes. You will read more about him in the Pralltown chapter. They lived in New Zion until her untimely death at the young age of 32 in 1939. From that union, my dad's father James Hayes Jr., was born in 1929.

---

23. New Health Camp for Fayette Colored Children Established. (1944, July 30). *The Lexington Herald*, p. 9.

Sometime in the year 2017, I took a visit to New Zion. After discovering who my family was, I wanted to set eyes on the place myself. Upon arrival, I walked up to the cemetery near the church and was looking at the headstones, trying to place where my ancestors were. I was able to locate a few of them. Nearby, an elderly gentleman was on a riding mower tending to a yard. He got off and approached and inquired if he could assist me. I told him what I was doing and he asked who my ancestors were. I mentioned the name Onnie Jewett and he told me that he knew him, then pointed down the street just a little bit and informed me that used to be his farm. Then he asked had I seen any pictures of them, to which I replied no. He unlocked the church and lead me inside to a room that had pictures of New Zion residents covering the walls. I was able to spot a few and get my first glimpses of this unknown family of mine.

Illustration 5: Mary Lillian Hayes(Jewett)

Illustration 6: Another pic of Mary Lillian. You can see that i took this photo with my phone, it was on the wall inside the church.

Illustration 7: Onnie Jewett

Illustration 8: Lucille Jewett (Smith)

Church

There was one church in the New Zion community. It was a Methodist congregation by the name of New Zion United Methodist Church. The church's beginnings are said to be in the year 1874. Members of the community grew tired of traveling to Lexington for service so they were able to form their own church.[24]

The current structure was built in 1924. However, at this time, it was just the walls and roof completed, which was sufficient enough to hold service, but it was not complete. Funding was lacking for the entire project. Several years passed before the church was officially finished.[25]

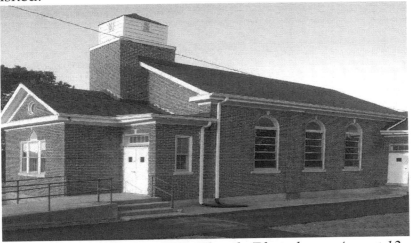

Illustration 9: New Zion M.E. Church (Photo by me August 12, 2017)

---

24. Community is States Oldest Black Settlement. (1997, February 28). *Lexington Herald-Leader*, p. 23.

25. New Zion Church Is Completed After 30 Years; Organ Installed. (1954, July 1). *The Lexington Herald*, p. 1.

New Zion Cemetery

Just behind the Church property lies the New Zion Cemetery, where nearly all who called it home and since passed on are buried. My family mentioned on previous pages are buried here, as well as the village founders Calvin Hamilton and Primus Keene.

Another individual buried in this cemetery is a man who at the time of his death in 1913, was one of Lexington's wealthiest black men, Charles Garner. He was born in Lexington on February 10, 1865 to Simon Garner and Charity Calvin. It was written that he attended school in his youth, just long enough to be able to write his name and then he went to work on a local farm. His salary was $3 per week.[26] He saved enough money to begin purchasing and trading livestock. This, horse breeding, along with farming, is how he amassed his wealth.

At the time of death, he had considerable property that included a two story brick home at 448 North Upper Street, a farm near New Zion on Newtown Pike that consisted of 153.2 acres, and another 46.4 acre farm on Mt. Horeb Pike in north Fayette County.[27] His estate was estimated to be worth $55,000 in 1913. Today, that estate would be worth $1,648,872.22. He was buried in the New Zion Cemetery in September 1913.

---

26. Nice Fortune, Amounting To Over $47,000 Left By Charles M. Garner, Colored, Who Made His Own Way To Success, Despite Discouragement. (1914, May 24). *Lexington Leader*, p. 6.

27. Public Sale of Farm Lands & City Residence: Monday, February 9, 1914. (1914, February 8). *The Lexington Herald*, p. 22.

Colored Farmers and Business Men's League

In 1904, several members of the community came together and established the Colored Farmers and Business Men's League, which held annual meetings to discuss everything from farming, business, banking, to all other community needs. Members of this organization included my 3rd Great Grandfather, Phil Jewett, New Zion founders Primus Keene and Calvin Hamilton, and Charles Garner, who was one of the three Vice presidents of the organization. Basil Black and Rev. J.H. Ross were the other two, while the President was Dr. L.M. Hagood.

Collectively, the members of this organization owned 800 acres of property. At each annual congress, various questions were posed such as farming questions like: How to raise onions? Potatoes? How to fatten hogs? How to use pasture land? And how to care for farming instruments? The answer to the latter was a presentation by my ancestor Phil Jewett. Each question and answer was presented by a different member of the group.

Other questions were: Can we have a bank? How to get rid of mortgages, was presented by Calvin Hamilton. Can we have a post office? Should we employ our own doctors and lawyers? And many many more.[28]

Now let's reflect for a moment. The majority of these black men were once enslaved. These are the types of questions and solutions they would get together to discuss among themselves for the advancement of our race.

---

28. Colored Farmers and Business Men's League Holds a Congress at New Zion. (1904, November 23). *Lexington Leader*, p. 5.

Not even 50 years removed from being in bondage. This within itself is amazing and should inspire those of us today. We really have no excuse. But let's not get sidetracked because that's a discussion for another book.

> **Grocery Business.**
> How get and manage?
> Copartnership and how manage?
> Credit System, how manage?
> Perishable articles, how save?
> **Dry Goods.**
> Ought we to have a store, how get it?
> The amount we spend for dry goods?
> Where shall we buy?
> **Millinery and Dress Making.**
> What We Spend for Hats?—Mrs. Julia Adams.
> Can We Make Our Own?—Mrs. Mollie Davis.
> Can We eGt a Teacher?—Mrs. Millie Smith.
> **Miscellaneous.**
> Can we have Water Works?
> Can we have a Post Office?
> Can we secure Telephone Service?
> Ought we employ our own Doctors?
> Lawyers too?
> The morals of our people and how we can improve them?

Illustration 10: Clipping of a portion of the article from the inaugural conference. These were a few of the topics discussed during that conference. (Lexington Herald Leader, 23 November 1904)

The purpose of the league, in a nutshell was, WE WISH TO HELP EACH OTHER:

> "Our object is to show the progress made by the race, the results of their own handicraft and what they have accomplished; to investigate failures and find the causes and then suggest remedy; to learning methods of farming and attending business matters and, if possible suggest better plans. We desire exhibits of all productions or purchases by our people – not that we do not welcome others than our own people – but to exhibit stock and productions in our name when owned by others will neither help us nor be a credit to ourselves. We wish to help each other."[29]

This congress was also attended by prominent black businessmen from Lexington such as W.H. Ballard, Dr. J.E. Hunter, Dr. T.T. Wendell, and Dr. P.D. Robinson, among others.

To bring this chapter to a close, the New Zion community still exists today. Most of the businesses such as the few grocery stores, garage and others no longer exist. Many of the homes were also razed but some still exist and are lived in by the descendants of the community's founders. New Zion also had a Rosenwald School that served the community for several decades before closing and the children attended the newly integrated Scott County Schools.

---

29. Industrial Conference of Best Element of Colored People of Fayette and Scott Counties: Annual Two Days Meeting At New Zion Church An Event More Than Usual Interest and Importance To The Negro Race. (1908, November 15). *Lexington Leader*, p. 2.

Rural Communities West

"The time has come for the Negro to forget and cast behind him his hero worship and adoration of other races, and to start out immediately, to create and emulate heroes of his own."

- Marcus Mosiah Garvey

Chapter 2 – Bracktown

Historically, black communities have always took on the name of the white landowner who platted the land and sold the lots. Bracktown is one of a few named after a black landowner. Initially, that was the case as well for the community known as Bracktown, Northwest of Lexington. At inception, the community was actually named Stonetown.

Robert Stone, the original land owner, sold lots to African Americans for $100 each and named it after himself. The northern part of the community was Stonetown. Frederick Braxton, founder of the Independent Baptist Church, began buying land in the area in 1867 and owned a good portion of the southern part. The residents began calling the entire community Bracktown, in honor of Braxton around 1887.

The community had a couple of small businesses, such as a blacksmith shop and a grocery store. Also a one room schoolhouse where black children were instructed up until the eight grade.

Bracktown First Baptist Church organized around 1880. A new church house would be built in 1931 and this building remains today. However, the congregation had a new church built in another part of the community in 2006. Victory Apostolic Church now holds services in the previous building.

Illustration 1: Teacher and students outside Bracktown Colored School (1901)

Illustration 2: Students, community members and teachers, outside the Bracktown School (Unknown date, believed to be before 1921)

Illustration 3: Students and teachers, Bracktown School (Before 1921)

Illustration 4: Music Students outside the Bracktown School (before 1921)

Frederick Braxton

It would be a disservice to the community to not include the history of it's founder. This history was previously written in my first booklet but we will reproduce it within this text, making the necessary omissions to avoid redundancy and fixing a few grammatical errors. It was written as follows:

African people have always been the most spiritual people upon this planet. This was before we were introduced to the Abrahamic faiths and even today, thousands of years after being introduced to them. In the days of American slavery, the role of the church was an intricate part of everyday life, it was the very center. It served oftentimes as the community center, the place to hold secret meetings, to plan rebellions, escapes, etc., so much more than just the place of worship. Many of the black schools of the day, were started by the churches.

The oldest black church in Kentucky and the third oldest in America was founded in Lexington, Kentucky by Peter Durrett, a former slave. It was established in 1790.

In 1815, Durrett and his congregation, which consisted of free blacks and slaves, were able to purchase the church's first property along High Street that used to be a cotton factory and deeded to First African Baptist Church trustees Rolla Blue, Jas. Polluck, Solomon Walker, and William Gist. This property was traded April 24, 1820, for a brick house on Limestone and Maxwell Street. By the time Durrett passed away in 1923, the membership of the congregation was upwards of 300. He was then succeeded by London Ferrill, a former slave who came to Lexington from the state of Virginia.

When a cholera epidemic struck Lexington, Ferrill became a hero, as he remained in the city preaching to and praying for the victims of the epidemic while many people were fleeing. About 500 people fell victim to Cholera, one of them being Ferrill's wife.

By 1834, the church bought the property on the corner of Deweese and Short Street. At that time Deweese St. was called Back Street. Ferrill preached here until his death in 1854. He is buried in the Old Episcopal Burial Ground on the corner of Third St. and Elm Tree Lane, where it is believed that he is the only black person ever to be buried there. During his tenure as Pastor, the congregation grew from around 300 to about 1820 members, making it the largest church in the state.

black or white. After his death, Frederick Braxton took over the church as it's pastor.

Rev. Braxton was born in slavery to parents Mark and Violet Braxton. He was a slave belonging to former vice president and Kentuckian John Breckenridge. A blacksmith by trade, he became a Reverend while still in bondage, but later gained his freedom.

Illustration 5: First African Baptist Church in 1926

Reverend Braxton was pastor of First African Baptist for about 8 years. The congregation grew to have over 2000 members by 1861 under Braxton's direction.

The following year, 1862, tensions arose among church members over political views, so Braxton with 500 members left the church and organized the Independent Baptist church. The name was changed to Main Street Baptist later on under the second pastor. It was established on land purchased from Mary Todd Lincoln's family, Mary Todd Lincoln being the wife of Abraham Lincoln. According to the Main Street Baptist Church website:

> "John DeGarris purchased the property in 1853 from the heirs of Eliza Todd, Mary Todd Lincoln's mother. According to the 1863 deed, John DeGarris conveyed the church property to Pastor Braxton as the trustee of the church for $3000."[1]

An article in the Lexington Herald Leader Newspaper dated August 12, 2012, written by Merlene Davis, stated about the Reverend Braxton that:

> "He ruled the church with an iron rod. Often excommunicated members a hundred or two at a time, but yet so powerful was his appeals that he soon supplied their number, and the church continued very strong up to the time of his death."[2]

The Reverend passed away in 1876 and was buried at the African Cemetery Number 2 on Seventh

1. *Our History*. Main Street Baptist Church. (n.d.). Retrieved September 27, 2022, from https://www.mainstreetbaptistchurchlexky.org/about-us/our-history

2. Davis, Merlene. "Main Street Baptist Church Celebrates 150 Years by Honoring Founding Pastor." *Kentucky*, Lexington Herald Leader, 22 Aug. 2012, https://www.kentucky.com/news/local/community/article44373360.html.

Street.

Several area churches who have congregations around today sprang up from the roots of Main Street Baptist and by default, the Reverend Braxton. These churches include: Shiloh Baptist, Greater Liberty Baptist, Mount Gilead Baptist, Bracktown Baptist Church and Maddoxtown Baptist.

Illustration 6: Rev. Frederick Braxton.

Chapter 3 – Little George-town, Fort Spring, & Frog-town

Among the many black communities in Fayette County, Kentucky, a number of them were outside of the city of Lexington, often adjacent to farms that the community members may have worked upon or even owned. Such is the case with the three little communities we will be discussing in this chapter. Each are in the same vicinity but we shall begin with Little Georgetown.

Little Georgetown

Little Georgetown sprang up on the South side of Parkers Mill Road, just off Versailles Road sometime in the late 1800's, exact date being unknown. There is much debate on precisely where the name came from. Many suggest that it was named after white landowner George Waltz, who gave 200 acres of land to his former slaves.

They may have lived on the property prior to the civil war and emancipation. The "Little" was added to the name Georgetown because north of Fayette County, in Scott County, the town of Georgetown, Ky, already existed.

Another story goes that the community was actually named after a formerly enslaved black man by the name of George Washington. He owned much of the land and sold lots to other African Americans. This is the story that the locals tell.[1]

One more narrative is told and that one is that two former slaves of the Parker family, in which Parkers Mill, is named after, founded the community. Their names are Ned and Caroline Lewis. The fact that Washington is shown as a landowner in the area on an 1877 map suggests that the narrative of it being named for him is likely. However, as you have read in this book, it's not uncommon for the communities to be named after the original landowner, often the white slave owner who sought to gain a profit after emancipation.

Whatever the case, at some point there was up to 90 people who called Little Georgetown home. The community had a cemetery, a church, a school and a general store. It's unfortunate but with most of the communities we discuss in this book, this rural community was impoverished. A 1971 Lexington Herald Leader article stated that about 73% of the buildings in the area were in substandard conditions.[2]

---

1. Smith, G. L., McDaniel, K. C., Hardin, J. A., & Powell, S. (2015). Little Georgetown, African American Community in Fayette County, Ky. In *The Kentucky African American Encyclopedia* (p. 331). essay, University Press of Kentucky.

2. Living Next to the Airport. (1971, July 22). *Lexington Herald Leader*

Although there was dissatisfaction with living conditions, it was home and most had no desire to leave the community that they were born and raised in. Again, it was home. When the Bluegrass Airport was built in the vicinity in the 1940's, noise from the airplanes and pollution became a problem and major nuisance. Not only that, but as the years went on, the Bluegrass Airport continued to expand, decreasing the size of the community and making life increasingly difficult for the residents of the community. A new runaway was built in the 1960's and "approach lights" were built directly in their backyard in the 1970's. By the 1980's, everyone was pretty much forced out with little compensation, if any at all. The general store was demolished in 1981.

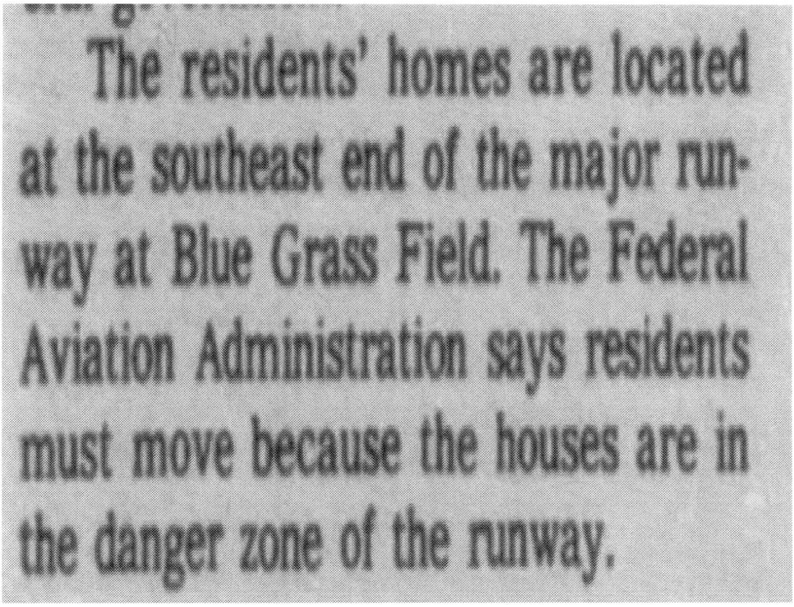

The residents' homes are located at the southeast end of the major runway at Blue Grass Field. The Federal Aviation Administration says residents must move because the houses are in the danger zone of the runway.

Illustration 1: A portion of an article in the local paper, explaining that the residents MUST move (Lexington, Herald Leader 18, Sept., 1979)

The airport is always wanting something for nothing when poor people are concerned. Little Georgetown is a perfect example of their dealings.

When dealing with the wealthy landowners they will spend just about any amount in the name of progress and what it is worth to airport needs and development.

A concrete example of their dealings with the poor was when land was obtained for the runway approach light towers. Little Georgetown people were paid next to nothing for their properties as compared with the wealthy landowners; keeping in mind that all of this land served the same purpose.

If any organization, be it federal, state, county or private, wants a person's land for some multimillion-dollar operation, they should meet the landowner's demand of price or relocation.

As to compensating for noise level, the airport should start sending retroactive payments to the people of Little Georgetown. If Little Georgetown had been anything other than a black community millions of dollars for rights of way and relocations would have been spent when the first expansion was deemed necessary.

WILLIAM S. SLEET
Lexington

Illustration 2: This article in the newspaper from a resident speaks for itself. (Lexington Herald Leader 24 Jan., 1979)

Today, only the church remains, Bethany Baptist

Church, located on Parker's Mill Road and possibly another structure or two but the community is gone. The church was organized in 1896. The original building burned down in 1992 but was rebuilt in 1993.

Briefly mentioned above was the tiny schoolhouse that the community had, but belonged to the Fayette County Public School system. There is not much available information about the schoolhouse but it held roughly 30 students. In those days, it was likely that the children's grades and age ranges varied as with majority of the little small schoolhouses.

Illustration 3: Little Georgetown Schoolhouse unknown date.

Illustration 4: Inside the Little Georgetown Schoolhouse, unknown date

Fort Spring

Fort Spring is another one of those communities where the name origin is debated and widely speculated about. Before we delve into the name, let's note that this community was just north of Little Georgetown, off of what today is Versailles Road.

Legend has it that in 1826, Thomas Shreshly gave some land to three of his former slaves just off of what was then Woodford Road and they created a community called "Reform." One source mentions that one of these formerly enslaved men was named Henry Clark. The others have been lost to history unfortunately. However, another source states that the land deeds show that

45

Shreshly sold 1 and ½ acres to Clark for $197.25 in 1826, suggesting that the above is unlikely to be accurate.

The name Reform was short-lived, if it ever truly was called such at all, because the community became known as Slickaway. Now, the origin of this name and the time that it originated is also up for debate. One version states that in 1826, Lewis O'Neil had built a stone tavern and then the community was born from that. This stone building is still standing today. This account further states that the name Slickaway started as slippery way. That name allegedly came about when a horse slipped on ice in the area and its rider was thrown into the Elkhorn Creek and died. Overtime Slippery Way became Slickaway.[3]

Another account in a 1901 newspaper article reads as follows:

> "A man named Morgan once conducted a saloon on a hillside there. While unloading a barrel of whiskey it slipped from his hands and slid down the hillside to the creek, the owner ejaculating "slick-a way!" Thus the name is said to have originated.[4]

The third account for the name Slickaway suggests that many enslaved black men would "slip away" at night to the community of Reform for recreation, drinking and other activities that they were not permitted to partake in.

---

3. Smith, G. L., McDaniel, K. C., Hardin, J. A., & Powell, S. (2015). Little Georgetown, African American Community in Fayette County, Ky. In *The Kentucky African American Encyclopedia* (p. 185). essay, University Press of Kentucky.

4. Fort Springs. (1901, September 15). *The Morning Herald*, p. 11.

It's unlikely we will ever know the exact origin but what we do know is that sometime later, the name was changed to Fort Spring. It is said that there is a spring under O'Neil's stone tavern and it was utilized by Union troops during the civil war, hence the name "Fort Spring." At any rate, this became a predominately black community following the civil war. Adjacent land owned by Mr. H. Worley, was sold to freed slaves and by 1883, roughly 150 black people called Fort Spring home.[5]

In 1901, the stone tavern was the restaurant and shaving parlor of black businessman Frank Allen.

If any of the above about Reform or Henry Clark starting the community is true, then that would make Fort Spring the first black community in Fayette County, Pre-Civil War, although I believe that this is one of those urban legends and there is very little truth to it, if any at all.

The community had a school, a church and a few area businesses. There are several articles in the newspapers of quarrels, stabbings and shootings between black men in the area, suggesting, saloons and other recreation, good and bad was accessible in Slickaway.

---

5. "Fort Spring (Fayette County, KY)," Notable Kentucky African Americans Database, accessed July 10, 2022, https://nkaa.uky.edu/nkaa/items/show/320.

Illustration 5: The Stone tavern built over a Spring which is said to be the birth of the name Fort Spring. Also used as a restaurant for a black businessman in 1901. It's still standing today.(The Lexington Herald 15 Jan., 1950)

Frogtown

Situated just west of the Fort Spring and Little Georgetown communities, off of Versailles Road and Parkers Mill, and near the Woodford County line, sits a small black community known as Frogtown. Not to be confused with Kirklevington in Southern Fayette County, which formerly was called Frogtown, and later Fayetteville. These two were mixed up at one time when a historical marker for David R. Atchison was erected near the Versailles Road Frogtown in 1967. Atchison was born in Frogtown in 1807 and became the president of the United

States of America for just one day in March of 1849 when president elect Zachary Taylor did not want to be sworn into office on a Sunday, so Atchison, a senator, was president pro tempore for half of Sunday, March 4 and half of Monday March 5, 1849. He was actually born near Tates Creek Road on his fathers farm, around that time, this area was known as Frogtown and as mentioned was renamed Fayetteville and then Kirklevington. The marker stood at the Versailles Road site known as Frogtown for twenty years until the mistake was discovered and it was moved to its proper location in 1987.[6]

The community never grew to be more than 25 to 35 residents. Children attended the nearby schools at Fort Spring and Little Georgetown. When those schools closed down, children were bussed to the city schools but had to walk at least one mile to catch the bus. A new bridge was built in 1981 that replaced an old bridge built in 1935, making it safe for the school bus and the mail trucks to drive directly to the homes of the residents.[7]
The community was prone to flooding in major rains, making it nearly impossible to get in and out of the area prior to the bridge being built.[8] Overtime, it became unsafe, thus the new bridge built in the eighties.

Frogtown had no running water up until the 1980's, residents often went all the way into town to get water, or the nearby spring, those that did not have wells.

Most residents were members of the New Vine

---

6. Edwards, D. (1987, August 28). Blooper Marks Tale of One Day President. *Lexington Herald-Leader*, p. 29.

7. Martin, M. (1981, September 8). Buses are Rolling Down Frogtown Lane. *Lexington Herald-Leader*, p. 4.

8. Frogtown Has Needed Bridge. (1935, March 24). *The Lexington Leader*, p. 20.

Baptist Church in nearby Fort Spring. Burials also took place at the cemetery near the church. Some Frogtown residents were native to Woodford County and were buried there in places like Huntertown, another black community just across the county line.

Some of the family surnames that lived in and established this settlement include: Byrd, Brown, Woodson, Waters, Beatty, Underwood, Hanley and Wilson.

Unfortunately, little has been documented about this small black rural community, making a book such as this one, all that more important, documenting the available information.

We will end this section with an interesting story that took place in this community in the 1920's. In 1923, there was a 13 year old black child who was said to be able to communicate with a spirit called "Job." The inhabitants believed it to be Job of the bible. The following was written in the local paper:

> "A 13 year old negro boy who talks with Job, rocks which fall on the roof of houses, thrown by an unseen hand; griddles which jump from the top of a hot stove and fly, buckets which leap from the floor and turn over in mid-air and spill their contents are among the mysterious manifestations of an unknown power which holds in its fearful spell the 25 or 30 inhabitants of the little negro village of Frogtown.
>
> .....The events of which they(the residents) tell with awe seem to concern one particular individual Harry Waters, 13 year old son of Green Waters, at whose house most of the disturbing sights are seen and the spirit voices are heard.
>
> Harry, in the presence of other members of his family, holds conversations with a voice

which seems to issue from the air above his head, a voice which proclaims itself that of Job, presumably the bible character of the many afflictions.

Sunday, a handful of silver money dropped thru the ceiling, the negroes say, and fell at Harry's feet. Saturday a slop bucket rose from the floor on the porch, where at least a half dozen people were standing, and turned over, spilling its contents on the feet of one of the women. The woman had just told Harry to go the spring for a bucket of water.

Nearly every action of the strange power benefits Harry in some way, or injures someone who has displeased him..."[9]

A month later the papers report that mediums and a priest were sent out to the residence and when the priest was attempting to pray, the "spirit of Job," told the priest to shut up.[10]

9. Frogtown People Held Under Spell of Spirit Power. (1923, September 26). *The Lexington Leader*, p. 1.

10. Colored Notes. (1923, October 2). *The Lexington Herald*, p. 13.

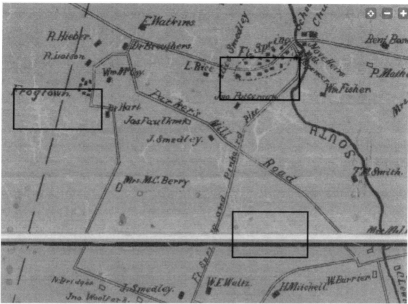

Illustration 6: The placement of each of these communities is shown in the rectangles on this 1891 Fayette County Map. Frogtown is to the Left, Fort Spring at the top and it's not listed on this map but Little Georgetown is in the vicinity of the bottom rectangle. The street shown at the very top of this map from left to right is Versailles Road, just to get an idea for those familiar with Lexington.

Rural Communities South

"History is a people's memory, and without a memory man is demoted to the level of the lower animals."

- Malcolm X

Chapter 4 – Jonestown & Coletown

According to biblical mythology, Bethsaida is the name of the city where the apostles Andrew, Peter, and Philip hail from. It is also the original name that a group of black people called their little community in southern Fayette County.[1] The community would later become known first as Jonesboro and then Jonestown. This was likely named after Thomas Jones who is said to have bought 50 acres and began subdividing the land and selling it to interested black buyers in 1893. According to one source, the first black buyer was Jonathan Hardy.[2] Anoth-

1. Defense of the People of Jonestown. (1906, January 16). *Lexington Leader*, p. 8.

2. *Our History*. BETHSAIDA BAPTIST CHURCH. (n.d.). Retrieved April

er source lists the first black buyer as Peter Owens and suggests that he purchased three acres.[3]

Although, Jonestown is officially recorded as beginning in the year 1893, records show that African Americans were in the area long before this date, possibly as the slaves of the white men who previously owned the land before Thomas Jones. An article in the Lexington Leader, dated January 16, 1906, suggests that there was a small hut being rented that served as a schoolhouse as well as the church, sometime before the community took on the names Jonesboro and Jonestown. This was around 1891. A book titled the Webster Family Album states that some of this land was owned by the Webster family. A deed in 1825 from Archilles Webster shows him donating land to a man called Atchison and it included something called the "Bethsaida Meeting House."[4] It is speculated that this was a house of worship for the enslaved populations in the area and it's likely that the Bethsaida church that was established in 1868, was from this meeting house. The small hut referred to in the 1906 newspaper article was more than likely the Bethsaida Meeting House.

The community in it's history, had over 30 homes, two grocery stores, a slaughterhouse, the church, a cemetery, and a school. One of the grocery stores was owned by Joshua P. Black. The other was owned by John Dou-

---

18, 2023, from https://www.bethsaidalex.org/our-history.html

3. Smithers, B. Y. (2001). Chapter 1. In *The Partial History of Jonestown, Lexington, Kentucky 40517* (p. 3). essay, Author.

4. Webster, R. D. (2005). The Bethsaida Baptist Church. In *The Webster Family Album* (p. 76). essay, R.D. Webster.

glas.[5] The stores closed in 1955 and in the 1970's, respectively.

Church

Rev. Isaiah Sailles is recorded as being the founder of the Bethsaida Baptist Church around 1868. It is unknown if he built a church from the ground up or if the "Bethsaida Meeting House," was the church building Sailles utilized, although evidence seems to suggest that it is. However, it's not recorded if that original church was a white congregation or a black one. Again, a deed record in 1825, mentions this building specifically. What is widely accepted is that this church once stood on the west side of Tates Creek Road(then called Tates Creek Pike,) directly across from the current church.

Little information exists about the Rev. Sailles pastorate or the subsequent pastors. There is a small blurb in the Golden Jubilee book about Rev. Sailles but that is it.

"Born in Jessamine Co., Ky. Attended the common schools of the county. Farmer and carpenter by trade. Ordained, 1882. Pastored nine churches; erected one; finished and dedicated one; baptized about 500 souls . Rev. Sailes[sic] is not pastoring now."[6]

According to this quote, Rev. Sailles pastored nine

5. Smithers, B. Y. (2001). Chapter 1. In *The Partial History of Jonestown, Lexington, Kentucky 40517* (p. 6).

6. Parrish, C. H. (1915). Rev. Isaiah Sailes. In *Golden Jubilee of the General Association of Colored Baptists in Kentucky: The story of 50 years' work from 1865-1915* (p. 224). Mayes Printing Co.

churches in total and built one. No names were given but based on everything, the one he built is likely the Jonestown Church.

No other pastor is mentioned on the church website until Rev. J.H. Mason in 1921. The current church was built during his tenure in 1922.[7] There are however, several obituaries from funerary services held at the Jonestown church prior to 1922. A few different pastors names were listed as conducting the services. These include Revs. Perry Smith, Louis Martin, J. H. Beatty, Isaac Fuller, O. Simpson and Thomas Harris. It appears that these men were pastors of other churches but likely were visiting pastors and sometimes held services at Jonestown, indicating that Jonestown may have been without a permanent pastor for some time. Joseph Henry Beatty died in 1912, and his obituary states that he was a reverend and his funeral services were held at the Jonestown church, so it is possible that he was the pastor there for an undetermined period of time.

The cemetery was on the church property but when the community dissolved in the 1990's, all of the remains were re-interred at the Lexington Cemetery. Nothing remains of the community except the Bethsaida Baptist Church at 3700 Tates Creek Road. My friend that I call my little brother, Charles Waples is from Jonestown. We met as teenagers around 1999. As a child, he attended this church with his mother. We visited his old stomping grounds in 2020 and I snapped the following photo.

---

7. *Our History.* BETHSAIDA BAPTIST CHURCH. (n.d.). Retrieved April 18, 2023, from https://www.bethsaidalex.org/our-history.html

Illustration 1: My teenage friend Charles "Dominic" Waples. He grew up in Jonestown. I took this photo of him at the Bethsaida Baptist Church in 2020.

School

Again, the old Bethsaida Meeting House was used not only as a house of worship, but as a school as well. And again, it dates as far back as 1825, possibly earlier. A former teacher, J. H. Johnson, stated that he taught at this school before the community was called Jonestown. He states it was fifteen years ago in 1904, so that places him there between 1888-1891, as he also indicated he was there for three years. There is not any further information about this school. He came back to teach at what then had been named Jonestown in 1904. John B. Caulder left that year and went on to teach in other schools, most notably Constitution Street Elementary. It is written elsewhere that Caulder himself opened the Jonestown School on July 20, 1902.[8]   But we have a newspaper article written two years prior in 1900, that states that Caulder's first year at Jonestown was then. It reads:

> "...The programme[sic] as a whole was well rendered and reflected much credit upon the teacher, Prof. J.B. Caulder.
>
> This was Prof. Caulder's first year at Jonestown and that his work was satisfactory, he has no better commendation than the love of his pupils and the praise and confidence of his patrons."[9]

It probable that Caulder made improvements to the school during his tenure, but he was not the schools

---

8. Smithers, B. Y. (2001). In *The Partial History of Jonestown, Lexington, Kentucky 40517* (p. 74). essay, Author.

9. Closing Exercises. (1900, March 25). *The Sunday Leader*, p. 4.

first teacher, unless a new building was dedicated that year and he was the first in that specific Jonestown school building. I have located no information to substantiate that however.

We do have information that a new high school was dedicated in Jonestown in the year 1917.[10] B.C. Green was the principal of the school. A position he held since 1915. The school closed for good in May of 1936. The church purchased the school building in 1938 and used it as a dining hall.

Joshua P. Black

Joshua P. Black, owned and operated a grocery store in the community. Originally from Keene, Kentucky in Jessamine County, Black's address on his World War 2 Draft Card is listed as Route 1, Tates Creek Pike, which was in Jonestown. On the same document his occupation is listed as "farmer" and that he was self employed. He owned a print shop, the Peerless Printing Company and he was the first district manager in Lexington of the black owned Louisville based Mammoth Life and Accident Insurance Company.[11] This company was founded in 1915 and had it's Lexington office at 269 East Second Street before moving to 149 Deweese Street around 1942. During the 1940's and 1950's, Mammoth was the largest black owned business in the state of Kentucky, employing over 750 people and assets upwards of 30 million.

10. Jonestown School, New Colored Institution is Dedicated With Interesting Ceremonies. (1917, February 20). *The Lexington Leader*, p. 5.

11. Swann, L. P. (2002, February 13). Legislator, educator got start at noted black owned business. *Lexington Herald-Leader*, p. 59.

The Kentucky offices closed in 1992 after a merger with Atlanta Life.[12]

Black also owned several pieces of property in Lexington, on North Broadway near Brucetown, Liberty Road and his store and home on Tates Creek Pike.

He lectured to young folks about doing for self, racial pride and racial loyalty.[13] He also rubbed shoulders with many of Lexington's black elite including pharmacist W.H. Ballard, businessman R. F. Bell, Dr. T.T. Wendell and more. He was secretary of the Colored Republican Civic League and all of these men were also founding members.[14]

Jonestown's Demise

The complete removal of a community is never an overnight process. It is always something that has been in the works, or at least in talks for ten to thirty years. Such is the case for this community.

It's destruction and the erasure of it's history began in the 1970's. This once rural community inhabited mostly by black tobacco and horse farmers, about four miles outside the city limits, was slowly being encroached upon by urban development. Jonestown at it's peak, was home to approximately 200 people.[15] By 1971,

---

12. "Mammoth Life and Accident Insurance Company," Notable Kentucky African Americans Database, accessed April 19, 2023, https://nkaa.uky.edu/nkaa/items/show/261.

13. Colored Notes. (1924, July 12). *The Lexington Herald*, p. 7.

14. Colored Notes: Colored Republican Civic League. (1915, July 13). *Lexington Leader*, p. 5.

15. Stafford, L. (1994, June 15). The Soul of the Community. *Lexington Herald-Leader*, p. 40.

that number had dwindled closer to fifty.[16] Today, the former site of Jonestown is home to several suburban homes and apartment complexes.   One street called Jonestown Lane is the only clue left that this community ever existed. That and the history remaining within Bethsaida Baptist Church.   Progress to some, is indeed devastation to others.

Coletown

Coletown is the southernmost community in Fayette County and was one of a very few communities to bear the name of a black landowner. It's named after a former slave Milly Cole. Sometimes spelled Millie, she was formerly enslaved to Horatio Johnson.   When he passed away, his sisters inherited his land and then his sister Sarah Johnson died in 1843.   She willed ten acres of land to Milly Cole and her descendants.[17] This makes Coletown one of the only black communities of Fayette County that was founded before the civil war. Located just off of Walnut Hill Road and Shelby Lane, the community's population was around fifty in the 1970's but I suspect it may have been a little bigger at earlier points in it's existence.[18] Probably always been less than one

16. Jonestown and Urban Gainesway. (1971, July 21). *The Lexington Leader*, p. 4.

17. "Coletown (Lexington, KY)," Notable Kentucky African Americans Database, accessed April 24, 2023, https://nkaa.uky.edu/nkaa/items/show/315.

18. Coletown's Future Is Grim. (1971, July 17). *The Lexington Leader*, p. 5.

hundred but I'm sure there were more than fifty at various points.

Members of the small community came together in 1913 and incorporated an organization called the "Pride of Coletown." This was the community grocery store. The incorporating members were: John D. Keene, William Henry Turner, Hizzy Elmore, Mitchell Searcy, Clay Parks, Walter Searcy, John Williams, Sr., Robert H. Williams, U. Jones, and John H. Scruggs.[19] William "Henry" Turner, according to his obituary, was also one of the founding members of the Greenwood Cemetery and Realty company, or what we know today as Cove Haven Cemetery. Turner was also a member of the "Good Heart, Sick and Death League" of Coletown, which as the name indicates, formed to take care of their sick and deceased.

Church

Each community had at the very least a church and a school. Coletown is no exception, however, at the time of this writing, I am unsure if there was ever a church within the boundaries of the Coletown community. In the newspaper database that I utilize for much information, you will see "Coletown Baptist Church" listed on two separate occasions. One in 1926, the other in 1937. It's highly probable that the alluded to baptist church is actually Mt. Gilead Baptist Church, which is a black congregation on nearby Jack's Creek Pike. Roughly two miles away from Shelby Lane, you will find this church. Many of the Coletown residents were mem-

---

19. $2,000 Company, The Pride of Coletown is The Latest Entry Into Mercantile Field Here. (1913, May 2). *The Lexington Leader*, p. 14.

bers here, which is the reason I suspect that Coletown Baptist and Mt. Gilead are one and the same.

Newspapers suggest that there was a white congregation called Mt. Gilead that was in the vicinity dating back to 1829. They sold the church to a black congregation in 1871, and they took on the same name. It's likely that they had some black membership and this group, formed their own church and bought the property no longer utilized by the white Mt. Gilead.

> "The Mount Gilead Baptist Church, on the Jack's Creek Pike, was erected in 1829. The congregation was divided however, in 1832, and many of it's members accepted the new faith advocated by Alexander Campbell., who was then visiting in Kentucky. The church was sold in 1871 to a black congregation by whom it is now used."[20]

In 1941, the church held it's 114th anniversary under the pastorate of Oliver Simpson. That places their beginnings around 1827, very close to the date given in the above quote, which stands to reason that they were at one time of the same congregation as the white church.

Klu Klux Klan set fire to a eight foot wooden cross at the door of the church in January of 1987, causing minor damage.[21] It is believed that it was in protest to the Martin Luther King Day celebrations that took place a day earlier.

---

20. Ancient Sanctuaries . (1901, September 1). *The Morning Herald*, p. 11.

21. Johnson, A. D. (1987, January 20). Crosses burned, 1 at church door. *Lexington Herald Leader*, p. 1.

School

There were two schools in the vicinity at various points. One being the Mt. Gilead School, which was located on Jack's Creek Pike. I can only make the assumption that this school was located inside or near the Mt. Gilead Church. It closed down in 1926 due to low attendance.[22] It is highly probable, due to proximity, that many of the students of Gilead merged with the newly built Rosenwald funded Coletown School in 1921, which is the other school alluded to. Neither of these schools show up on the 1891 map of Fayette County, so it's likely that both schools formed sometime after that year. The earliest mention that I'm able to locate in the newspaper database is 1902 for Gilead and 1907 for Coletown. This does not necessarily mean that they didn't exist prior to these dates, just the earliest I have found at this time.

In 1910, community members came together and extended their school period another two months themselves, after recognizing a need to do such. They called themselves the "Coletown Pay School." The public schools of Fayette County let out on February 23 of that year and the community wanted the children to receive instruction for a longer period. They had hoped to inspire the other black schools in the county to do the same.[23]

On Friday, October 19, 1920, a new schoolhouse was dedicated in Coletown.[24] The original was likely a

---

22. Colored Teachers To Hold Meetings. (1926, September 8). *The Lexington Leader*, p. 2.

23. Coletown Pay School. (1910, March 4). *The Lexington Leader*, p. 4.

24. Colored News Notes. (1920, October 31). *The Lexington Herald*, p. 11.

one room schoolhouse. This one however, was designed to have two teachers, with two rooms. The total cost to build the school was $3,800. Julius Rosenwald himself donated $800 of those funds. The Coletown community donated $300 and the remaining $2700 came from the general public.[25] The school closed it's doors around 1947 and was used as storage until it was sold and converted into a home in 1961.

---

25. Turley-Adams, A. (1997). Appendix I - Rosenwald Schools in Kentucky. In *Rosenwald Schools in Kentucky, 1917-1932* (p. 44). Kentucky Heritage Council.

Rural Communities East

"The forces that unite us are intrinsic and greater than the superimposed influences that keep us apart."

- Kwame Nkrumah

Chapter 5 – Cadentown

Genealogy, the study of families, family history and their lineages can teach us about some of the places our ancestors lived. The Census records, death records, military records, and many other records often contain the street names, neighborhood names and cemeteries where our families are buried. Such is the case for me personally, when I discovered some of my ancestors lived and are currently buried in a cemetery in Cadentown. Being born and raised in Lexington, I had never even heard of Cadentown until I was doing my genealogy research and found my family there around 2012-2013.

Behind whats now a private home, that was originally the church, at 705 Caden Lane, you will find the cemetery. Only 2 or 3 headstones are there but you will see several sunken indentations that indicate there were burials there. Death records show that several of my ancestors are in this cemetery.

My 3rd Great Grandfather George Baltimore, born in 1854, was buried in this cemetery August 30, 1918. His wife, my 3rd Great Grandmother, Minnie Baltimore's burial was here in 1925. Their daughter, Mattie Baltimore, which is my 2nd Great grandmother was buried here in 1914. Another set of grandparents I have recently discovered are buried here as well. Mattie Baltimore was married to Robert Ray, who is my 2nd Great grandfather, his mother Belle Maupin was buried here in 1911. I have been unsuccessful in finding when her husband, my 3rd Great Grandfather Red or Fred Maupin, passed away but whenever it was, I suspect his burial was also in Cadentown. Finding these records is what sparked my interest in this little community.

Tucked away off of Old Todds Road near Man O War Blvd, you'll find what was the 43 acre rural community of Cadentown.

The community was named after Irish immigrant Owen Caden, who in 1869 sold plots of land to African American families, who were recently freed from slavery following the civil war. The cost of each acre was $100.[1] With the influx of newly freed African Americans following emancipation, many white landowners seized the opportunity to sell their land.

Cadentown consisted of about 24 families, a cou-

---

1. Smith, G. L., McDaniel, K. C., Hardin, J. A., & Young-Brown, F. (2015). Cadentown, African American community in Fayette Co. In *The Kentucky African American encyclopedia* (p. 87). essay, University Press of Kentucky.

ple of grocery stores, three churches, a benevolent society, a cemetery and a school.

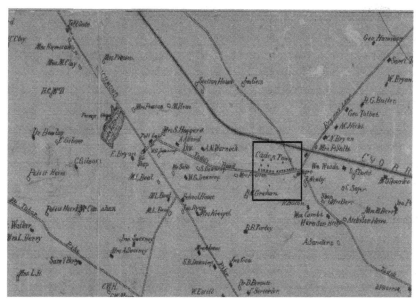

Illustration 1: 1891 Fayette County Map. Location of Cadentown is in the rectangle.

Cadentown One-Room Schoolhouse

The original Cadentown schoolhouse was built around 1879 and was standing until 1922 when a new schoolhouse was built. This building, the Rosenwald Fund School is still standing today and is now on the National Registry of Historic Places since 2006. It opened for operation in 1923.[2]

Julius Rosenwald, a philanthropist, organized a fund to match donations for the construction and creation of African American schools. One of which was the

---

2. National Registry of Historic Places, *Cadentown School*, Lexington, Fayette, Kentucky,

Cadentown Rosenwald School, also called the Rosenwald Fund School. The building, a 22 feet wide, 43 feet long rectangular structure was designed by local architect firm Frankel and Curtis Company. The cost was $3000 and $500 came from the Rosenwald Fund.

The Rosenwald Fund idea came together after a 1911 meeting between Julius Rosenwald and Booker T. Washington in Chicago. Washington was there raising funds for the Tuskegee Institute and along with the General Education Board, they formed an alliance.[3]

By 1917, the Julius Rosenwald Fund was incorporated as a non-profit. The purpose was for Rosenwald to help African American communities that "exhibited a strong financial and social commitment to education," build schools in their communities. There were five Rosenwald schools built in Fayette County and the Cadentown School is the only one that is still standing.

The Cadentown Rosenwald school was in operation from 1923 until 1947 when it closed its doors. After the schools closing, the Cadentown Baptist Church used the building as an activity center. Sometime later, the property became a vacant building on a privately owned lot because the original church moved to a new location and sold the property.

---

3. Turley-Adams, A. (2007). Julius Rosenwald (1862-1932). In *Rosenwald schools in Kentucky: Exhibit guide* (p. 8). essay, Georgetown College.

Illustration 2: Photo of the Original Cadentown School. The teacher on the original file states the name as J.W. Durett, however its actually John Weldon Jewett. It's dated 1901 but likely earlier because Jewett resigned around 1898.

Illustration 3: Cadentown Rosenwald Schoolhouse. Photo by me 5/19/2023

Illustration 4: Cadentown Rosenwald School (Library of Congress)

In section 8, page 1 of the National Register of Historic Places, the registry's statement of significance for the Cadentown school states:

> "The Cadentown School (FA-1007) near Lexington, Fayette County, Kentucky meets National Register Criterion A and is significant within the National Register Areas of Significance Black Ethnic Heritage and Education. It is an important part of the history of Cadentown specifically and the African American community of Fayette County in general.[4]

John Weldon Jewett

Beginning in 1890, John Weldon Jewett taught at the Cadentown School. Grades 1-6 were taught in this one room schoolhouse. In William Decker Johnson's 1897 book "Biographical Sketches of Prominent of Negro Men and Women of Kentucky," he has this to say about John Weldon Jewett and his tenure at the Cadentown School:

> "From the beginning the school grew in numbers, enthusiasm and usefulness and it is now one of the best rural schools in the South, and has sent out a larger number of regular graduates in the course of study prescribed for the Common Schools than any other Negro school; and, at the Midwinter Exposition, 1895, he was awarded a beautiful silk banner for the superior excellence of the displayed work of his

---

4. National Registry of Historic Places, *Cadentown School*, Lexington, Fayette, Kentucky, p. 1

pupils."[5]

As Johnson noted in the quote, the Cadentown School was one of the best Negro Schools in the south. This is one of the reasons they were awarded the Rosenwald Fund to build a new school in later years. Cadentown "exhibited a strong financial and social commitment to education," thanks to Jewett's leadership, work ethic and dedication to the education of his pupils and the work ethic and dedication of the teachers that succeeded Jewett at the school. Some of those pupils included some of my family. That family that I speak of is George Baltimore Jr., my 2nd great-grand uncle, who we will discuss later in this section, and his sister, who is my 2nd Great-Grandmother, Mattie Baltimore. They both were students of Jewett and graduated from the Cadentown school in 1896.[6]

Professor Jewett resigned from teaching after about seven or eight years and worked for the Internal Revenue Service until his death in 1905 at the age of 37 but remained involved in teaching in some capacity. His death certificate suggests that he was interred at the African Cemetery No. 2.

One incident of note occurred at the old schoolhouse a few years after Jewett's resignation and a Grandparent of mine was involved. In August of 1901, schoolteacher W. C. Martin was removed and replaced with

5. Johnson, W. D. (1897). John Weldon Johnson. In *Biographical Sketches of Prominent Negro Men and Women of Kentucky: With introductory memoir of... the author, and prefatory remarks showing the diff* (p. 34). The Standard Print.

6. Colored School Was Held At The Courthouse Last Night. (1896, June 18). *The Morning Herald*, p. 2.

H.W. Graves to the dismay of the community. The citizens stated that Graves was unfit to teach their children and that the move to appoint him was political. Several members of the community nailed the door to the school shut to prevent his entry. They were calling for Martin to be reinstated. Twelve were eventually arrested and charged under the Klu Klux law, which was "confederating and banding together to intimidate Graves."[7] One of the twelve was Belle Maupin, who lived in Cadentown and was my 3rd Great-Grandmother.

Illustration 5: John Weldon Jewett

7. Negro Schools Scenes of Riot in the County. (1901, August 21). *The Morning Herald*, p. 1.

Cadentown Cemetery

On the first page of this section, I mentioned genealogy research led me to Cadentown when I discovered Grandparents lived in this community that I never heard of. One Saturday morning in 2013, I jumped on my bike and rode from East End to Cadentown in the rain. I was determined to learn of this place where my ancestors lived. It was around this time that my love for black cemeteries was born. Prior to, I began venturing to the African Cemetery No. 2 on Seventh Street. I had learned of some ancestors buried there.

My first visit, I met a lady known around Lexington as the "Cemetery Lady," Ms Yvonne Giles, who is an authority on Lexington black history. As I scanned the headstones looking for my family, she tending to flowers on a grave, approached me and asked whom I was looking for. I explained who, and she told me she wasn't familiar with those names. She had studied this cemetery for years and knew just about everything about it. She even published a book "Stilled Voices Yet Speak," about the cemetery. She also explained to me that there were hundreds buried there in unmarked graves and it's likely my progenitors were among those. She explained her love for the cemetery began the same way as mine, finding family there. We talked for nearly an hour and I recall her telling me she was so excited to see young black people take interest in their roots, as I was doing.

When I left the cemetery, I felt inspired to continue the work that she started. This is what led me to riding a bicycle all the way to Cadentown days later. All of the places my people lived and are buried, if within reach, I felt obligated to visit and learn about.

So on that 2013 day, I approached the old baptist church and stood there for a while, contemplating knocking on the door and asking for permission to walk back there or just going anyway. I chose to go anyway. There are only two markers in the ground but several sunken in places, which marked areas where people were buried. None of my foreparents had markers, so I don't know the exact location. The same dilemma occurred when I searched the African cemetery for George Ray, Helen Ray and Lula Williams, other grandparents in unmarked graves. George Ray is the son of Robert Ray and Mattie Baltimore, both from Cadentown. George Ray is my paternal grandmother's father. He passed away in 1935, when she was just 3 years of age. His parents and grandparents are in the Cadentown cemetery, as well as several great aunts and uncles and their offspring.

The Find a Grave Website, a resource for locating the burials of ancestors, lists 35 names of people buried here. Only one of which is any of the above in my family, Mattie Ray, who was buried there in 1914. Again, I have found five that I know of in this cemetery. This suggests to me that the listing is incomplete. Browsing numerous newspapers under the keyword Cadentown, I found many obituaries of those buried here. I would estimate that there are over one hundred, possibly two hundred, but I have no way of knowing precisely how many.

One of the only legible markers, ironically, is of my girlfriends great-grandmother, Henrietta Harris. She was buried there in 1978. I had done some genealogy research for her as a birthday gift and discovered her family and mine in the same community and were members of the same church.

Chapter 5 – Cadentown

Around 2001, the cemetery was under threat of erasure by a nearby church, the East End Church of Christ, a white congregation. The building was built in 1978 at 3055 Old Todds Road.

The church had plans to build an auditorium but outcry from Cadentown's remaining citizens forced the city to deem Cadentown a historic zone and ultimately blocked the churches plan. Initially, planning officials ignored the outcry of Cadentown citizens, stating they "would have better luck if Cadentown was in a more affluent part of town."[8] That's basically a polite way to suggest that the history and concern of poor negroes does not matter. This dispute occurred in 2002. Nonetheless, it was granted its historic status and the church was forced to alter it's plans. Thankfully! The church even went as far as to suggest that one of the headstones was moved closer to the church property in an attempt to prevent the church from expanding.[9] Personally, I think that's an absurd assumption that only one who lacks empathy for the African American plight would make.
That's a very common mindset among the enslavers children, when it comes to preserving our history.

With that said, I noticed the lack of care from the black community at large, about our history. It seems we only cry out once the other community decides to get rid of something of historical value. But this is a whole other topic, so I will leave my words as they are and offer nothing further, except to say the same occurred with the

---

8. Matthews, P. (2002, November 16). Historic Label Complicates Dispute. *Lexington Herald-Leader*, p. 27.

9. Meehan, M. (2001, May 10). UK Archaeologist Consulted. *Lexington Herald-Leader*, p. 21.

African Cemetery, that suffered years of neglect and only when plans to remove it were enacted, did the black community make a push to preserve it. It shouldn't be a reaction to urban development's erasure but rather a CONSISTANT ACTION on our part to preserve our history, as a COLLECTIVE COMMUNITY. At present, it's small pockets of black people who do the work, the majority appear indifferent. Back to Cadentown Cemetery.

As it stands today, the cemetery remains. The last burial took place in 1993 when William Henry Brown was buried here. He was married to my future wife's Aunt Della Brown(Harris)

Archaeologists from the University of Kentucky have even found evidence of African burial practices in the cemetery.[10]

Oral tradition of those in the area states that there was a larger cemetery adjacent to Cadentown cemetery and that African Americans throughout Fayette County were buried there.[11] This further marks the sites importance. The African Cemetery on Seventh Street was established in 1869, making it the first official cemetery exclusively for African Americans in Lexington, however African Americans have been here prior to that date. It's possible there was a spot designated for the enslaved. We have to remember, in the eyes of the dominant class of man, these enslaved individuals were not people but rather property, thus the fact that records were not kept. Some were buried in the old Presbyterian Cemetery on

---

10. Rogers, F. (2001, August 11). Preserving Fayette's Black Cemeteries. *Lexington Herald-Leader*, p. 11.

11. Meehan, M. (2001, May 10). UK Archaeologist Consulted. *Lexington Herald-Leader*, p. 21.

Limestone but many lived in rural areas, so one can reason that this spot was designated for that purpose.

If the elders suggest that that's what took place, it's
a more than likely scenario. They heard it from their elders who may have had loved ones and friends that were
buried there.

*Illustration 6: On this map, the address at the bottom is the
East End Church.; The circled area is the one room schoolhouse behind the original baptist church at 705 Caden Lane.
The arrows indicate where the cemetery is located. It likely extends more towards the church.*

Churches

There were three churches of different denominations in Cadentown. At one time, each congregation shared the same building, alternating Sundays for service. Some members attended the services of the other denominations while others only attended the services of the congregation that they belonged to.

The Baptist Congregation was established in 1868 by Rev. Alfred Thomas, D.W. Seals, John Snowden and others. Nine people were given baptisms and the church was born.[12] In 1978, the church moved into a new church house that was built on property given to them by a black woman named Elizabeth Ember. The location was 2950 Cadentown Road, Liberty Road at the time. The congregation is presently active and remains in the same building now under the name Cadentown Missionary Baptist Church.

The Methodist congregation which organized as the Haven Methodist Church, was established around 1871. A newspaper article mentioned the Haven Church celebrating their 66th anniversary in 1937, placing their origins in 1871.[13] They would have their own church house built years later in 1901, just down the road from the Baptist church and the address was 626 Caden Lane, on the corner of Old Todds Road. It was designed by Ulysses Grant Seals, who on a personal note, was the brother in law to my Great-Grand Aunt Bertha Baltimore

---

12. Beatty, C.M. (1978, November 06). Interview by E. Owens. Black Church in Kentucky Oral History Project. Louie B. Nunn Center for Oral History, University of Kentucky Libraries, Lexington.

13. Colored Notes. (1937, November 22). *The Lexington Leader*, p. 12.

Seals. She was married to his brother Garnet Seals, they however divorced in 1937. There was an error printed in the Herald Leader that states U.G. Seals designed the church in the 1870's,[14] however, according to his death record, he was born in 1864, so its unlikely that he designed it at that date. The Property Value Assessment website of Fayette County shows the property originally deeded to Haven Methodist Church in 1901. Not to mention, they were sharing the building with the Baptist church throughout the late 1800's. One other thing to note, when you search the newspaper database, the earliest mention of Haven Methodist Church dates back to 1901, the same year as the deed. With that said, this does not diminish their historic value, it's just about accuracy of information and for any readers, I welcome further correction if that information becomes available.

The Haven Methodist congregation became defunct in the late 1980's or early 90's. Members likely joined the Wesley United Methodist Church, who owned the Haven church property from 2002 to 2006. The building still stands and is now a private residence.

The third church was the Power Society congregation organized by Roxy Turner of Goodloetown. Some of the Cadentown Baptists such as Rev. Jesse Slaughter and about twenty others converted over to the religion of Turner and held services at the church. They had plans to turn the church into a Power church. However, this did not go over well with the majority of the baptists and a dispute among them was born that lasted several years.[15]

14. Wilkinson, D. (2001, May 20). A Tour of Fayette County's Black Communities. *Lexington Herald-Leader*, p. 64.

15. The Power Society: Leads To a Split in a Colored Church at Cadentown, Fayette County. (1894, February 13). *The Kentucky Leader*, p. 4.

"A religious war has again broken out at the Cadentown Colored Baptist Church, which culminated yesterday in a suit by Berry Smith[Baptist] and others to recover possession of the church from John Givens, Mat Nelson, and others[Power] who have been in control for some time. Each side claims that the other has wandered from the true faith and is unworthy to be classed with the anointed."[16]

Their services would last for days, often resulting in the police being called, due to how loud the service would get. One reporter for the local paper wrote the following:

"and the chief aim of that church and it's members seems to be to make as much noise as possible and in this respect they are supremely proficient."[17]

Residents of the various neighborhoods where the Power Society were present, often filed noise complaints, stating that the group would be singing as late as midnight, four to five times a week, preventing them from a quiet nights rest.[18]

The Methodist congregation of Cadentown had a lawsuit against the Power Church due to some property

---

16. Religious War breaks out in the Cadentown Baptist Church-Fiscal and Police Courts. (1896, June 2). *The Lexington Herald*, p. 2.

17. Sister Roxey: Holds Salvation Army Services on Mechanic Street. (1898, August 13). *The Daily Leader*, p. 3.

18. Power Band Ordered to Cease Their Midnight Vigils, As A Result of Protest of Citizens. (1910, October 19). *Lexington Leader*, p. 2.

damage during one of the services in their church building.

In 1908, John Hawkins of Cadentown, transferred a tract of land to the organization so they could build their own church.[19] The church would be known as "St. Mary's Tabernacle, C.F.B.." and their first service in the new church house was held in December of that year.[20] The C.F.B. Stands for Christian Faith Band, which is one of the several names the church group went by. Other names included Star of Bethlehem Church, Power Society, and the Power Band Church of God. The last mention of this church in the local papers was in 1929. Whether the church consolidated with another or disbanded altogether is unknown. However, the Pentecostal Power Church on Second Street is still in existence today and was an extension of this group. See the Taylortown-Smithtown chapter for more on that organization.

Reverend George Baltimore

George Baltimore Jr., is my 2nd Great Grand Uncle. He was reared in Cadentown and was a member of the Baptist congregation before he moved to Indianapolis, Indiana. There he served as Pastor of the New Bethel Baptist Church for ten years. Prior to that he, was associate pastor for twelve years. While pastor, he remodeled the old church in 1935 and built the new building seven years later in 1942. Before joining the ministry, Baltimore ran a grocery store for 20 years in Indianapolis.

---

19. Unique Deed Filed. (1908, September 13). *The Lexington Herald*, p. 4.

20. Colored General Notes. (1908, December 13). *Lexington Leader*, p. 10.

He passed away in 1948.[21]

Illustration 7: Rev. George Baltimore (1882-1948)

Decline

Once a quiet rural settlement 5 miles outside of Lexington, is now a busy section with traffic passing through to the nearby shopping centers and developed areas. The majority of the original structures are nonexistent. The former Methodist church, the former Baptist church and schoolhouse exist as well as the building at 2922 Cadentown Road that housed the former Union Benevolent Society No. 7 and a grocery. That is all that is left of this predominately black community that formed

---

21. Rev. George Baltimore, Baptist Pastor, Dies. (1948, November 13). *The Indianapolis Star*, p. 15.

immediately following emancipation. Now, there are several near mansions being built in the community and it's a shell of it's former self.

The old baptist church building dating back to the 1870's, was converted into a private residence. It was purchased in 1978 by Danny LaFollette, a white male. He was charged with cultivating marijuana inside the old schoolhouse in the 1990's and the property was seized. The U.S. Marshall service received an order to sell the property. Alvin Seals, president of the Cadentown Association and other members of the community attempted to purchase the property. Unfortunately, they were outbid. They were however, successful at this time, getting the property on the National Registry of Historic Places and getting a clause in the deed preventing any future owners from altering the outside appearance of the structures.[22] The same was granted for the old Methodist Church down the street.

By the 1970's, the community was about two-thirds white. Many of the original inhabitants either moved away into the city seeking employment or passed away. Descendants, oftentimes, could not afford the property taxes and were forced to sell their parents and grandparents land.

The last known structure to exist that was in my family was the home at 662 Caden Lane. It was owned by Amos Carter and his wife Isabelle Carter(Baltimore) who was my 2x Great-Grand Aunt. The home was razed in 2016.

22. Xiong, N. (1998, July 31). Buyers Pledge to Respect Site. *Lexington Herald-Leader*, p. 4.

Chapter 6 – Willa Lane

Willa Lane is a community east of Lexington that formulated much later than the majority of communities that this book discusses. Situated just south of Avon off of Haley Pike, Willa Lane prior to formation was farmland owned by J. Madison Jackson, whose wife sold 103 acres after his passing around 1920 to a fellow called Good-paster. He subsequently sold the land he divided into 5 acre lots to Willa Stevenson who then sold the lots to black buyers in 1924, officially forming the community.[1] It was originally called Stevenson Subdivision. In 1932, a new street was paved and called "Willa Street." Then it became Willa Lane. By the 1960's, the official street name was changed to "Willow Street."[2] This was possibly from some sort of error, likely the same error that oc-

---

1. Ockerman Jr., F. (2021). Recovery and Redefinition. In *New history of Lexington, Kentucky* (p. 78). HISTORY PRESS US.

2. Unusual Customs Part of Settlements Rich Past. (1985, August 11). *Lexington Herald Leader*, p. 1.

curred with Dewees Street becoming Deweese. A mix up that stuck.

When I learned of Willa Lane, I scoured the internet to find information but came up empty every time. Willa Lane is one of those sections where there is just not much written information about the community. What we do know is it was a community of about 40 people. There's one mention in a book that I used as a reference several times. The book "A New History of Lexington, Kentucky." On page 78, there's a few paragraphs about small black enclaves that developed on the outskirts of Lexington. One of them was about Willa Lane. It explains the transfer of land and the very beginning of the community. You see the name Willa B. Stevenson as landowner but who was she? No sources ever gave specifics, only her name. I have discovered who she was. I have also found discrepancies with some of the information so before we talk about who she was, let's explain those and how I've reached the conclusions that I have.

During my investigation into who the Willa B. Stevenson that was mentioned in the Foster Ockerman Jr. authored book was, I indeed found a woman with that name selling property on Haley Pike, just as was stated in the book. I automatically assumed it was a white woman because the majority of these communities that I've written about were named after the white landowner. I was wrong. There is a black man named "W.H. Stevenson," with adjoining property along Haley Pike. Papers also show a "Willie B. Stevenson" transferring property along Haley Pike. It's clear that "Willie" and "Willa" are one and the same. To further illustrate this point, "Willa," is mentioned as early as 1910 performing instrumental solo's at Asbury M.E. Church, the same church "Willie" was a member of and was also performing. So is there a Willie and a Willa? I think not. One further point before we move forward, a 1915 paper advertises "Willa B. Stevenson" organizing a music club at her home. The given address is 822 South Limestone Street. When you look at the census records for that address, you find the head of household named W.H. Stevenson, a wife Lucy A. Stevenson, and a 17 year old "daughter" named Willie B. Stevenson. This is sufficient evidence to conclude that "Willa B." is "Willie B." There was no mention of Willa B's musical accomplishments in the short paragraph about Willa Lane in Ockerman's book, accomplishments you will read about in the coming pages.

Now, let's explain the discrepancy. It is minor but it's our duty to provide this information as accurately as possible. Other scholars lay the groundwork. Then there are others who come along that simply adds the missing pieces. This is what I am doing. None of these sources have linked "Willie B. Stevenson" to the Willa Lane community. I am doing that very thing.

There exists an Encyclopedia that is exclusively about Kentucky African American History. A very wonderful resource. On page 480, there's a section about Willie Belle Stevenson but no mention at all of "Willa Lane" or her involvement in Real Estate. Nor does it mention that her father was a reverend. In it, it shows her father as "William H. Stevenson" and mother as Lucy Allen Stevenson. This further validates my findings because "William H." is in fact head of household on the census we previously mentioned. What I strongly feel is incorrect however is the date of birth. It's listed as November 8, 1904.[3] Yet the 1910 census records state that she was 17 at the time it was taken. If she was born in 1904, she would've been 6 in 1910. She was actually performing in 1904 as you will see. The 1920 census also contains an inaccuracy with her birth. It has her listed as being 20, placing her birth in the year 1900. While there are child performers, it's unlikely that she was performing in those churches at 4 and 5 years old and her age not being mentioned in the papers. One more, on her death record, she is listed as "about 70." At her time of death, that would place her birth around 1889. I am suggesting it to be about 1894, nonetheless 1894 or 1889 make more sense given the year she graduated school. One last thing, the encyclopedia states that "the place and date of her death are unknown."[4] However, I have her death certificate.

The conclusions I've reached come from the multitude of newspaper articles I've read about Willa and Willie. Each of which is in footnotes as you read on thru this section, so there was no need to add additional ones when explaining my findings. Anyone who fact checks me, as you SHOULD, will see the same things.

Now that we have established that this is whom the community was named after, who exactly was Willie B. Stevenson(Willa)?

Willa Belle Stevenson was a young black woman from Lexington. Again, her parents were the Reverend William H. Stevenson and Lucy A. Stevenson. Willa was educated at the all black Chandler Normal School, just

3. Smith, G. L., McDaniel, K. C., Hardin, J. A., & McDaniel, K. R. (2015). Stevenson, Wille Belle . In *The Kentucky African American encyclopedia* (p. 480). essay, University Press of Kentucky.

4. Ibid., p. 480

off of Georgetown Street, graduating in 1909.[5] The 1910 census record finds the family living at 822 South Limestone Street and has her listed age at 17, indicating her birth roughly around 1893.

During her schooling, it is clear that music was her passion, singing and composing classical, gospel and negro spiritual music. She was also a pianist, organist for various church choirs as well as a poet, winning 1st place for a poem she presented in San Francisco at the Golden State Anthropology Exposition.[6] With a Reverend father, she was regularly performing at the city's black churches such as the now defunct Asbury M.E. There she performed on two separate occasions at a music recital organized by Roy W. Tibbs in 1904 and again in 1905. Tibbs, a native of Hamilton, OH., was founder of the Howard University Glee Club and husband of Madame Lillian Evanti, a world renowned black opera singer.[7] Other churches where Willa held her performances were the Historic St. Paul A.M.E., the Historic Pleasant Green Baptist, First African Baptist and the defunct Gunn Tabernacle.

In the year 1915, February the 18th, Miss Stevenson organized a musical club called the "Orpheus Choral

5. At Opera House Chandler Exercises are Held. (1909, June 4). *Lexington Leader*, p. 9.

6. Dunnigan, A. A. (1982). Willie B. Stevenson. In *The Fascinating Story of Black Kentuckians: Their Heritage and Traditions* (p. 311). Associated Publishers.

7. Morris, J. (2015, January 15). *Roy W. Tibbs: Founder of Howard University Glee Club*. Anacostia Community documentation initiative. Retrieved October 16, 2022, from https://cdi.anacostia.si.edu/2015/01/15/roy-w-tibbs-founder-of-howard-university-glee-club/

Club." The purpose was to study classical music. Stevenson was founder and president. The club existed at least a decade or more. We find more mentions of it in a few 1924 newspapers and it listed her still as the president. The Orpheus Choral Club stopped being mentioned in any of the local papers by 1925. However, you see the emergence of a couple more music clubs in which she is the organizer and president. One of them being called the "Roland Hayes Choral Society."[8] Named after the talented negro tenor Roland Hayes, who is said to be the first African American man to ever gain international fame as a performer. Roland even performed in Lexington several times and this club bearing his name was in attendance. The other music club would be a local branch of the National Association of Negro Musicians, and they took on the name "Lexington's Harmonic Promoters Club." Other organizers of this club included news reporter and educator D.I. Reid, Professor John B. Caulder, local activist Lizzie Fouse and more.[9] This meeting was held in her home at 822 South Limestone Street, which also served as her office for the various organizations that she was a part of. The people listed above are all prominent black men and woman of Lexington, so it is clear that she was in the same circles with Lexington's best of our race.

February 3, 1925, she held a performance at the Opera House, captivating the crowd. She composed a piece titled "Can't Hide" which was sung by George L. Johnson "in a manner that won great applause," the pa-

8. Colored Notes. (1926, December 29). *The Lexington Leader*, p. 13.

9. Colored Notes. (1925, May 13). *Lexington Leader*, p. 7.

per read.[10]

It's apparent that 1925 was a busy year for Miss Stevenson because by August, she received a teaching certificate from Chicago's Musical College under the tutelage of world famous pianist and Australian born music composer Percy Grainger who taught a piano class at the college.[11] While there, she was the only black woman in her class and earned a Percy Grainger Scholarship after winning a piano contest.

Just two short years later, the Colored Notes section of the local paper indicated that in 1927, she owned a music studio where she herself taught music to several students.[12] She taught voice, music theory and her specialty, the piano.[13]

The 1930's began a new decade but we find Miss Stevenson still heavily active within the music scene of black Lexington, creating musical festivals with the Asbury M.E. Church and heading several organizations centered around music. On March 5, 1931, she was appointed to the state manager position of the Kentucky branch of the International Music Foundation where she was to supervise all of the state managers within the organization.[14]

While all of this was going on, she remained involved in real estate. We began this section talking about

---

10. Colored Singers in Fine Concert. (1925, February 3). *The Lexington Leader*, p. 11.

11. Colored Notes. (1925, July 6). *The Lexington Herald*, p. 11.

12. Colored Notes. (1927, April 11). *The Lexington Herald*, p. 9.

13. Wins Musical Honors. (1925, August 30). *Lexington Leader*, p. 15.

14. Colored Notes. (1931, March 5). *The Lexington Leader*, p. 16.

her buying land and selling it to other African Americans. You see deed transfer after deed transfer in the newspapers that lists her name, sometimes it says Willa, other times, it says Willie. Besides Willa Lane, the family had property throughout Lexington. Willa and her father sold property in various other locales such as Taylortown on Campbell Street, a lot on East Third and Chestnut (357 E. Third Street), and a lot on Robertson Ave in the Irishtown section. They also owned the home at 822 South Limestone that the family shared together, which was razed sometime in the early 60s and stood in the vicinity of the Kentucky Clinic.

Other notable organizations that she was a member of or affiliated with is the Songwriters Guild of America, which was founded in 1931 and locally she was music director at the Phyllis Wheatley Center, the Y.W.C.A. For a short time, she also taught music, vocal and instrumental, at the all black Western High School in Paris, Kentucky.[15]

Willie a.k.a. "Willa" Belle Stevenson was clearly a remarkable, multi-talented, musician, music teacher and highly respected woman among the citizens of black Lexington. Even if she never achieved national or international success with her music, the citizens of black Lexington loved her and sought out her leadership in various respects. I am thankful that in spirit, she chose me to be the one to tell her story.

With that said, we all have a death date. Her death came on February 28, 1959. She was buried at what is now Cove Haven Cemetery on Whitney Ave. She had

---

15. Dunnigan, A. A. (1982). Willie B. Stevenson. In *The Fascinating Story of Black Kentuckians: Their Heritage and Traditions* (p. 311). Associated Publishers.

two brothers, Charles Stevenson and Dr. Chaplain Mc-
Cade Stevenson. Dr. McCade lived in the family home
on Limestone and Charles resided at 419 Oak Street in
Forest Hill.

Willie never married and did not have any children.

WILLIE BELLE STEVENSON

WILLIE BELL STEVENSON

A woman who has accomplished so much and was a great talent, must've had a great upbringing and parents who pushed to ensure their children were set up for success and to achieve great things. So who are her parents?

Her father was the Reverend William Henry Stevenson, a man very active in the religious, educational and the business institutions of black Lexington. The Lexington Herald describes him as "one of Kentucky's best known citizens."[16]

One can surmise that he taught his children how to purchase and profit from the sale of land and property. There is record of each of them doing this very thing. There is also record of the family, in particularly the three children, Charles, Chaplain and Willie, investing money into the Lexington Investment Company when they were children in 1899.[17] If I have her year of birth correct at 1893, that means his children were investing at a very early age because she was only 6. And this is the earliest account found in the newspaper. Its possible, it was occurring months to years before 1899. Before they even understood what investing was. This suggests teaching the children financial literacy and proper investing was a priority. It also suggests the family resided in Cynthiana, Kentucky in Harrison county that year.

W.H. Stevenson was the financial secretary at Simmons University in Louisville, Kentucky.[18] Simmons was an all black college founded in 1879 named in honor of its former president, Rev. William J. Simmons, who was also pastor at First African Baptist in Lexington from 1879-1890.[1920] Stevenson held another position in finance as the Financial Agent of the Freedman's Aid Movement

16. Colored Notes (1934, August 31). *Lexington Herald*, p. 16.

17. Lexington Investment Co. (1899, April 5). *The Daily Leader*, p. 5.

18. Colored Notes (1934, August 31). *Lexington Herald*, p. 16.

19. Smith, G. L., McDaniel, K. C., Hardin, J. A., & Hudson, J. B. (2015). Simmons College of Kentucky. In *The Kentucky African American Encyclopedia* (p. 452). University Press of Kentucky.

20. McIntyre, L. H. (1986). The Sixth Pastor. In *One Grain of the Salt: The First African Baptist Church West of the Allegheny Mountains* (pp. 43–44). L.H. McIntyre.

of the M.E. Church.[21] With that said, it makes perfect sense that he would teach his children finance and investing.

Rev. Stevenson preached at a number of black churches in Lexington. Consolidated Baptist, Evergreen Missionary Baptist, First African Baptist, Willard Street Baptist Church, and Shiloh Baptist to name a few. It's clear that he was connected with the pastors of nearly every black church in the city, just as his daughter performed and led choirs at the various churches throughout the city. His home church was the M.E. Church in Hamilton, Oh but he was instrumental in the organizing of about 7 different churches from Lexington, to Cynthiana and Cincinnati.

Lastly, September 29, 1924 addition of the Lexington Leader suggests that he was in the process of creating an organization called the Stevenson-Gregory Cooperative Fire Insurance Company with about 25 other black men from around the state of Kentucky. The Articles of Incorporation were filed on September 26, 1924 and Stevenson was the president. His son Dr. C. M. Stevenson would serve as the Assistant Treasurer and lastly, the central focus of this chapter, Miss Willa would serve as the secretary.[2223]

The Reverend would pass away in 1934 and was buried at the African Cemetery No.2.

I was unable to find much on his wife Lucy Allen Stevenson. It does appear that she is the sister of one of

21. Old Hospital Building. (1910, July 14). *Lexington Herald Leader*, p. 1.

22. Fire Insurance Co. to Open Offices Here. (1924, September 28). *The Lexington Leader*, p. 2.

23. Colored Notes. (1924, September 29). *The Lexington Leader*, p. 9.

Lexington's prominent black doctors Dr. J.M. Allen. The names Lucy Stevenson and Dr. Allen are listed as siblings to a "Parolee Barnett," from a 1925 obituary.[24] Lucy's maiden name is Allen. Parolee is likely a misspelling of "Pearlie." If this is accurate, then this means that Willie comes from a distinguished black family, that values education on her maternal side in addition to her paternal.

Lucy succumbed to illness in 1941 and was interred at Cove Haven Cemetery.

To sum up the chapter, although the Willa Lane community is small and virtually unknown to nonresidents, I felt it was of great significance to document who the community was named after. Especially considering the fact that the overwhelming majority of these communities discussed in this book were named after white people. May the descendants of those who called Willa Lane home read these pages and take great pride in their communities progenitor and her accomplishments.

---

24. Cochran, L. J. (1925, November 26). Colored Notes. *The Lexington Herald*, p. 11.

Chapter 7 – Uttingertown, Columbus, Nihizertown, Centerville, & Pricetown

The majority of the well known black communities are within the city limits of Lexington, as Fayette County's black population is largely concentrated there. However, there are several rural communities that developed following the civil war and they remain rural areas today. A few already written about in earlier chapters, were rural in their beginnings but are now within city limits. Enclaves like Cadentown, Jonestown, and Warrentown were just outside of Lexington and with expansion throughout the city's 247 year history, they are now in the city.

Little has been written about these rural communities, most exist in name only. Overtime, the people who called these communities home, migrated to the city seeking opportunity, or they left the state altogether. The church and a cemetery are whats left in most of these communities and with the available information, it is my intention to write as accurately as possible the history of these places, beginning with two adjacent communities called Uttingertown and Columbus.

Uttingertown/Columbus

Uttingertown formed just North of Winchester Road and East of Lexington on Royster Road in 1869. Samuel L. Uttinger, a white man who owned the land began selling two acre plots of building land on his farm to black buyers. Each acre was sold for $100.[1] Today that would be $2,182.41 per acre. Uttingertown was about 32 acres in total and by the 1970's, had a population of about 49.[2] The majority of the residents worked on the nearby farms.

The adjoining community was established around 1893 when Clarence H. Crimm began selling his land to black families seeking to build a home. This community literally next door to Uttingertown on Royster Road was originally called Columbiatown but was called Columbia as well, and lastly referred to as Columbus. The common theme was to name the community after the landowner as you have read throughout this book but Crimm took

1. Ockerman Jr., F. (2021). Recovery and Redefinition. In *New history of Lexington, Kentucky* (p. 78). HISTORY PRESS US.

2. Two Communities on Royster Road. (1971, July 30). *The Lexington Leader*, p. 4.

another approach. He chose Columbiatown after the Columbian Exposition, a World fair held in Chicago that celebrated the murderer and rapist Christopher Columbus' 400th anniversary of "discovering" America. There is so much to be said about that as indicated by the verbiage used and quotes around discovering, but that's beyond the scope of this book. Columbiatown was bigger than its next door neighbor Uttingertown in acreage as it totaled about 50 but the population was smaller with 42 residents in 1971. This same year, according to a survey done in the area, 78% of the homes in these two communities were in substandard condition, which is typical of poor black neighborhoods where the inhabitants often could not afford minor repairs, nor did the city or county government truly give a damn about improving the conditions of these communities.

Uttingertown had a school that children from both sections attended. It was known as the Uttingertown Rosenwald School for 3 years between 1917-1920.

When Rosenwald no longer funded the school, it remained operable until the year 1952 when it was abandoned.[3] Prior to the Rosenwald funding, its not exactly known when the school opened, the earliest mention is in the Kentucky Leader and it covered Fayette County's first commencement of black schools which was held on June 1, 1894 at the courthouse. The Uttingertown graduates were Sallie Coleman, Cora B. Simpson, Mary Greene and Coleman Greene.[4]

This two room schoolhouse remained standing

---

3. Fayettes Last One-Room School, Which Opened Thursday, May Be in Its Final Year. (1955, September 2). *The Lexington Leader*, p. 8.

4. Commencement. (1894, June 2). *The Kentucky Leader*, p. 7.

abandoned, dilapidated, missing half of its roof until it was razed in 2002. At this time, it was one of the two remaining one room school buildings in Fayette County.

Illustration 1: School children outside the Uttingertown School (1901)

The family of Jimmy Winkfield came from Uttingertown. Winkfield was among the African American jockeys who dominated the sport of horse racing for several decades, winning the Kentucky Derby in 1901 and 1902.[5] His great niece Artemesia Winkfield Brummell, a schoolteacher, was born and raised in Uttingertown on her family's farm. Her father was George Winkfield, who was the son of Jimmy older brother August. She taught at the Lincoln Institute in Shelby County, which was ran by

5. Brown, D. (2007, November 21). *Jimmy Winkfield (1882 - 1974)* BlackPast.org. https://www.blackpast.org/african-american-history/winkfield-jimmy-1882-1974/

Whitney B. Young Sr., and was an all black boarding school. The school operated from 1912 to 1966. She also taught at the all black Douglas High School in Lexington before relocating to Louisville and teaching at a couple of the schools there.[6]

Only the church, Uttingertown Missionary Baptist and a few homes remain along Uttinger Lane and neighboring Columbus Lane.

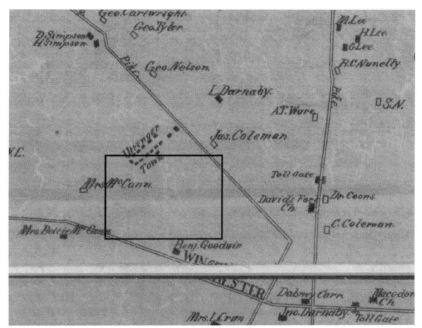

Illustration 2: Rectangle depicts Uttingertown. Columbus is not shown but it is directly next to Uttingertown, along the same street and inside the rectangle.

6. Lexington Obituaries and Memorials. (2004, July 9). *Lexington Herald Leader*, p. 16.

Nihizertown/Pricetown/Centerville

Much like the two aforementioned communities, Pricetown, Nihizertown, and Centerville, were neighboring rural black communities that were birthed following emancipation. The exact date that these communities formed is not known but the earliest deed records date back to 1873.[7] Pricetown bears the name of Dr. Sanford Price who subdivided parts of his land and sold it to the formerly enslaved seeking housing. Pricetown as well as Nihizertown were located on Todds Road in Eastern Fayette County, to the West of Cleveland Road, whereas Centerville is to the southeast of these communities, off of Cleveland Road. Nihizertown took on the name of John Nihizer who sold two acre plots of his property to former slaves as well. Not to be confused with a town with the same name in Bourbon County, Ky, nothing could be found on the origin of Centerville. The only thing known is it's in close proximity to Nihizer and Pricetown, and the residents likely shared the available amenities, such as the general store that existed, Mount Calvary Baptist Church on Pricetown Rd and the Pricetown Colored School.

The three communities combined had a population of 105 and the total acreage was approximately 77.[8]

Mount Calvery Baptist church, which still exists today, was started by Rev. Matthew Garner around the year 1881. They held services out of members homes and

7. "Pricetown, Nihizertown, and Centerville (Fayette County, KY)," Notable Kentucky African Americans Database, accessed October 16, 2022, https://nkaa.uky.edu/nkaa/items/show/334.

8. Ockerman Jr., F. (2021). Recovery and Redefinition. In *New history of Lexington, Kentucky* (p. 78). HISTORY PRESS US.

the schoolhouse until the completion of their church building. The original church burned down in 1965 but by November 1966, the current church building was completed.[9]

The genesis of the Pricetown school is unknown. One newspaper account stated that in 1904, Pricetown was an "old" school, suggesting that its been around for some time, possibly a decade or more.[10] A new two room schoolhouse was built in 1933 and consisted of two rooms. One was used for lunch and the other, four grades were taught out of simultaneously, something the instructor Lena Mae Howard says wasn't as difficult as people may think.[11] Between 1955-56, the school closed down and the property was sold.

Only "one-room" school in Fayette County, the present Pricetown schoolhouse was built in 1933, several hundred yards down the Todds Road from the original school opened before 1900. (Leader photo).

Illustration 3: Pricetown School 1955 (Lexington Herald Leader)

9. *Mount Calvary's history: Mt. Calvary MBC: Lexington, KY*. Mt. Calvary MBC. (n.d.). Retrieved October 16, 2022, from https://www.mtcalvarymbcky.org/mount-calvary-church-history

10. Fayettes Last One-Room School, Which Opened Thursday, May Be in Its Final Year. (1955, September 2). *The Lexington Leader*, p. 8.

11. Ibid., p 8

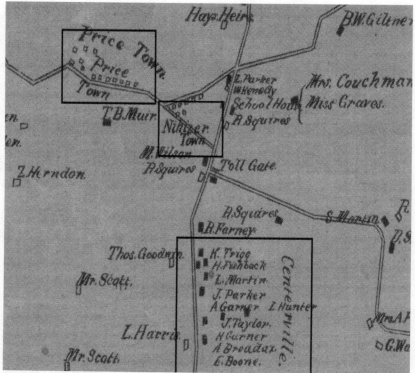

Illustration 4: Location of each depicted by the rectangles on the map.

Downtown

"Educate your children, economize your earnings, acquire property, become part owners of the soil of your country."

- Thomas T. Henry

Chapter 8 – Branch Alley & West Water Street

Story time! Once upon a time there existed a small section in downtown Lexington that was inhabited by mostly African Americans. This section was considered an eye sore to the city and the conditions were unsanitary. The tenement houses were dilapidated and mostly deemed inhabitable. In 1915, a group from the "Clean City Club," inspected some of the dwellings and had this to say about their conditions:

> "A number of the joists and sills have decayed, allowing the floors to settle and in some places the joists rest upon the ground, thus causing the floors to become damp in wet weather. The front steps have been allowed to

get into such a dilapidated condition that at the present time, they are dangerous. The door-ing[sic] in some of the rooms is very bad, boards being rotten and an occasional hole was found in same"[1]

Another dwelling was described as follows:

"Situated in the rear of 156 Branch Alley is a dilapidated frame shed, at one time possibly used for a kitchen, but now falling to pieces and full of garbage and rubbish. The entrance to the kitchen at the present time is thru this shed. In the yard is an old abandoned cistern, about half full of rubbish with the top left uncovered making a trap for someone to fall into and injure themselves."

"Near this cistern and at the rear of the lot is located one of the most dilapidated and dangerous privy vaults that I have ever seen. The floor is partially gone and the building itself is about to fall down."[2]

There was no running water in the section, water was retrieved at a nearby hydrant, however water and other conveniences were supplied on Main Street, just a street over. With that said, this "slum district" was home to some of Lexington's poorest citizens and this was all that they could afford. It was not exclusively an African American community, there were whites who owned businesses and lived here as well. In fact, most of the property owners were white but they rented their

1. Wants Inspection of Houses Kept Up. (1915, January 27). *The Lexington Leader*, p. 6.

2. Ibid., p. 6

units that were in substandard condition out to African Americans. One particular white woman had a notorious reputation. Margaret Dobbs aka Mag, owned a brothel and it was common place for fights to occur at her place as well as shootings, stabbings and robberies. She was arrested quite often for a variety of offenses along with her sister, Phoebe Dobbs. Phoebe was described as a very large woman, weighing over 320lbs. She killed herself in 1898 by overdosing on morphine. It was said the cause was because she could not choose between two lovers.[3] Article after article, you will find these two involved in an affray of some kind. Eventually Dobbs moved her operation out of Branch Alley to Megowan Street or what is now called Eastern Ave.

We will not focus too much on Dobbs in this section, only wanted to give you a glimpse of what it may have been like to live on Branch Alley and from what I've read she is one of its most notorious characters. During my research into this community, it was her name that appeared time and time again.

---

3. Phoebe Dobbs. (1898, November 4). *The Morning Herald*, p. 5.

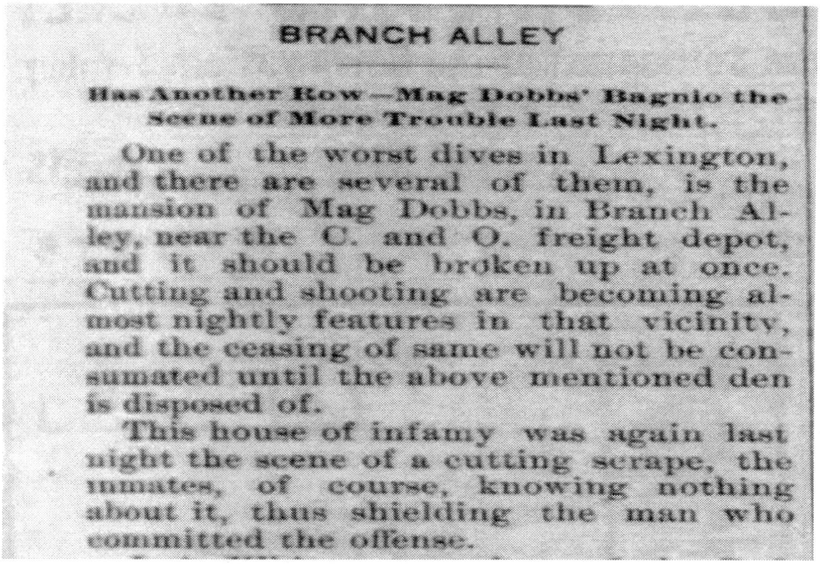

BRANCH ALLEY

Has Another Row—Mag Dobbs' Bagnio the Scene of More Trouble Last Night.

One of the worst dives in Lexington, and there are several of them, is the mansion of Mag Dobbs, in Branch Alley, near the C. and O. freight depot, and it should be broken up at once. Cutting and shooting are becoming almost nightly features in that vicinity, and the ceasing of same will not be consumated until the above mentioned den is disposed of.

This house of infamy was again last night the scene of a cutting scrape, the inmates, of course, knowing nothing about it, thus shielding the man who committed the offense.

Illustration 1: Illustration 1: Lexington Herald-Leader August 14, 1888

There was a high level of lawlessness and chaos within the community. Shootings, fighting, stabbings, robbery, etc were a common sight in Branch Alley as a whole, not just at Dobb's place. Those who ventured to go there were just asking for trouble. Especially, if you were from out of town, you were easy prey for the wolves. Many men, white and black alike would enter a number of the brothels in the area, only to be robbed of their possessions by the women who operated and worked out of them.

With that said, where exactly was this infamous Branch Alley?

SHOOTING ATTEMPTED IN POLICE STATION.

Charged with attempting to shoot Henry Johnson, colored, while the latter was seeking protection in the police station, James Washington colored, living on Branch alley, was arrested by Capt. McCarty and Lieut. Harkins Wednesday night in the police station. Johnson had come in to notify the police that Washington had been shooting at him while on Branch alley and a few moments later Washington walked in and, according to the statements of the officers, drew a revolver and started to shoot Johnson. The officers seized Washington in time to prevent the shooting and he is now held to await trial on charges of maliciously shooting at without wounding and of carrying concealed a deadly weapon. Washington later declared that he had come to the police station to get protection from Johnson, who, he said, had been throwing rocks at him and trying to enter his house when he did the shooting on Branch alley.

Illustration 2: 1912 article depicting the kind of things that occurred regularly in Branch Alley (Lexington Herald-Leader July 11, 1912)

Branch Alley was the section on East Water and Vine Street that was bounded by Limestone to the west, Rose Street to the East, Main Street to the North and High Street was it's southern border. It was the alley directly behind the Phoenix Hotel and the Union Station. Today, the Central Branch of the Lexington Public Library and Phoenix Park rest on the site of the Phoenix Hotel and the Fayette County Clerk's Office is located where the Union Station used to be.

According to the Lexington Herald-Leader, in 1791, there were two Water Streets. The following was written:

"Both Water and Vine streets were
known as Water Street in Lexington's 1791 plat.
After the market house was built from Limestone to Upper, the Water Street of today was
called Market Street, then Pearl Street. In 1836,
when Hunt's Row was built, the two streets
were referred to as the northeast and southeast
divisions of Water Street."

"As to when Vine Street was so named,
or why, is a puzzle. Vine Street, when opened
east of Limestone, was called Branch Alley...."[4]

There where a number of businesses in Branch
Alley and on Water Street. West Water Street started at
Limestone and extended as far west as Merino Street.
Where Rupp Arena and Triangle Park sit today, that was
part of West Water Street. These businesses included ev-
erything from restaurants, various warehouses, saloons,
to barbershops, not to mention several brothels, then re-
ferred to as disorderly houses, dives and bagnios. The
Odd Fellows "Colored" masonic lodge was also along
Water St.

The name Branch Alley comes from the Town
Branch Creek, which once was above ground and flowed
directly behind the neighborhood, between Vine and Water St. It's a part of the South Elkhorn Creek that is all underground through downtown Lexington but surfaces on
Manchester Street and flows through Scott County. The
city's origins are near the intersection of Mill Street and
Main, near the Town Branch when a group of settlers
chose to settle here in 1775.[5] The branch was a steady

---

4. Two Water Streets. (1952, January 13). *Lexington Herald-Leader*, p. 51.

5. Ranck, G. W. (1872). Chapter 6 – Settlement of Lexington. In *History
of Lexington, Kentucky: Its early annals and recent progress* (p. 24). essay,
Clarke.

source of water for these Europeans who named their settlement "Lexington," after the battle of Lexington and Concord in Massachusetts, that took place the same year.[6]

By the time Lexington was a little over one hundred years old, this ever growing city needed a central location for a train depot due to the increase in businessmen and visitors to the city. The booming horse racing industry brought travelers from around the country to the bluegrass. After much deliberation that began in the 1880's, a site was chosen. The Railroad companies had their sites on a specific location and needed the assistance of city officials to obtain it.

> "The fact that the Louisville Southern is coming into this city over the K.C. Road from where it enters the city, makes just that much stronger the tendency to a union depot somewhere between Vine and Water Streets. This can probably be easy if steps are taken to that end. The managers of the K.U. Road should see that their plans are made with a view to this. When that is secured, the C.S road will probably come into the arrangement...."[7]

Main Street, to the immediate west of the viaduct that connected Main to High Street, and over the town branch, was to be the location. The Union Station would open up for business in 1907. Union Station became literally the backyard of those whose residences were in

---

6. Ranck, G. W. (1872). Chapter 4 - Discovery and Naming of Lexington. In *History of Lexington, Kentucky: Its early annals and recent progress* (p. 19). essay, Clarke.

7. Can't We have A Union Depot? (1889, February 12). *The Kentucky Leader*, p. 4.

Branch Alley. Overtime, more tracks were laid and encroached on the neighborhood more and more to the dissatisfaction of the residents and property owners.

With the abundance of travelers coming through Lexington via the depot, they were exposed to this eyesore of a community in the heart of downtown and the everyday violence and murders that would take place just a literal stones throw away.

> "It is generally an ill wind that blows no one good and this shooting emphasizes more than ever that that disreputable outfit ought to be wiped out. Whats the use of advertising the beauty's and advantages of Lexington and then greet all comers arriving at the Union Station with the sights they see on the South Side of Branch Alley?"[8]

Health officials, city government officials and officials from the various railroad companies were all complicit in seeking a way to rid downtown of this community. By July 1914, there were raids conducted, vagrancy charges were handed out, locks were placed on the doors and orders to vacate were given. On the 23rd a total of 28 men and women were arrested. The houses were inspected and subsequently condemned after these conditions were described:

> "In the second house, garbage was piled in the yard. Water and slops had been cast out on the ground which was covered with a filmy scum. The outhouse is about six feet from the

---

8. One Killed and Two Injured in a Shooting. (1914, July 23). *The Lexington Herald*, p. 4.

door of the house. The outhouse is broken down and the floor is broken in , but is still in use."

"In another house the flooring was rotted out of a lean-to or kitchen in the rear of the house, and a pile of ashes and garbage was in the corner. The tenant said it was that way when she moved in."[9]

The property owners such as Joseph Dinelli, Annie Nottnagle, T. Granducci, and Sallie Adams were indicted on charges of "maintenance of a nuisance."[10] They were given notice to repair the homes and provide water and other necessities and according to the papers, these orders were ignored. Likely because the owners could not afford to do so. Over the next few months more homes were found to be unsanitary and the same charges were given.

Lawyers for the property owners placed the blame on the railroads and city officials for the conditions of the units. The argument was that the railroads intended to make the neighborhood unlivable in order to buy up the property at the lowest price. Lawyer George S. Shanklin argued:

"The railroad has worked its way an inch at a time across Water Street, over the Town Branch and now is at the very doors of these houses with its tracks completely shutting off egress. The city has stood idly by watching this encroachment. It is within the city's rights to permit the use of the streets by railroads, but it has no right to give a railroad such occupancy

9. Police Raid Cleans Branch Alley Houses. (1914, July 23). *Lexington Leader*, p. 1.

10. Ibid.

that the property along the street is entirely deprived of a thoroughfare."

"It is for this reason that the property in Branch Alley cannot be rented to white people and the papers are authority for the statement that as soon as colored people move back there they will be pulled."

"That is the kind of agitation that the railroad wants, in order to make it so unpleasant for the property owners that they can get this property for next to nothing......"[11]

The railroads in question were "Lexington and Eastern," "Louisville and Nashville," and "Chesapeake and Ohio." The mayor J.E. Cassidy stated that their only concern was to make the properties livable and they were not in bed with the railroad companies. However based on the history of southern cities and negro neighborhoods, I have no doubts that behind closed doors, they were indeed working together to get rid of this neighborhood. To their credit it was in very inhabitable conditions but you will see this same story in another chapter of this book with the University of Kentucky and Lexington's 40+ year attack on the black community of Adamstown.

Ultimately, the Chesapeake and Ohio railroad company got what they wanted. Shortly after 1914, they gradually began buying up the property in Branch Alley and removing the shacks. By the 1920's the shacks on Branch Alley were completely gone. Today, you will find in its old location the Lextran Bus Terminal, the Kentucky Utilities company, and the Rose Tower Apartments.

---

11. Commissioners Hear Branch Alley Protest Aired. (1914, July 27). *Lexington Leader*, p. 1.

"The company[C&O] has for sometime been gradually acquiring this property – not that it had to have it for any especial purpose, but the old frame shacks which for years have lined Branch Alley, have long been regarded as a nuisance and an eyesore, located as they were across from the Union Station, and the company officials figured that if this property could be acquired and the buildings removed, the ground could be devoted to a better purpose."[12]

After the demolition of the shacks and this district was no longer a concern of the city and railroad, what happened to the Town Branch? The stream that early settlers began building the town around? The stream that "rolls slimily and turgidly through that delectable neighborhood" and "was a stream of almost living filth?"[13] The stream that became the dumping ground for sewage and other waste that is extracted out of business and residential necessity? The rains created flooding problems that brought this sewage to the doorsteps of it's citizens and the reminder of Lexington's 1833 cholera epidemic that killed 502, was ever present on this growing city that was missing an adequate sewage system. So, they did the best thing they could do at the time, enclose the stream underground in a brick tunnel. This took place around 1934.[14] This stream continues to flow underneath Vine

12. C. & O. To Clean Up Around Station. (1918, February 20). *Lexington Leader*, p. 7.

13. The City's Shame: The Town Branch a Mass of Corruption and Filth. (1888, October 13). *The Kentucky Leader*, p. 2.

14. Soper, K. (2015, August 24). *Town Branch is the famous creek that*

Street as I type this. There are plans to resurface the Town Branch in the near future.

Illustration 3: Workers at Town Branch underneath the city. (Lexington Herald-Leader April 12, 1935)

Asbury M.E Church

The Asbury Methodist Church, a black congregation organized and has it's beginnings in Branch Alley. In the location of the Lextran Bus terminal today, near the intersection of Beck Alley and Vine St., sat the Asbury M.E. of yesterday. At this time it was called the "Old Branch Church." This church's origins are said to go back to 1830 when it was known as the "Colored Charge," and they were holding their meetings in various rented buildings.[15] In the 1850's, the Old Branch Church, was built by

runs underneath downtown Lexington Ky. ExploreLexingtonKY.com. Retrieved October 22, 2022, from https://www.explorelexingtonky.com/blog/town-branch-is-the-famous-creek-that-runs-underneath-downtown-lexington-ky/

15. Smith, G. L., McDaniel, K. C., Hardin, J. A., & McDaniel, K. R.

Rev. George Downing and several others such as Rev. Henry Hopkins Lytle, George Perry and others.

Illustration 4: Old Branch Church 1850

(2015). Lytle, Henry Hopkins. In *The Kentucky African American encyclopedia* (p. 342). University Press of Kentucky.

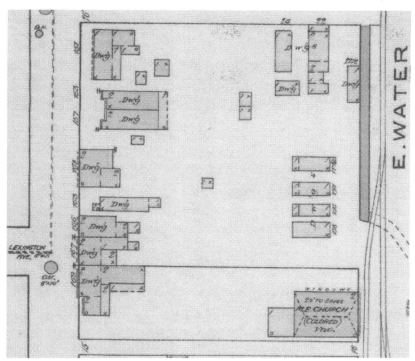

Illustration 5: The 1886 Sanborn Fire Insurance map. It shows a portion of Water Street, Branch Alley and at the bottom right sits the M.E. Church. At the bottom of this map is Beck Alley, the top is Ayres Alley(now the MLK bridge that connects Main to High Street.

(1886) *Sanborn Fire Insurance Map from Lexington, Fayette County, Kentucky.* Sanborn Map Company, May. [Map] Retrieved from the Library of Congress, https://www.loc.gov/item/sanborn03200_001/.

The original church building was on a lot that had an old carpenters shop. The church committee purchased this lot and the shop for $500. The carpenters shop was converted into a temporary place to hold service until their permanent church house that was being built was completed. And this lasted for 5 years, the "Old Branch

Church was completed in 1854.[16]

By 1886, The Old Branch aka Asbury, purchased a new lot on the Northeast corner of Mill and High Street. The old church around the block was then purchased by the railroad company and used as a storehouse.

Rev. Downing is credited with establishing another church due to the crowding of the growing Old Branch Church. In 1875, the Gunntown Mission was established.[17] Also called the Gunntown Tabernacle Methodist Church, this church opened in the Gunntown section of Lexington, just off of Deweese Street and a short walk from Branch Alley. Some congregants joined the new church while others stayed.

These two congregations who started out as one, would merge after 88 years in 1963. With this merger, a new name was chosen, Wesley Methodist Church, after the founder of the Methodist denomination.[18] They worshiped out of the Asbury location on High Street and the location on Deweese was to be sold.

The Rev. Downing was born in slavery in Virginia but was brought to Kentucky by his parents in his early childhood. At the time of this writing, I am unable to track down any information about his life outside of these church organizations or his death. According to one source, he is buried at the African Cemetery No. 2.[19]

---

16. Seals, W. T. (1955). History of Asbury. In *Asbury Methodist Church Anniversary Album 1830-1955* (p. 12). essay, Asbury Methodist Church.

17. Historic Churches End 88 Year Separation. (1963, June 9). *Lexington Herald-Leader*, p. 18.

18. Ibid., p. 18

19. Reid, D. I. (1935, May 25). Colored Notes. *The Lexington Herald*, p. 14.

Illustration 6: Asbury M.E. Church, High and Mill Street

Illustration 7: Gunn Tabernacle on Deweese Street (Lexington Herald-Leader June 9, 1963)

Robert Charles O'Hara Benjamin

In this section, I would like to reproduce a text that I published in April 2020 about a man I feel is one of the great black men of the 1800's. The reason its being reproduced here is because his place of death was on the corner of Water and Spring Streets, making it relevant to this chapter, this neighborhood.

His accomplishments, travels, and voice is one that should be among those spoken of in the black history discussions, when we speak of Dr. King, Brother Malcolm X, the Honorable Marcus Garvey, Martin Delaney and so many others. He's right there with them when it comes to his fight for his race of people. With that said, the succeeding paragraphs are the said reproduction, but with additional information added.

Robert Charles O'Hara Benjamin, better known as "R.C.O." was born on the island of St. Kitts, March 31, 1855. He was a prominent figure in the black liberation fight of his time. As a writer and journalist, his editorials were fierce and very critical of the white power structure. Not only that, but very critical of black folks who wanted to emulate white people and not support other black folks. A giant of a man based on his body of work and the multitude of hats he wore. In his life, he is credited with several black firsts that will be covered in this chapter. A Lawyer, an author, a journalist, a poet, a teacher and newspaper owner, as well as an outspoken freedom fighter, the "hat" that eventually cost him his life in 1900.

Little is known of Benjamin's early life on the islands, but it is said he traveled to England and studied at several schools while he was there. Those schools being

Oxford University and Trinity College.[20] After leaving Oxford, he traveled the East Indies for two years but upon his return to England, he was soon off across the Atlantic to the States. New York City was his destination. He arrived April 13, 1869, but left days later on a ship, upon which he worked as a Cabin Boy. The ship sailed to Venezuela, Guyana and to the West Indies. He returned to New York in the fall of that year.[21]

While in New York, he met Henry Highland Garnet, who was a black abolitionist that had escaped from slavery during his childhood. It's believed that Garnet helped him get a job as a salesman of the New York Star newspaper. It wasn't long before he would move beyond sales and became a reporter and editor of a New York based, African American newspaper called the "Progressive American." In 1876, Benjamin hit the campaign trail for Republican presidential candidate Rutherford B. Hayes, who went on to win that election. Due to his work on the campaign trail, he was awarded a position at the New York City Post Office. A position he didn't remain in very long because he left and landed in the state of Kentucky. Once in the bluegrass state, he taught school for a while in a small town called Hodgenville. It was here where Benjamin began studying law. It is said that he befriended a local white lawyer named David Smith, who began teaching him law.[22] With law, he discovered

---

20. Smith, G. L., McDaniel, K. C., Hardin, J. A., & Farrington, F.D. (2015). Benjamin, Robert Charles O'Hara. In *The Kentucky African American encyclopedia* (p. 40). University Press of Kentucky.

21. Thompson, Rico (2020). Chapter 2 - R.C.O. Benjamin. In *Sankofa Lexington* (p. 14). Afrakan World Books n Moor.

22. Simmons, W. J. (1887). R. C. O. Benjamin, Esq. . In *Men of Mark; Eminent, Progressive and Rising* (p. 992).

his passion and would study vigorously after school hours.

Next, he would accept a position as a principal in a Decatur, Alabama high school but remained studying law. From Alabama on to Brinkley, Arkansas where he would teach some more. According to sources, he was forced to flee from Brinkley, Arkansas due to some of his fierce editorials he wrote in local papers, that were critical of whites and the racist southern laws.[23]

This well traveled gentleman would next appear in Memphis, TN. At this pit stop, Benjamin would be admitted to the Tennessee bar, officially becoming a lawyer. This in January 1880.[24] When we say it was a pit stop, that's what we mean because by 1882, he had a law practice in Evansville, Indiana[25]

Continuing his nationwide law practice, 1883 finds "The man of a thousand titles," practicing law in Staunton, VA., becoming the first black man to do so in the state,[26] and in Pittsburgh, PA.[27]

Local papers make a brief mention of Benjamin opening up his law practice here in Lexington in 1885.[28]

23. Thompson, Rico (2020). Chapter 2 - R. C. O. Benjamin. In *Sankofa Lexington* (p. 15). Afrakan World Books n Moor.

24. Simmons, W. J. (1887). R. C. O. Benjamin, Esq. . In *Men of Mark; Eminent, Progressive and Rising* (p. 993).

25. An Evansville Colored Orator. (1882, July 15). *Evansville Courier and Press*, p. 2.

26. Colored Lawyer in Staunton. (1883, July 24). *Staunton Spectator* , p. 3.

27. The Coastline Railroad. (1883, January 11). *The Wilmington Morning Star*, p. 1.

28. Lewis, G. A. (1885, December 19). Local and Societal News. *The Frankfort Roundabout*, p. 1.

However, he did not remain here permanently at this time, because in 1888, he became the first black lawyer in the state of California, when he was admitted to the bar in the city of Los Angeles.[29]

One final "first" within his legal career that we would like to introduce to the readers would be that he along with black men Henry Clay Smith and John Henry Ballou, created the first black law firm in the state of Alabama in 1891.[30] There were a total of 12 states in which he practiced law with Rhode Island(1894), Texas(?) and Kentucky (1897-1900) being three additional states not previously mentioned.

While in Birmingham, he was even involved with the creation of an all black school. In 1887, the Robert Brown Elliott School of Technology was incorporated. The listed members were: A.L. Scott, Samuel Roebuck, W.R. Pettiford, Geo. Turner, J.H. Thompson, Sandy Goodloe, D.A. Williams, A.T. Walker, J.T. Jones and Mr. R.C.O. Benjamin himself. This school was said to be the first of it's kind in the country.[31]

Prior to returning to Alabama in 1891, Benjamin spearheaded an organization that attempted to purchase land in California and relocate up to 40,000 southern black people to the west coast. He was the president of the California Colored Colonization Society. This land was to be purchased in the counties of Fresno and Shasta.

---

29. Personal and Literary. (1888, February 17). *The Wichita Daily Beacon*, p. 3.

30. Smith, J. C. (1993). Chapter 5 - The Southern States. In *Emancipation: The Making of the Black lawyer, 1844-1944* (p. 272). University of Pennsylvania Press.

31. News Nuggets. (1887, April 2). *Western Appeal* , p. 1.

They were to supply each family with a small tract of land, where they could make a home and a life away from the southern hostilities that they were subjected to.

In an interview conducted, Benjamin explained his intentions as such:

> "Our object in bringing negroes to California is to supplant the Chinese. The celestial are not citizens, or voters and the colored people are both. We have already signed contracts in our possession, which will guarantee employment to all the people we bring here. We have secured 50,000 acres of excellent land situated in Fresno and Shasta Counties, all of it may be irrigated. This will provide homes for an immense number of colonists."[32]

However, this did not go over well with California's white population, who stated that they already had enough Chinese in the state and did not want more Negros, especially southern field hands who are barely literate.[33][34] On the following page, we present an article found in an Oakland newspaper that called the project "nonsense," while going on a racist tirade about why the Negro is not wanted in California.

---

32. Negros For California: A Project For Wholesale Colonization of Southern Colored People. (1891, August 19). *The Wilmington Messenger*, p. 4.

33. Minor Mentions. (1891, August 27). *The Wilmington Morning Star*, p. 2.

34. Colored Men For California. (1891, August 13). *The Philadelphia Inquirer*, p. 4.

NEGROES FOR CALIFORNIA.

An Oakland Paper Says the Colonization Scheme Is Nonsense.

In discussing the New York Herald's article advocating the colonization of negroes in California, printed in THE TIMES yesterday, the Oakland Times says:

"The New York Herald's assertion that 50,000 negroes can find work immediately in California shows how much farther and how much faster silly notions can travel than common sense. It shows, too, the evil done by thoughtless newspaper proprietors who open their columns to irresponsible men having in view no good purpose. Had there been no notice taken of the wild vagaries of one R. C. O. Benjamin by the press of California, there would have been no proposition to flood California with colored paupers broached in so high a place as the generally reliable columns of the Herald. California has no need for 50,000 negro laborers—nor for fifty. It is a fact that California cannot furnish steady employment to all the white laborers now here. There are thousands of idle men and boys in San Francisco and in the other large cities of the State. What California needs is capital to develop her natural resources, that employment may be given to the laborers already here. It is true that the State is growing and prospering—but there is always room for more growth and greater prosperity. And California has had her lesson in cheap labor by a servile race. She has been, for a few years past, getting rid of the Chinese, and as fast as they have gone their places have been taken by white men. There has been some negro immigration, but it has been only the national proportion. The negroes here are of the class common in the Northern States, educated and self-sustaining. In past years one or two attempts have been made to flood the State with colonies of ignorant field-hands, but these attempts have been abortive. The conditions here are not favorable to the Southern negro. The Californian persists in looking upon the negro as a man who has to earn his own living, not as a child who is to be humored and cared for. The negro cannot thrive under these conditions, for as a race he is dependent. He has not the remotest idea of the meaning of the word "rustle." The man who cannot "rustle" in California is apt to starve, despite the glorious richness of the State and its abundant yield of everything needed to supply the wants of humanity."

Simultaneously, while practicing law in the various states, Benjamin also owned and edited several newspapers. You can be sure that at every city we have mentioned him relocating to, he either edited papers in those cities or owned them outright. It was mentioned earlier in this text that he started his career working for newspapers upon arrival in America. He is believed to be the first black man to become editor of a white newspaper, The Daily Sun, in Los Angeles, CA, around 1888. Some of the newspapers around the country Benjamin edited or owned were: The Chronicle in Evansville, Indiana, The Colored Citizen in Pittsburgh, PA, The Los Angeles Observer, The San Francisco Sentinel, Free Lance in Nashville, TN, under the pen name "Cicero," the Negro American in Birmingham, AL, the Washington Bee and lastly the Lexington Standard in 1897.[35] The latter being considered the leading negro paper in the south.[36]

Cicero's writing style was brash, fearless, and brutally honest, very critical of the country's white power structure, but also critical of his own race when necessary. Benjamin believed that the problems of the negro race should be solved by the negro race. Taglines printed in the Lexington Standard included "Men, Not Party; Principle Not Party Name," "Fearless, Independent, and Honest," and also "The Standard publishes what it pleases...."

His critiques of the injustices and mistreatment of blacks in the south often forced him to flee the city he

---

35. Thompson, Rico (2020). Chapter 2 - R. C. O. Benjamin. In *Sankofa Lexington* (p. 15). Afrakan World Books n Moor.

36. On Behalf of Editor C.C. Moore. (1899, February 18). *The Morning Herald*, p. 3.

was in at the time. Most notably, Brinkley, AR in 1879 and Birmingham, AL in 1887.[37] That could possibly explain why he moved around as much as he did, but this we can not be certain of. Many of his editorials called for blacks to arm themselves and defend themselves against racial violence.

While he was writing for the Washington Bee in 1887, Benjamin was very critical of the coverage of the murder of black men by whites in Galveston, TX. He stated, "Knowing how white papers distort the dispatches, and suppress the news that will bring the crimes before the eyes of the public..." but given the fact that he was there at the time of the incident, he also explained what really occurred and how the white media attempted to justify the incident.[38] Furthermore in 1898, while writing for the Lexington Standard, Benjamin's column about William Littlefield, a black man that killed three white officers in Mississippi, caused quite a stir and much controversy when he wrote:

> "If we had more Littlefields there would not be quite so many negroes arrested on suspicion. An eye for an eye, tooth for a tooth is our motto. Shoot and shoot, kill and kill, and fight and fight, curse and curse, damn and damn is the series of resolutions the negroes must adopt or be lynched, burned at the stake and be totally annihilated by the white man. Hurrah for William Littlefield."[39]

---

37. Thompson, Rico. (2020). Chapter 2 - R. C. O. Benjamin. In *Sankofa Lexington* (p. 15). Afrakan World Books n Moor.

38. Benjamin, R. C. O. (1887, October 8). Texas News: Negroes Shot Down in Cold Blood. A Correct Report of the Inhumane Butchery By One Who Visited The Scene. *The Washington Bee*, p. 1.

39. An Incendiary Paper: Much Comment in Lexington Over An Article

The Negro who thinks he is "actin' like de white fo'ks" and who refuses to patronize Negro establishments, is a fool. A white man patronizes his own race first. Who ever heard of a white woman talking about not allowing a white dressmaker to sew for her, or a white shopper refusing to buy at a white store, or a white teacher refusing to read a white newspaper? Nobody, and nobody ever will. White people have sense. They know blood is thicker than water, and so knowing, they act along this line. The Negro does not need to talk so much of race love; he needs to shut up and work, and subscribe for his race paper.—The American Guide,

* * * * *

Written By A Negro Editor. (1898, June 1). *The Courier-Journal*, p. 1.

Our brother Benjamin in his busy lifetime, also found the time to write several books. Starting with a book called "Poetic Gems," in 1883. In 1888, he wrote a biographic book about Haitian Revolutionary T'ouissaint L'Oventure called "Life of T'ouissaint L'Oventure: Warrior and Statesmen..." Next, he published a book called "Don't: A Book for Girls" in 1891. This book was basically an advice book for young black women of the day. The next one published was "The Negro Problem, A Method Of It's Solution," which was an address given at the AME Zion Church in Portland, OR, June 3rd 1891, published the same year. In 1893 The Zionist Methodist was published. After that we have Southern Outrages: A Statistical Record of Lawless Doings, in 1894. "Benjamin's Pocket History of The Negro" was published, also in 1894. And in 1896 he published "Light After Darkness: Being An Up to Date History of The American Negro." While in Lexington, he published a black business directory that listed all of the black businesses within the city. (1899)

Several other books are listed as being authored by Benjamin although I have not been able to locate the publishing year of the following works: The Boy Doctor, The Defender of Obadiah Cuff(those 2 were fiction,) History of The British West Indies, The Southland, Lectures on Africa, Hope of The Negro Life, Future of the American Negro and Historical Chart of the Colored Race.

The Murder of Benjamin

Within these pages, we have done our best to document and share this brothers life story as accurately as the records reflect. With that said, it's clear that brother

Benjamin was highly respected among our race, throughout the United States. Some of the newspapers referred to him as "the greatest colored orator," some boasted about his feats as a lawyer, a journalist, a school teacher, a poet, a historian, an author, a well sought after preacher and as an "extreme race man," dedicated entirely to the enrichment of the black race. His motto was "My race first and my best friends next."[40] A well traveled man who after witnessing the countless lynchings and atrocities committed upon his people across the country, created the "American Liberty Defence[sic] League in 1894. The purpose of the organization was:

> "1. To encourage and assist Miss Ida B. Wells in her anti-lynching crusade by seizing the opportunity while public attention is directed to the subject to keep someone in the field to agitate and emphasize our demand for justice.
> 2. To publish necessary literature to and statistics for distribution.
> 3. To keep detectives in the field to investigate every lynching, get the negro side of the stories, and the real facts for our English friends, our northern sympathizers, and for ourselves; to employ counsel to defend those charged with heinous offences[sic], and secure the conviction and punishment of those who participate in lynchings."[41]

Its such a tragedy that a man who accomplished so much, would lose his life, at a young age and in such a

---

40. Thompson, Rico (2020). Chapter 2 - R. C. O. Benjamin. In *Sankofa Lexington* (p. 15). Afrakan World Books n Moor.

41. The American Liberty Defence League. (1894, October 20). *The Washington Bee*, p. 2.

violent manner. Much like Malcolm X, Martin Luther
King, Medgar Evars, Nat Turner and countless others, he
died in the service of his people.

The day was October 2, and the year was 1900.
Benjamin took a group of black men to a precinct to register them to vote. The official questioned the registrants
and Benjamin felt it was unnecessary, creating a heated
dispute. Instead of me attempting to recreate the narrative in this text, its best to give the eyewitness accounts
that were documented. The following are the quotes directly from those who were there, Mr. Allen, a precinct
challenger, explains the confrontation that lead up to the
shooting:

> "R.C.O. Benjamin came in the morning
> and registered peaceably. In the afternoon, about
> 5 o'clock, he came back with three or four col-
> ored men, in whom he seemed interested in
> having registered. After presenting one of them
> to the window, they questioned him consider-
> ably, and during the conversation John Doyle
> questioned him at great length. Benjamin said
> that that was not necessary, as that was not the
> law. He showed that he was much interested in
> having the negro registered, and broke into the
> conversation several times, to which Mr. Mike
> Monyhan seemed to object. The first thing I
> knew is Mr. Monyhan drew his pistol and made
> a break at Benjamin and hit him over the head
> two or three times. Mr. Benjamin showed no re-
> sistance.
>
> John Doyle went out to tell Mike Mony-
> han to stop, and succeeded in getting him away
> from Benjamin two or three times but he would
> always break back and hit him, Benjamin, show-
> ing no resentment and making no resistance fur-
> ther than holding up his hands to ward off the

blows. I went out, took hold of Benjamin, lead him away up Spring Street towards Main, and told him to go on home. At that time Benjamin had a pistol in his hand. I told him to give up the pistol and go on home. He refused to give me the pistol, but said he would go on home. He said "I want my pistol but I am going home."[42]

John Doyle, the same man who was questioning the black men, stated that the fight occurred around 5 or 6 pm, and that later between 7 and 8pm, he heard shots, saw Benjamin run by and turn down the railroad where he was shot in the back.[43] Benjamin's body lay cold and lifeless behind Speyer's junkyard along the railroad. Today, this would be in the vicinity of Triangle Park(then Water and Spring Street.)

SHOT IN THE BACK.

At 8 o'clock a Herald reporter called at Ross & Williams', the undertakers where Benjamin's body was taken after he had been shot. There were two bullet holes in the body, the fatal one entering just below the left shoulder blade from behind. This bullet penetrated the left lobe of the lung and broke the breast bone, from which it protruded in a lump, without breaking the skin. Another bullet, evidently of the same caliber, entered the right arm from in front. The right eye was bruised from the blow which Monyhan is alleged to have struck Benjamin in the afternoon. When the clothing was first removed blood trickled from the wound in the back

42. Benjamin Killed. (1900, October 3). *The Morning Herald*, p. 7.

43. Ibid

Stories conflict but at some point, the two men were face to face yet again and had an argument. Witnesses state that they heard men shouting and then shots go off but didn't actually witness the shooting.

Moynahan claimed self defense, but Benjamin was shot in the back and his pistol was found in his right pocket.[44] He may have cursed the murderer but it's unlikely that he fired first or even brandished his weapon.

There was an an abundance of evidence to show that the murderer did not act in self defense, most notably, the gun in Benjamin's possession had not been fired in considerable time. Nonetheless, Moynahan was found not guilty.

Moynahan had a clear pattern of violence because just a year prior, he assaulted another black man viciously, who was attempting to vote. And then again, a month after his murder charge was dismissed. This time, he was charged with assaulting his cousin, who he was angry with for employing Negros.[45]

Illustration 10: L to R, Benjamin's father in law, Daughter Lillian Allen, Wife Lula, Son Robinson and R.C.O.

44. Ibid,. p. 7

45. In Trouble Again: Mike Moynahan Arrested in Charge of Assault and Battery. (1900, November 1). *The Daily Leader*, p. 1.

The photo on the previous page was taken just days before he was killed. And, it also shows that he had a family. He met his wife, Lula Robinson while in Alabama. His son, 3 at the time, was born in Xenia, Ohio and daughter Lillian Allen was born in Lexington. She was several months old. Lula took over the Lexington Standard newspaper for a while but in July 1901, she sold it to Wade Carter, due to health concerns. After which, she left Lexington and went back to Alabama.[46] She passed away months later in Birmingham.

Robert Charles O'Hara Benjamin was buried at the African Cemetery No. 2 on Seventh Street. In 1910, a distinct marker was placed at his burial site and it is the marker that graces the cover of my first book.

Illustration 11: Benjamin's marker, photo by me 2020

---

46. Standard Changes Hands. (1901, July 10). *The Morning Herald*, p. 6.

Laura "Dolly" Johnson

Laura "Dolly" Johnson, was a cook from Lexington who gained national fame as the Head Chef for then President Benjamin Harrison, that began in 1889. After her tenure at the White House, she returned to Lexington and opened up restaurants in various locations throughout downtown. One of them was located on Water Street, which is the reason her story is placed in this chapter.

There are varying accounts as to her place of birth. Some suggesting Lexington, her death record states she was born in Scott County, and other sources say she was born in Louisville.[47] Her death certificate also suggests that her parents were William Johnson and Emily Miller. At her time of death, she was approximately 65 years old, placing her year of birth around 1853. Of course slavery officially ended in 1865, so she was around 12 at that time. Whether she was born free or enslaved is unknown.

The year 1889 saw Dolly accepting a position as head chef at the White House under the Benjamin Harrison Administration. Sources vary as to how she got the attention of the President but nonetheless, we know that she did. After Harrison's tenure, she worked for Grover Cleveland as his chef, but stayed briefly.[48]

The Courier Journal, out of Louisville, KY, states that she was the cook for William Henry Harrison and that she left after three months because in her words, "I couldn't stand it....they were stingy and I cant cook for

47. Smith, G. L., McDaniel, K. C., Hardin, J. A., & Powell, S.L. (2015). Johnson, Laura "Dolly". In *The Kentucky African American Encyclopedia* (p. 281). University Press of Kentucky.

48. Ibid,. p. 281

anybody like that."[49] This is a mix up because William Henry Harrison was the president in 1841, before she was born. It's likely that they confused him for Grover Cleveland, because we know she left the White House after a very short stay during his presidency. The Harrison name may have been the confusing part.

At any rate, upon her return to Lexington, she opened up restaurants in several locations. In 1900, her restaurant, "The Maryland Restaurant," was at 69 Water Street, at the west end of the section of Water known as Branch Alley. That's in the proximity of the Jeff Ruby Steakhouse in the new City Center. In 1906, she was located on South Broadway and then in 1910, "Kentucky's Premier Colored Cook," operated her restaurant "The White House," on North Broadway, across from the Opera House.[50]

Downtown's Central Hotel became her next stop in 1911, when she closed her restaurant and became head chef there. Then almost yearly, she moved to another location and opened her restaurant. Those being 203 South Upper Street, 152 South Limestone and 314 North Upper Street.

Regardless to which location, her dishes were highly sought out. Prominent businessmen and politicians always made it a point to visit her location while in town. She would also do catering for a number of esteemed citizens of Lexington.

Dolly was married to another chef by the name of Ed Dandridge, who was a former horse trainer. Both

---

49. Gratz Park; Rosa Gave The Park Color and Dash. (1955, September 11). *The Courier Journal*, p. 124.

50. Amusements. (1910, February 10). *Lexington Leader*, p. 3.

passed away in the year 1918 and both are buried at the African Cemetery No. 2.

Illustration 12: Dolly Johnson around 1891 in the White House Kitchen

Dennis Seales & Daniel Seales, Sr

"Negroes in the early days just after the war owned valuable city property in the downtown district of Lexington," reads a 1920 newspaper article. It further states "They owned such property as the following: The southwest corner of Main and Limestone, the northeast corner of Market and Short, a stretch of property from the corner of Mill and Short, west towards Broadway and considerable property on Vine Street."[51] Some of that Vine Street property was owned by Dennis Seales, the father of Daniel Seales Sr. The elder Seales, a black man,

51. Negroes Growing With Lexington: Owned Valuable Property. (1920, December 26). *The Lexington Herald*, p. 34.

born free in Kentucky around 1784, owned a stable on Vine Street, in the vicinity of Branch Alley, where he housed the horses he sold. He was also a jockey.[52] His home in an 1859 city directory was on the north side of High Street, in between Mulberry(Limestone) and Upper Street. Vine Street is a street over from High Street so it's likely that his stable was directly behind his home. Dennis Seales passed away in March of 1863 at the age of 78. His obituary stated he died a wealthy man and was well respected among whites and blacks.[53]

Daniel Seales, the son of Dennis was born in 1821 in Lexington. He left the city in 1840 to attend college at Oberlin College in Ohio, returning to Lexington a few years later and opening a school. The school however was short-lived as it closed in 1849. It is likely that his brother Enoch Seales, was a teacher here. A Memphis newspaper suggests that he was teaching school in Lexington at some point but no specific date was given:

> "Far back, as thirty years ago, colored people were being educated in the state of Kentucky. Enoch Seals taught them in Lexington and William Gibson taught them in Louisville, while Berea College stood with open doors to receive them."[54]

Shortly after the schools closing, Seales left for

---

52. Daniel Seales: An Old Time Kentucky Negro, Here on a Pilgrimage. (1898, May 24). *The Daily Leader*, p. 7.

53. Dennis Seales. (1863, March 10). *Chicago Tribune*, p. 2.

54. The Colored Schools Again. (1887, September 25). *The Memphis Daily Avalanche*, p. 2.

California amid the gold rush of the day. It was in California where he made a name for himself and amassed quite a fortune. He is one of San Francisco's early pioneers, buying and selling significant property therein. He stayed in California until about 1868 when he headed East. In his own words on how he became known nationwide as "the Black King of Finance:"

> "I quit working for anybody after I put in three years at the Custom-House, and I ought to have quit before. That's what I should advise all young men to do. I built several buildings on various properties and accumulated money fast."
>
> "In 1868, times got bad here and I sold some of my property and went east. I bought real estate in Chicago, Cleveland, Lexington, East St. Louis, Indianapolis and other places, making it a business. In Chicago, I bought the southeast corner of La Salle and Monroe Streets, and at different times a good deal more in other places besides the west side, where I still own considerable......I have felt that real estate in the right cities was always a good thing, and this is why I have stuck to it."[55]

Seales, describes how he was able to get to California, borrowing the funds from his father Dennis. Upon arrival he also explains what he did to cut expenses, which enabled him to save his money and begin purchasing property:

> "I arrived here first on the ship Panama

---

55. Black King of Finance, Arrival of Daniel Seales, Who Owns Property in Many Cities. (1895, December 6). *The San Francisco Call*, p. 5.

on January 2, 1852, and immediately got a job at $120 a month in the warehouse department of the Custom-House. My father, who, fortunately, was never a slave, was an owner of horses at Lexington, Ky. I had no money, but, as I had the California fever, I borrowed $700 of him and got off. Transportation, you know, was then very high."

"I had $100 left when I arrived, and I immediately sent that back. In six months I had made the other $600, and I sent that on too and paid the whole thing up in full."

Seales and two white men rented three rooms and he took the attic at $25 a month. In order to avoid this expense, he states he would make up the beds of the two white men and sweep their rooms. He would also do his own cooking to cut down on the expense of food as well as buy bottles of maple syrup to mix with water to make drinks. Then he began buying property:

"I bought at Dupont and Green Streets, then on the southeast corner of Union and Kearny; at Calhoun and Union, at Union and Dupont, on Valparaiso Street; where the Unitarian Church now is, and also where the Fourth Congregational was. I also bought other property as I could and paid for it out of my rents."

This brilliant strategy worked because in 1884, he had $200,000 worth of real estate and $40,000 in his bank account.[56] Combined, that would be over $7 million dollars today.

---

56. Wealthy Colored People. (1884, September 4). *Daily Nevada State Journal*, p. 1.

COLONEL DANIEL SEALES.
[*Sketched by a "Call" artist.*]

Illustration 13: A 1895 sketch of Daniel Seales, Sr.

Black King of Finance, Arrival of Daniel Seales, Who Owns Property in Many Cities. (1895, December 6). *The San Francisco Call*, p. 5.

Despite his wealth and rubbing shoulders among Americas wealthiest citizens, white and black, Seales would often be denied service at various places solely because of his race. He would respond by filing lawsuits for discrimination and winning.

Daniel Seales and his family permanently settled in Cleveland, Ohio. He had four children, one of which Daniel Jr, graduated from Yale.

Senior passed away in 1905.[57]

---

57. "Seales, Daniel, Sr.," Notable Kentucky African Americans Database, accessed January 1, 2023, https://nkaa.uky.edu/nkaa/items/show/2516.

Urban Communities North

"There is no agony like bearing an untold story inside you."

- Zora Neale Hurston

Chapter 9 – Brucetown

One of the best sources of information regarding the past would be the newspaper. The newspaper reported on what was occurring in a community at that particular time.   It's a way to time travel so to speak, or we can even say it's a form of time capsule.   It helps you to understand the circumstances that your direct ancestors may have had to face and in some cases can even give you clues as to why you were raised the way you were. Because for the most part, our fore-parents did their best with us, but had a limited means of doing so. Some were illiterate and had limited skills due to being the offspring of the enslaved class. These papers just help further illustrate what was going on with them in their day. It can give us small clues to the achievements and brilliance of many of our progenitors as well. Some things were even reported across the nation and in other countries, in small blurbs such as this 1876 story of one young African American girl, who was not named, that had the amazing ability of recall. This young girl lived in the Brucetown community. The following quote is directly from a newspaper in Scotland:

> "A Kentucky newspaper, the Lexington Gazette, says there is a negro girl in Brucetown, about nine years of age, whose memory is truly marvelous. Her wonderful powers were first brought to the notice of a white man who keeps a grocery in that part of the city about two weeks ago. He had been reading aloud in her presence the day before and accidentally heard her repeat, word for word, what he had read from the paper, though twenty-four hours had intervened. After this he tested her memory frequently, and has found her capable of repeating thirty or forty lines from a book after hearing it read once over."[1]

Unfortunately, no name was ever attached to this individual, likely due to her race. The way that this was reported is almost as if the negro is not supposed to have any intellect whatsoever, and, when he or she does, it's an anomaly and something to marvel at. With that said, the newspapers, although great sources of information from the past, were not without their own racial biases and quite often misinformation. A black Pralltown resident once made the remark in 1894:

---

1. Girl With a Remarkable Memory. (1874, April 21). *North British Daily Mail*, p. 2.

Chapter 9 – Brucetown

> "It is strange that when the newspapers write up anything about negroes they try to make them appear to the public as thieves, liars, and cowards."[2]

This was in reference to an incident that occurred with a wild animal on the loose in Pralltown. The newspapers reported that the negroes in that vicinity were afraid and this citizen responded to that article stating that it was in fact, white people in the area who were the ones afraid.

Now in regards to misinformation, there is a story of a lynching that reportedly occurred in or near Brucetown and was reported in newspapers throughout the country. I have information that the location may have been elsewhere but before we get to that, let's introduce you to this community called Brucetown. The section titled "Mob Violence," will continue this story.

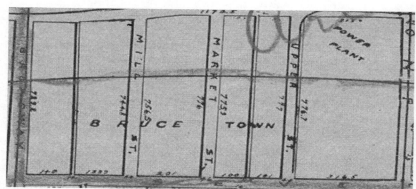

Illustration 1: 1912 map of Brucetown. On the map you see Market Street, which today is Florida Street and you also see Mill, which is Dakota. Far left is North Broadway, far right would be Limestone. And the bottom is Seventh Street and lastly you have what is Idaho ave at the top.

2. A Pralltown Negro: Protests that the "What is it" Did Not Terrify His Race. (1894, July 12). *The Kentucky Leader*, p. 8.

Located in North Lexington, between Seventh St. and a railroad, is the neighborhood called Brucetown. The streets that make up the neighborhood are Florida, Dakota, Idaho, N. Upper and Jenkins Alley. See the map on the previous page for the former street names. This bottom land tract was owned by W.W. Bruce. Bruce was the son in law of millionaire and local merchant John Wesley Hunt. Bruce owned and operated a Hemp factory that stood on Seventh St. and North Limestone.

In 1865 following emancipation, Bruce began selling homes on 183 lots, that he had built for his newly freed slaves and other poor citizens who were looking for affordable rents. These former slaves were employed at his factory. In the 1850 census, he is listed as owning thirty four persons, ranging from the age of fifty all the way down to two. One of these thirty-four was a young girl named Catherine about 13-15, that he purchased from Henry Clay.[3] The 1850 Census or Slave Schedule, did not list the names of those held in bondage, only their ages and gender.

Prior to the shotgun homes being built, the area was just a low lying field that was likely not meant for habitation. Shotgun styled homes, of course, were the dominant structure type in all of these poor urban communities. In an effort to keep employees nearby, Bruce had these homes built on the field anyway, not only profiting from their labor but from their need for housing too. By the year 1880, Bruce's Addition, as it was originally called, had 562 residents, 513 of them were

---

3. Curious Agreement for Slave Purchase: Executors of Henry Clay Sell Negro to W.W. Bruce of Lexington. (1906, June 3). *The Lexington Herald*, p. 7.

black.[4]

The community was prone to flooding and often had drainage problems that left a terrible stench permeating the air within the community. There was a sewage vault on Seventh and Limestone that drained into a nearby pond, albeit drained poorly. This, the city made a few attempts to remedy but was very problematic. Citizens complained that their water may soon become polluted, and that they would file suit against city officials if this is not taken care of.[5] The neighborhood suffered major floods a multitude of times over the years, April 1, 1908, being one the worst.

> "That whole section of lowland in the vicinity of Eddy and Seventh Streets presented the appearance Wednesday morning of a huge lake, several feet deep,"[6]

These problems existed for several decades before proper drainage and a sewer system was installed in the area.

Many of the residents, as noted above, worked in the nearby hemp factory but the majority were farm hands. The women were typically relegated to domestic servant roles, cooks and washerwomen.

---

4. Thomas, H. A. (1973). Victims of Circumstance: Negroes in a Southern Town, 1865-1880. *The Register of the Kentucky Historical Society, 71*(3), 258

5. Unsanitary Conditions. (1914, May 6). *Lexington Leader*, p. 1.

6. Heavy Rains Cause Flood. (1908, April 1). *Lexington Leader*, p. 1.

Church

The central community church was Evergreen Missionary Baptist Church. It's roots are with Pleasant Green Baptist Church. Evergreen Baptist began in 1865 with George Dancer. After baptizing numerous individuals into the fellowship of Pleasant Green, Dancer became head of a mission that took on the moniker Evergreen Baptist Mission. By 1869, it grew and became an established church but with no official building until around 1872. That year a lot on Market St was purchased from William W. Bruce and the first church house was built.[7] The congregation would encounter many growing pains, various pastors would come and go over the years. A few years, the church had no pastor at all. Today, the church is located at 749 Florida Street in Brucetown.

Roxy Turner also had a sect of her Power Society holding their service in the community. More on Mrs. Turner in the Goodloetown chapter.

Mob Violence

The story of the lynching that was alluded to previously was said to have occurred in Brucetown. We will give you the account of what occurred, followed by the conflicting reports in the newspapers. There is no conflict of the details of the event however, only the location is questioned.

In 1878, an event that reportedly occurred in Brucetown made national headlines. On January 15,

---

7. Church, E. (n.d.). *Evergreen Missionary Baptist Church History.* Evergreen Missionary Baptist Church. https://www.embchurch.com/content.cfm?id=306.

three black men, suspected of involvement in the murder of a white man, were killed. Two weeks prior, it is said that a black man named Stivers was the culprit. He was hung immediately. Not satisfied, that Wednesday evening, a white mob descended on Brucetown to the home of Tom Turner. Turner was ordered to leave the home and go with the mob but refused. The mob opened fire on Turner, striking him four times, in front of his wife. In a nearby field, two other black men were found hanging from a tree. They were Edward Claxton and John Davis.[8]

This was circulated by the New York Times and was sourced in a few books, however, the Courier Journal of Louisville, Kentucky states another location:

> "On arriving at Simpson's Woods, about eleven miles from Lexington, on the Tates Creek road, they found the dead bodies of Ed Claxton and John Davis, both colored, hanging from two trees about 13 yards apart."[9]

The article further states that Edward Claxton was of a medium build and approximately thirty years old and John Davis was about sixteen or seventeen. The other sources state that the man shot, Tom Turner, was shot in

---

8. Smith, G. L., McDaniel, K. C., Hardin, J. A., & Powell, S. (2015). Brucetown, African American community in Lexington, KY. In *The Kentucky African American Encyclopedia* (p. 72). University Press of Kentucky.

9. Hellish: High Handed Outrage Committed in Fayette County, About Eleven Miles From Lexington. Two Negroes Hanged to Trees and Another Shot to Death, One a Mere Youth. (1878, January 18). *The Courier-Journal*, p. 1.

his home in Brucetown, however, this same Courier-Journal article has this to say:

> "Going a mile farther on the Jacks Creek Road, the dead body of Tom Turner(colored) was found in a cabin on the farm of Mr. McIsaacs, where he and his wife lived, being employed by Mr. McIsaacs.[10]

Jacks Creek and Tates Creek Road are in the southern part of Fayette County, outside the city limits, while Brucetown is in North Lexington. Unsure how, the confusion came about, what we do know for sure is that four unfortunate black men lost their lives. Another article gave a more detailed account of what happened. The article suggests that the murdered white man's name was "Shootman," father being a man named Jacob Shootman. There was a warrant for the arrest of Claxton and Davis. They were apprehended by the authorities and housed in the East Hickman School, under the guard of several men. Around midnight, unknown masked men barged in to the schoolhouse and took Davis and Claxton, which resulted in them becoming some of the strange fruit Billie Holiday sung about.

Prior to this, the men made their way to the home of Tom Turner, broke the door down and demanded he put on a blindfold and go with them. He stated that if he was to be killed, then they must do it right there because he would not leave with them or be blindfolded. So with that, he was shot about four or five times and instantly killed.[11]

---

10. Ibid,. p. 1

11. The Kentucky Lynchings. (1878, January 19). *St, Louis Daily Globe-Democrat*, p. 5.

Another rumor suggested that a fifth man, a black preacher was also hung, but this rumor was never substantiated. Long live the four black men we are certain lost their lives.

Bess Coleman

In a bit more positive news, the first licensed black woman to practice Optometry in the United States, called Brucetown home in the 1930's. Bess Francis Coleman, originally of Harrodsburg, Ky, was born in August of 1893. Coleman would first become a school teacher in 1910. She taught at the same school she graduated from, the West Side Colored School. She would meet and marry Pharmacist John Coleman in the year 1923. John was also of Harrodsburg. The couple would leave for Chicago two years later. In Chicago, at an eye appointment with her husband, Bess believed that was something she could pursue. Her husband sent her to study at Northern Illinois College of Optometry. She graduated from the college on June 1, 1934 at 40 years of age. By May 1935, Bess Coleman returned to Kentucky. However, her husband would remain in Chicago, operating the pharmacy they owned. The couple would visit each other frequently but lived separately. Her practice was at her home which was located at 685 North Upper Street. Health complications would shorten her career and she retired early. By 1941, the family was residing in Denver Colorado. Bess Coleman passed away in 1967, she is buried at Maple Grove Cemetery in Harrodsburg, Ky.[12]

---

12. The Exemplary Life of Bess Coleman, O.D. *Hindsight: Journal of Optometry History*, *51*(2), 37–50. https://doi.org/10.14434/hindsight.v51i2.30279

Illustration 2: Bess Coleman

Daniel Isaiah Reid

Daniel Isaiah Reid, who at one time was a school principal and journalist, lived in the Brucetown community with his wife Cora. They had a home at 705 Dakota Street. Reid was born in Lexington in 1879 to parents Edward and Lizzie Reid. Reid would become principal of a school that only lasted a few years in 1907 until 1910. This was the Forest Hill School, more on that in a later chapter. Reid was also a journalist, penning editorials for the Lexington Herald Leader's Colored Notes section, one of the first black men to do so. He was involved in a lawsuit filed by W.D. Johnson, author of Biographical Sketches of Prominent Negro Men and Women of Kentucky, 1897 and owner of the Lexington Standard, the cities black newspaper. This lawsuit was in 1909. Reid was a member of the black democratic party while Johnson was a republican. The suit was also against Wade Carter. While editor of the Standard, the newspaper plant was being leased from Wade Carter and after the election of President William Taft, Johnson was assigned to an office in Washington D.C. During a visit to Lexington, he discovered that Carter had turned the plant over to Daniel Reid and that Reid was using the newspaper as a publication for the Democratic party. This would ultimately become the demise of the paper altogether. The suit prevented Reid from further publications of the paper and Johnson was unable to continue because the building was used for other things during this time and neither were permitted to continue publication. Reid did attempt to start the paper again in 1911 as a solely democrat paper but it failed. In 1912, Reid created another paper, the Lexington Weekly News but closed it a year later. One more paper was created by Reid that year, the Colored Citizen. Reid passed away in 1950 and was interred at Greenwood cemetery.[13]

African Cemetery No. 2

I could not write this book without including a section for one of my personal favorite historic places in the city of Lexington. Numerous people we have discussed in this book are buried here. It is the oldest of the two major black cemeteries in the city. Although not in the Brucetown community, it is a literal stones throw away, just to the East of Brucetown.

The problem I encountered when trying to find the proper placement for this section is its locale. It's kind of the North side being a 2 minute walk from Brucetown, but it's kind of the East Side as well, being a two minute walk from the former site of East End's Bluegrass As-

---

13 "Reid, Daniel Isaiah," Notable Kentucky African Americans Database, accessed September 25, 2022, https://nkaa.uky.edu/nkaa/items/show/2525.

pendale Housing Project. Let's just say, its both, North-East Lexington. For that reason, I was unsure, if I was to add it to this chapter or to that one. Obviously, I decided it's better for this chapter, so here we are.

In the Cadentown Chapter, I made mention of a lady I met in a cemetery named Yvonne Giles. It was in this cemetery where I met her and it was this encounter that sparked my quest to document as much of our history as I can. She is the inspiration for this book. In fact, my journey into genealogy, began almost the exact same way she stated that hers did. In short, I met her there when looking for my family. She inquired about my quest and a conversation began about history and the cemetery. Hers, in her own words, was as follows:

> "I returned to No. 2 Cemetery on a Sunday afternoon to take pictures of and record information of the few markers my mother had identified. While there, Thomas Mundy came into the site. He introduced himself as a volunteer board member of African Cemetery No. 2, the organization that was responsible for restoring and maintaining the cemetery. He asked what I was doing. I launched into telling him about my quest to find the burial locations of family members. He understood perfectly for he had taken the same journey."[14]

Thomas Mundy understood what she was doing, just as she understood perfectly, what I was doing.

---

14. Giles, Y. (2009). Introduction. In *Stilled Voices Yet Speak: A History of African American Cemeteries in Lexington and Fayette County, Kentucky: Volume 1, Benevolent Society No. 2 cemetery, Ladies Auxiliary Society Cemetery* (p. ix). Essay.

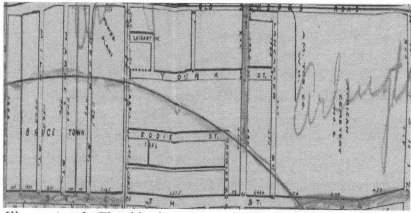

Illustration 3: The blank space at the far right of this map image is the African Cemetery. The far left is Brucetown. The space in between, which consists of Eddie Street and York Street, is in a section called Neale and Prall's Addition. The cemetery itself is a part of Neale and Pralls Addition. This image is to show the proximity.

In the year 1852 on October 20, a group of black men, all of whom were slaves, came together with the shared purpose of "caring for the sick, burying the dead and performing other acts of charity."[15] The organization organized under the name Union Benevolent Society No. 2. In November of 1869, they purchased four acres of land on what was then the outskirts of Lexington, for the purpose of creating a cemetery. This location is what today is Seventh Street. The group paid one thousand dollars to Michael and Rebecca O'Mara for the property, beginning with five hundred down. The remainder was paid by 1871. Four years later, another four acres of adjoining land was purchased for eight hundred. The Benevolent Society Cemetery No. 2 was established. Other names for the cemetery included: Seventh Street

---

15. Ibid., p. 2

Cemetery, Colored Cemetery No. 2, and African Cemetery No. 2, the latter becoming its name much later. On some death records, in the section for where the deceased was interred, sometimes you will just see "No. 2," indicating the burial took place in this cemetery.

Some of the original members of the group, recorded on the deed are Leonard Fish, Jordan C. Jackson, Lewis Page, Sam Breckinridge, and Henry King, among others.[16][17]

It is estimated that over five thousand burials took place at the cemetery but there are only about six hundred markers. About three hundred of these individuals were originally buried in the Old Presbyterian Cemetery on Limestone Street. However, when that cemetery was removed in the late 1800's, they were re-interred at the No. 2 Cemetery.[18] See, the Taylortown chapter, under the section "Harry Street," for more on this.

A couple of these individuals buried here in unmarked graves include my Grandmothers' parents and her great grandmother. My Grandmother Mary Louise White, was born June 15, 1932, to George Otis Ray and Helen Lyons. Both of my Grandmothers' parents passed away when she was very young. George Ray, my Great Grandfather passed away at the age of 27 from Tuberculosis on December 11, 1933 and was buried in this cemetery two days later. His wife, Helen Clay Lyons, was 24 when she succumbed to the same illness on July 8, 1935.

---

16. Ibid., p. 95

17. A Prosperous Society: The Colored People Manage Their Finances to Good Advantage. (1892, February 3). *The Kentucky Leader*, p. 2.

18. "Presbyterian Cemetery (Lexington, KY)," Notable Kentucky African Americans Database, accessed January 23, 2023, https://nkaa.uky.edu/nkaa/items/show/2511.

She is also buried in the No. 2 Cemetery, as well as her mother Lula Williams. Lula met her demise after a battle with Tuberculosis on August 29, 1926, at the age of 35.

There's a host of other great aunts and uncles who were buried here as well and I suspect even more great grandparents, whose death records I haven't been able to locate.

The most famous individual that was buried in this cemetery would be the world's greatest jockey Isaac Murphy, who was born in slavery but went on to win the Kentucky Derby on three different occasions, in 1884, 1890, and 1891. He was the first to win consecutive derby's and his 44% winning percentage remains tops among all jockeys today.[19] Murphy also a 5x winner of the Latonia Derby, passed away in 1896 from Pneumonia and was buried in our beloved Cemetery No. 2. Seventy-one years later in 1967, Murphy's remains were removed and re-interred at a site off Russell Cave Road. Then again several years later, his remains were moved to the Kentucky Horse Park, where they remain today.[20] In 2015, a new monument for Isaac Murphy was unveiled at Cemetery No. 2, in the approximate location of his original burial. In my opinion, I believe Isaac should have never been moved in the first place. He was buried in No. 2 Cemetery and that's where he should remain.

Murphy was not the only Kentucky Derby winner to be buried here. The very first Kentucky Derby winner, Oliver Lewis, who won the 1875 Derby aboard the horse

19. "Murphy, Isaac [Burns]," Notable Kentucky African Americans Database, accessed January 23, 2023, https://nkaa.uky.edu/nkaa/items/show/667.

20. *Isaac Burns Murphy*. Kentucky Horse Park. (n.d.). Retrieved January 22, 2023, from https://kyhorsepark.com/equine-theme-park/park-memorial-s-statues/isaac-burns-murphy/

Aristides, was buried here in 1924. The horse Aristides was trained by African American horse trainer and former slave Ansel Williamson, who passed in 1881, and is believed to be buried here. That burial however, has not be substantiated. James "Soup" Perkins is another black Derby winning jockey, whose burial was at this cemetery in 1911. He won the derby in 1895.

The cemetery and the organization prospered up until the 1930's, when a period of neglect and decline began. By that time, nearly all of the members of the Benevolent Society No. 2 had passed away and there was no one left to care for the eight acre burial ground.

During it's thirty to forty year period of neglect, weeds were overgrown, the grass was over six feet high, vandals desecrated grave sites, trash littered the property and there were rodents everywhere. In the 1970's, it was labeled abandoned, as no owner ever came forward to claim the property. The mayor at the time, considered removing the graves and building apartments on the site.

> "The Old Seventh Street Cemetery could be converted into a low rent housing project area, a new park, or cleaned up and left as open space."[21]

Members of the black community decided to take action and fight to preserve the historic site. In 1978, they formed the African Cemetery No. 2 Corp, whose sole purpose it was to restore the cemetery. In May of 1981, the cemetery restoration was complete.[22] They successful-

---

21. City May Take Over Old 7th Street Cemetery. (1973, April 18). *The Lexington Leader*, p. 46.

22. Martin, M. (1981, May 20). A Cemetery Restored, For Their Labor, Citizens Group Wins Deed To Historic Site. *The Lexington Leader*, p. 3.

ly raised $140,000, the total cost of the project. Some of the funds came from community donations and the rest of the funding was grant money. A monument for those who are buried in unmarked graves, such as my Great Grandparents, was unveiled on this day and the monument remains today. It's one I visit when I go to pay respects to my deceased family.

Illustration 4: Photo by me in the cemetery (2021)

Illustration 5: Noticed some vandalism at the cemetery on my visit May 31, 2022

Ladies Auxiliary Society Cemetery

There was another cemetery adjacent to the African Cemetery. This cemetery was organized by a group of black women. In 1883, one acre of land was purchased by the Ladies Auxiliary Society, founded by Mary Breckinridge, Lizzie Starling, and Belle Robinson and others. The purchase was from James and Sarah Grimes and the cost was $200.[23] This one acre was in the northwest corner of the African Cemetery. With the two cemeteries combined, it created an "L" shape.

In the 1980's during the period of neglect, many of the burials were supposedly removed from the one acre site to the back of the African Cemetery. By that time, a Automotive junkyard had been operating on the site. One notable burial that took place in the Auxiliary cemetery was a man by the name of Harry Slaughter. I published information about a slave insurrection in my book Drapetomania. Slaughter was a part of this "insurrection." There is just one problem with the chapter, and it's a huge blunder on my part. This next section will explain in detail.

Harry Slaughter

In my previous publication, there is a chapter titled "Harry, Shadrick, and Presley." In this chapter, I told the story of the 1848 "slave insurrection," which was

23. Giles, Y. (2009). Ladies Auxiliary Cemetery. In *Stilled Voices Yet Speak: A History of African American Cemeteries in Lexington and Fayette County, Kentucky: Volume 1, Benevolent Society No. 2 cemetery, Ladies Auxiliary Society Cemetery* (p. 116).

more of an attempted escape by many enslaved black men of Lexington. I erroneously stated that three of the men were hung. One of them actually was not. Since I began this chapter explaining newspapers and inaccuracies in some of their reporting, it's only fitting that I explain my own inaccuracy and correct the error. How ironic that I have to do it in this chapter? Before we explain the accurate account, we must republish that chapter in this book, followed by the correction. The chapter was short and went as follows:

In the year of 1848, there was an attempt by a number of slaves in Lexington to get free.

Led by a white man Patrick Doyle, also called "E.J," the 42 escapees were handed pistols and other weapons and marched on, heading north towards Ohio. They made it to Bracken county, Kentucky, nearby Cincinnati. Maysville, Ky was likely their next destination.

After facing hunger and thirst and extreme fatigue, many of them went to a nearby plantation and surrendered. Not only did they surrender, they gave up the location of the remaining fugitives. It is always one of our own who turns on us and spoils the plans.

The men in pursuit attempted to overtake the group of men, when the freedom seekers, armed with pistols opened fire on the enslavers. A heavy gun battle commenced. This gunfire was brief however because the pursuers fled. One individual was wounded, Charles Fowler.

After calling in reinforcements, the pursuers attempt to overtake the fugitives once more. Again, gunfire is exchanged. Hundreds more seeking the $5000 bounty, happened upon the scene and scoured the area in search of the fugitives, all of them were eventually captured. Patrick Doyle was arrested and went to trial, where he was found guilty of "enticing slaves to run-away." He was sentenced to twenty years in the state penitentiary.

It is likely that Doyle did not act out of the kind-ness of his heart and was not much of a friend to the slave at all. He was motivated by money. He was arrest-ed prior in Louisville for attempting to sell two free ne-gros into slavery. One can reason that if this revolt was successful and they made it to Ohio, he would turn them over to slave catchers for the reward money. Given how many joined him, it would've been a large amount.

Three of the fugitives were hung in Bracken Coun-ty. Harry, Shadrack and Prestley. May their descendants read this book and smile with joy, knowing their ances-tors didn't go down without a fight![24]

This is what I published verbatim. All of the infor-mation is correct except for the last paragraph. All of the accounts stated that this was the case, that all three were hung, thus me writing it as such but, there is a newspa-per article from 1897 where "Harry" was interviewed and told the story of what occurred himself.

> "I was in my prime going on 32 years old, when a man by the name of Doyle came to me and told me that he would pilot me across the Ohio River for $100 and guarantee me safe conduct. All my family were free, and the girl whom I was engaged to be married was free

---

24. Thompson, Rico (2022). Chapter 16 - Harry, Shadrick, and Prestley. In *Drapetomania: Kentucky's Runaways and Rebels, The Good Troublemakers* (pp. 193–194). Sankofa Lexington.

born."[25]

He goes on to state that he was owned by a woman named Miss Sidney. She treated him well but he desired to be free. He wanted to marry the love of his life as a free man. He goes on further into the account:

> "On a Saturday night, the first week in August, 1848, Doyle and forty-five of us negroes left Lexington by way of the Russell Cave Pike. We were armed with pistols and bowie knives. I carried an old fashioned pepper box revolver and a large bowie knife. Many of the boys had nothing but single barrel pistols."

The men vowed to fight to the death if they were approached by white men and these men made any attempts to apprehend them. Something they actually did do when they were spotted by two young boys. The boys went and told of a group of negroes hiding out. Several men came in pursuit.

> "Men came after us, but we frightened them off with our pistols. Firing many shots. They fired at us a number of times, but did not hurt us, nor did we wound any of them. While they were gone for re-enforcements we left the place and ran as fast as we could along Brookville Road. We distanced our pursuers, and escaped when night came on, but our band was scattered. Doyle left us early in the day, and we were without a leader. I was chosen to lead, but we only had about twenty men, and we were nearly worn out with our long march, during which time we had nothing to eat. We fled

---

25. Old Slave's Story, He and Others made A Strike For Freedom. *The Miami Helmet (Miami, OH)*, July 29, 1897, p. 4.

through the broken country into bracken county
and on Tuesday morning, we were within five
miles of the Ohio River."

The band of freedom seekers started off as a group
numbering forty-five. As others fled, that number dwindled down to twenty and then down to two. Men fled in
all directions. Slaughter states that only one man remained by his side by the time the other pursuers located
them. That man was Shadrick or "Shad" as they called
him. He unfortunately was hung when it was all said and
done but Harry, he put up a fight, all 214lbs of him. He
was a man with a "remarkable physique," standing six
feet, two inches and was said to have been the best phys-
ically fit man in Fayette County at the time.[26]

"Well Shad and I continued our flight
alone, and swam the Licking River. We had not
gone far after crossing the river till we saw a
man leaning against a tree. He seemed to be
asleep, but after we had passed we heard him
fire his pistol, and before we knew what had
happened, ten or a dozen white men had sur-
rounded us.
They quickly captured Shad and tied
him, but I was determined they should not take
me. Well, the men tried to take me, and as fast as
they would come within striking distance I
would knock them down."

Harry Slaughter fought the men for about five
minutes more before a man called "Mayor" approached
and convinced him that if he went with them that he

26. "Last Survivor: Old Lexington Darkey Tells An Entertaining Life History." *The Messenger (Owensboro, KY)*, 14 Aug. 1897, p. 2.

would not be hurt or killed. He conceded and went with the men to the Brookville Jail.

> "I was charged with being one of the ringleaders of the insurrection, but Madison C. Johnson, Maury Pindell and Judge Graves came down to Brookville and interceded in my behalf. They proved that we were not insurrectionists, but we were simply trying to obtain our freedom. Well, I was taken back to Lexington and put in Pullman's negro jail. I was kept there a month or more."

He was soon released and Miss Sidney allowed him to purchase himself and he was then officially a free man. The others again, suffered that unfortunate fate.

Upon his new freedom, he married his bride, bought a home in Lexington and lived out the remainder of his days a free man. He passed away in 1906 and was interred at the Auxiliary Cemetery.

Chapter 10 - Taylortown, Smithtown & Wolf's Row

Taylortown, Smithtown and Wolfs Row are three communities in north Lexington where predominantly African Americans resided. There seems to be some confusion as to the specific borders of Taylortown. Several sources state several different things and I will explain them all as we move forward in this text. If one source is correct, that would mean that Smithtown and Wolfs Row are in Taylortown, yet they are their own small community, similar to Chicago Bottoms, Gunntown and Goodloe all being Goodloetown.

In Bossism and Reform in a Southern City, author James Duane Bolin places Taylortown between Fourth and Fifth Street, and Broadway and Upper.[1] In a 1968

1. Bolin, J. D. (2000). It Is a New Lexington! In *Bossism and reform in a Southern City: Lexington, Kentucky, 1880-1940* (p. 6). University

Lexington Herald Leader News Article, James Sleet, who resided at 415 Kenton Street and was a representative of the Taylortown Action Group, expressed his concern over poor lighting in the community, particularly Kenton, Campbell, Upper, Broadway and Limestone Streets.[2] Kenton Street is in fact between Fourth and Fifth as indicated in Bolin's book, so we can be certain, that area is a part of Taylortown. Mr. Sleet extends it further east to Limestone in the newspaper article. The Notable Kentucky African American Database extends the borders even further west to Jefferson Street.[3] And the Northside Neighborhood Association creates even more borders when they state that Taylortown is from Second Street to Sixth Street. This would put Smithtown directly in Taylortown.[4] The NNA also states that the Negro Catholic Church, St. Peters, on the corner of Fourth and Jefferson is Taylortown while Smith Street in Smithtown is just a street over. The 1912 Slade Map of Lexington, which we have used throughout this book, indicates that Taylortown is between Fourth and Fifth Street as Bolin wrote but it also erroneously places Smithtown between Kenton and Upper as you will see in the first illustration.

On the following pages, we will show you the borders of each of these sources using the 1912 Slade

Press of Kentucky.

2. Johnson, K. W. (1968, March 11). Official Proceedings. *Lexington Herald Leader*, p. 8.

3. "Taylortown (Lexington, KY), " Notable Kentucky African Americans Database, accessed September 28, 2022, https://nkaa.uky.edu/nkaa/items/show/336.

4. Association, Northside Neighborhood (n.d.). *History*. History of Northside Neighborhood Lexington KY. Retrieved September 28, 2022, from https://www.northsidelex.com/history.html

son, Broadway, Sixth and Fourth Streets. These two sections were settled in the late 1860's and were expanded over the next couple of decades.[5] Smithtown was mostly residential, but there were a couple of saloons and stores in the area throughout it's history.

The year 1899, saw the formation of a black baseball league in Lexington. Smithtown and Taylortown both had teams in this league. The Smithtown Reds and the Taylortown Sluggers. At some point, the two teams combined to form one. The other Lexington teams were: All-Stars, Bums, Brucetown Heavy Hitters, Chippewa Indians (Native Americans), East End Club, East End Violets, Ellerslie Avenue Team, Fort Springs, The Gem Theaters, Maddoxtown Blues, Hamburg All-Stars, Hill Boys, Lexington Goldberg, Lexington Hard Hitters, Lexington Heavy Hitters, Lexington Heavy Hitters Jr., Lexington White Sox, Lexington Reos, Loafers, Lexington Hustlers, Mechanic Street Blues, Pralltown, White Plume, and Yellmantown.[6]

Surrounding towns that had teams in the Bluegrass Colored Baseball League include Danville, Centerville, Frankfort, Georgetown, Lancaster, Mt. Sterling, Nicholasville, Paris, and Versailles.

The Lexington Hustlers were the most famous team from this league. The same time that Jackie Robinson was making headlines for "breaking the color barrier" in Major League Baseball, the Hustlers became the

5. Kellogg, J. (1982). The formation of black residential areas in Lexington, Kentucky, 1865-1887. *The Journal of Southern History*, 48(1), 21. https://doi.org/10.2307/2207295

6. "Blue Grass Colored Baseball League, " Notable Kentucky African Americans Database, accessed September 29, 2022, https://nkaa.uky.edu/nkaa/items/show/2627.

first integrated team in the South, when this black owned, managed and operated team added the white future Kentucky Senator, Bobby Flynn to their roster in 1947.[7] They often played games against white teams and even had Satchel Paige pitch a game for them in 1950.[8] Hank Aaron and Negro League great Josh Gibson, had games against the Hustlers.

Illustration 4: Smithtown/Taylortown Sluggers 1940's

---

7. "Lexington Hustlers Baseball Team, " Notable Kentucky African Americans Database, accessed September 29, 2022, https://nkaa.uky.edu/nkaa/items/show/164.

8. Smith, G. L., McDaniel, K. C., Hardin, J. A., & Powell, S. l. (2015). African American Baseball. In *The Kentucky African American Encyclopedia* (p. 3). University Press of Kentucky.

One can not mention the Smithtown neighbor-hood and not also mention that former Major League Baseball Player and coach John Shelby hails from there. T-Bone, as he was called, was born in 1958. He played 10 years in the Majors from 1981 to 1991, winning two World Series Championships with two teams, the Balti-more Orioles in 1983 and the Los Angeles Dodgers in 1988. After his playing career ended, Shelby would spend the next two decades coaching in the Majors.[9]

Wolfs Row was a section in Taylortown. Today, we know it as Toner Street but in the late 1800's and early 20th Century, this was Wolf Street. The majority of the homes here were small cottages, none of which survive today. There was also a German Lutheran Church on the corner of Fifth and Wolf Street.

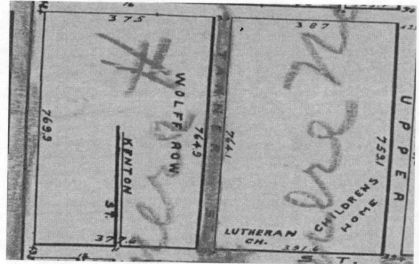

Illustration 5: Wolfs Row. On the map, you see Tanner Street, it's actually Toner Street. Sits between the streets of Fifth, Sixth, Broadway and Upper.

9. Allen, M. (2022, June 15). *John Shelby*. Society for American Baseball Research. Retrieved September 29, 2022, from https://sabr.org/bioproj/person/john-shelby/

Harry Street

Harry Street, is a section nearby to Taylortown. Depending on the specific borders, you could say that Harry Street is in Taylortown. This streets origin is different than any of the communities and streets within that we have discussed in this book. What makes it so interesting, different and worth noting is because it was built where a former cemetery once stood.

The Presbyterian Cemetery was the primary cemetery of Lexington for many years. This burial ground owned by the First and Second Presbyterian Church was located on Limestone Street, between Sixth and Seventh. The last burial took place in 1879 and the cemetery fell into disarray after years of neglect. It became a nuisance to the city so in 1887, it was sold and the bodies were removed and interred to other cemeteries.[10] The whites were reburied at the Lexington Cemetery on Leestown Road and the black folks were buried at the African Cemetery No. 2 on Seventh Street. An estimated 300 persons of African descent were removed and placed at this new location. After the removal of the burial ground, this section was called "Waverly Square." Harry Street became an official street in 1900.

Not all of the bodies were removed however. Eight years later in 1895 during excavation, a coffin containing the remains of a young girl, about 10, was found. The name engraved on her coffin was A.D. Taylor.[11] In 1910, a coffin was found when construction crews were digging

---

10. "Presbyterian Cemetery (Lexington, KY)," Notable Kentucky African Americans Database, accessed September 30, 2022, https://nkaa.uky.edu/nkaa/items/show/2511.

11. Found a Coffin. (1895, August 2). *Lexington Herald Leader*, p. 8.

to lay the foundation for new housing.[12]

Aaron Dupuy

One person of interest that we know was buried in the old burial ground was a former slave of Kentucky Statesman Henry Clay, Aaron Dupuy. Originally of Virginia and born around 1788, Dupuy was likely owned by the Clay family since birth. There is not a lot known about his life but one event that occurred was recorded and recollected by another slave, who was hired out to Clay. Apparently, Aaron loved to drink alcohol, something that annoyed Clay's wife. He was their driver and on this particular day, Aaron indulged and made himself unfit to take Mrs Clay to her destination. Henry Clay or-dered the overseer to whip him. When inside the car-riage house with the overseer, the overseer instructed Aaron to remove his shirt. Aaron, obviously intoxicated urged the overseer to remove his as well. In amusement, the overseer obliged. Peter Still, who was enslaved and hired out to Clay at the time writes the following in his slave narrative:

> "But behold! No sooner had he lifted his arms to pull his shirt over his head, than Aaron seized the garment and twisting it around his neck, held him fast. Then catching the whip, he applied it vigorously to the overseer's naked back, raising the skin at every stroke. His victim screamed, and threatened him with vengeance,

---

12. Coffin Found in House Excavation. (1910, April 29). *Lexington Herald Leader*, p. 1.

but all in vain; the blows fell hard and fast."[13]

According to Still, nothing came of this other than laughter from Clay and the remark "there had been whipping enough.[14]

Illustration 6: Aaron Dupuy c1852

Aaron was a married man. Sometime in 1806 he met and married an enslaved woman named Charlotte.

---

13. Still, P. (1995). The Separation. In K. E. R. Pickard (Ed.), *The Kidnapped and the Ransomed, The Narrative of Peter and Vina Still after Forty Years of Slavery* (p. 63). University of Nebraska Press.

14. Ibid., pp. 64

She was working downtown Lexington in a Tailor shop.[15] She has a very interesting story of her own. In fact, chapter five of my first book was written about her. That short chapter will be reproduced in the next section with alterations. Aaron passed away February 6, 1866 and as you have learned, was buried in this old cemetery.

Charlotte Dupuy

The most famous case of a slave taking his owner to court in an attempt to gain freedom was the Dred Scott vs Sandford case. Scott was held in captivity in St Louis, Missouri. After some time in a free territory with his owners and on return to Missouri, Scott believed his time in the free territory automatically earned him the right to freedom. So he sued in 1856. The decision came down in 1857, the courts ruled that Scott will remain a slave. Under the constitution of the United States, a black man has no rights as a citizen in this country. The Supreme Court Justices stated:

> "We think that [blacks] are not included, and were not intended to be included, under the word "citizens" in the Constitution, and can therefore claim none of the rights and privileges which that instrument provides for and secures to citizens of the United States. On the contrary, they were at that time [of America's founding] considered as a subordinate and inferior class of beings who had been subjugated by the dominant race, and,

15. The Henry Clay Estate. (n.d.). *Aaron Dupuy* . Henry Clay - Ashland. Retrieved September 30, 2022, from https://henryclay.org/mansion-grounds/enslaved-people-at-ashland/aaron-dupuy/

whether emancipated or not, yet remained subject to their authority, and had no rights or privileges but such as those who held the power and the Government might choose to grant them."
— *Dred Scott*, 60 U.S. At 404–05.

A little known case very similar to the Dred Scott Case took place in Washington, D.C., 17 years prior. This was the case of Charlotte "Lottie" Dupuy. Dupuy would sue her owner, Secretary of State, Henry Clay, in 1829 for freedom.

Lottie was born into slavery in Cambridge, Maryland, sometime around 1787 to George and Rachel Stanley. Her then owner, Daniel Parker, sold her to a tailor named James Condon for $100. She was eight years old at this time and was forced to leave her family. In 1805, Condon brought her to Lexington, Kentucky. She met a young man named Aaron Dupuy in 1806 and they would soon wed. Aaron Dupuy was owned by Secretary of State Henry Clay and lived on his plantation famously known as "Ashland." Ashland is located on what is now Richmond Rd/Main St. May of that same year, Condon sold Lottie to Henry Clay for $450, allowing the couple to live together. Two children were produced from this union, Charles and Mary Ann. The Bill of Sale from Condon to Clay states the following:

> May 12, 1806
> "I have this day bargained sold and delivered, and by these presents do bargain sell and deliver, to Henry Clay, for and in consideration of four hundred & fifty dollars, a negro female slave named Charlotte, aged about nineteen,

which said slave I warrant & defend to said Clay against the claim of all & every person whatsoever; and I likewise warrant her to be sound.

Witness my hand & seal this 12th May 1806

(signed) Jas. Condon {L.S}

Teste.

Isaac Wells"

In 1825, Henry Clay became Secretary of State under John Quincy Adams and moved his family to Washington, D.C. Lottie, Aaron and their children would join them there. They lived with Clay at his home, 'The Decatur House', located at Lafayette Square, across from the White House. The home was originally built for United States Naval Officer Stephen Decatur, hence the name. Lottie had relative freedom to move about in D.C., often visiting family along the Eastern Shore, as she was originally from Maryland.

Clay's service as Secretary of State was ending in 1829 and he was preparing to move the family back to Kentucky. Dupuy sought out the courts to file a petition to be granted her freedom. At some point, her previous owner Condon had promised her freedom, as he had granted her mother, so this was her justification. Being around free family and friends while in D.C., anyone enslaved would desire that same freedom to move about as they please.

She found a lawyer to represent her in the suit and on February 13, 1829, Attorney Robert Beale wrote a petition to the D.C. Judges. The petition to have her remain in D.C. while her lawsuit was ongoing was granted. While Lottie was able to remain in D.C., Clay took her husband and children back to Kentucky with him. She remained in the Decatur House and would become employed by it's next resident, newly appointed Secretary of State, Martin Van Buren. Van Buren would eventually become the 8th President of the United States.

Her lawyer argued that Lottie and the children were entitled to their freedom because of the promise her former owner had made her. He stated that if Clay was allowed to take her back to Kentucky, she would be held as a slave for the remainder of her life. The petition for freedom would be denied but Lottie refused to return to Kentucky. Clay reported to his agent that:

> ". . . her conduct has created insubordination among her relatives here, I think it high time to put a stop to it, which can best be done by her return to duty,"

She was jailed in Alexandria, Virginia where she remained until Clay was able to arrange for her return. Clay decided to send Lottie to his daughter and son in law in New Orleans. She would remain there 10 more years. October 12, 1840, Henry Clay would grant Lottie and her daughter Mary Ann their freedom. Four years later he granted her son Charles his. Charles was used on many occasions as sort of a "prop" for obedient servitude, as he would often accompany Clay to various states. Clay wanted to show off how well his slaves were treated. The contradictory Henry Clay while publicly denouncing slavery, remained a slave holder until his death. In 1852, her Husband Aaron Dupuy gained his freedom.   The couple were reunited and remained in Lexington their remaining days.[16]

Schools

There were a couple of city schools in Taylortown. The original Dunbar High School opened up in 1923 at 545 North Upper Street. Named after the great black poet Paul Laurence Dunbar, the school became the first black school in Kentucky to be admitted to the Southern Association of Colleges and Secondary Schools. Only eight all black schools were ever admitted. This school operated from 1923 until closing in 1967 due to integration.

During it's existence, Dunbar produced one of Kentucky's most legendary high school basketball coaches, Sanford T. Roach amassing a win/loss record of 512-142 from 1943 to 1965. During that span, Dunbar won 2 Kentucky High School Athletic League State Championships and 6 regional titles. After retiring from coaching, S.T. Roach would become the first black principal at an integrated school when he became the principal at George Washingtion Carver Elementary between 1965-1966. He was inducted into the National High School Sports Hall of Fame in 1996. Kentucky Athletic Hall of fame In 1988, and the Kentucky State University Hall of Fame in 1977.[17] This year, 2022, he received entry into the newly formed Lexington African American Hall of Fame

16. Thompson, Rico (2020). Charlotte Dupuy. In *Sankofa Lexington* (pp. 39–47). Afrakan World Books n Moor.

17. *Sanford T. Roach's biography.* he History Makers. (n.d.). Retrieved September 30, 2022, from https://www.thehistorymakers.org/biography/sanford-t-roach-39

alongside his entire Dunbar High School Bearcats 1959 team and John "T-Bone" Shelby of Smithtown. He passed away at the age of 94 in 2010.[18]

After the Dunbar school closed in '67, it became a community center by the early 70s and managed by Parks and Recreation. Youth basketball leagues held games here. Even I played in one in 1994.

Illustration 7: Dunbar Class of 1934 (Courtesy of Lexington Public Library)

Another school in Taylortown was The Fourth Street Colored School. This school located on the same block as Dunbar was established sometime in the 1880's and was one of four city schools for black children. By 1895, it was suggested to change the name in honor of it's principal, Green Pinkney Russell. The name change was

18. Lexington African-American Sports Hall of Fame. (n.d.). Lexington African-American Sports Hall of Fame. Retrieved September 30, 2022, from https://laashof.com/

accepted and at that moment, the Russell School was born.

Green Russell was born in Logan County, Ky in 1861 on Christmas day. He attended Berea College, originally studying law but changed it to education during his six year enrollment, graduating in 1885. After graduation he taught at the Chilesburg Colored School before being invited to become Principal at Fourth Street. The year 1912 saw him accepting the position of President of Kentucky Normal and Industrial Institute for Colored Persons(now Kentucky State University) in Frankfort, Ky. His tenure at KNIICP wasn't without conflict and turmoil and in 1929, he succumbed to pressure and resigned.[19]

Green P. Russell passed away in 1936 and was buried at Greenwood/Cove Haven Cemetery.

There was also a school ran out of the St. Peters Claver Catholic Church on Jefferson and Fourth Street. This was the only Catholic Diocese for African Americans in Lexington and it was established around 1887 as the St. Martin Deporres Center.[20]

In the early 1900's, there were talks of building another school in the Smithtown community called the "Bethesda Normal and Industrial School" It opened at 534-536 Alford Street in November of 1906 and was established by Reverend O.L. Murphy.[21] Alfred Street today

---

19. Hardin, J. A. (1995). Green Pinckney Russell of Kentucky Normal and Industrial Institute for Colored Persons. *Journal of Black Studies*, *25*(5), 610–621. http://www.jstor.org/stable/2784634

20. *St. Peter Claver Parish*. Cdlex. (2022, September 23). Retrieved September 30, 2022, from https://cdlex.org/stpeterclaver/

21. Bethesda Normal School Looks Like a Go. (1906, December 11). *Lexington Herald Leader*, p. 1.

is Willy Street, just off of Smith St. and Bourbon Ave.

Rev. Murphy, alongside Dr. W.H. Stevenson, purchased the old Good Samaritan Hospital building at 333 East Short Street near Goodloetown in 1910. Stevenson represented the larger branch of the Bethesda School out of Columbus and the plan was to convert this old hospital building into the new Bethesda School. The purchasing price was $14,000. It was even said that Booker T. Washington himself would attend the grand opening of the school.[22]

It is unknown as to the reasoning but by September, 1910, Rev. Murphy, was no longer associated with the school and the name was changed to "Lexington Normal and Industrial College." I have found that the two men were arrested in Cincinnati for soliciting money under false pretenses. Stevenson's lawyer was J.A. Chiles and he stated that it was false. However, shortly after that, it was announced that Rev. Murphy was no longer apart of the project and the name was changed. One can reason that he was doing some shady business of some sort, but I have not confirmed that.

The new project was under the management and direction of First African Baptist Church pastor W. Augustus Jones.[23] By October, he himself was no longer connected to the school. The project was unsuccessful and the school was never opened in this location and the likely cause was lack of funding.

This former hospital building was up for public auction by 1920 and was purchased by W.T. Woolfolk,

22. Old Hospital Building. (1910, July 14). *Lexington Herald Leader*, p. 1.

23. New Corporation, Lexington Normal and Industrial College. (1910, September 28). *Lexington Herald Leader*, p. 10.

who operated his coffee company from this location for the next couple of decades[24] This building remains standing today.

The Rev. Murphy was an interesting character himself, known around town as a "power preacher." Preaching a new gospel similar to that of Roxy Turner who founded the Power Society Church in Goodloetown. He preached on the streets of Lexington and before long garnered a large enough following that he established a church in Smithtown, possibly the same locale as the Bethesda School. Healing the sick, casting out evil spirits and performing other miracles were the Reverend's claims of what he was able to do.[25]

He was also within the management of the Pentecostal Power Church that today is on East Second Street. They branched off from Roxy's organization and incorporated in 1909. Roxy's group was also called the "Christian Faith Band" and R.A. Murphy, his wife and Wellington Saunders, were members. Rev. Murphy, his wife and Saunders names are on the articles of incorporation.

24. The Kaintuckeean. (2015, November 4). *The Old Protestant Infirmary grew to become Samaritan Hospital.* The Kaintuckeean. Retrieved September 30, 2022, from https://www.thekaintuckeean.com/protestant-infirmary/

25. Ugly Charge Sworn Out by Woman Against the Power Preacher. (1904, August 25). *Lexington Herald Leader*, p. 1.

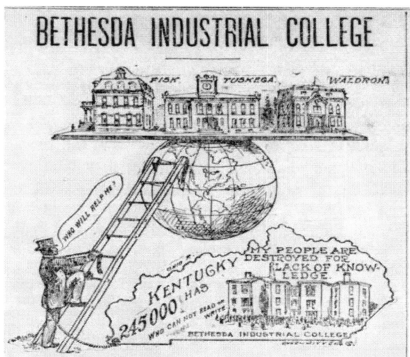

We have purchased the old Good Samaritan Hospital property, on East Short street, for the opening of a large industrial school and plant to be devoted to the development of the character and industrial education of the young men and women of the colored race, and are now making strenuous efforts to raise money to pay the purchase price and remodel the buildings. We hereby appeal to the friends of morality and industry to help us. The business men of Lexington have pledged us $1,640, and we need now $3,666 before we can open our school.

We have struggled on a smaller scale for years at this work for our race, and each year have been crowned with some degree of success. Now we are ready to enlarge our facilities and open in Lexington one of the representative Negro industrial schools of the South.

Help us to carry Bethesda Industrial College to success, and it shall be among the glories of the Blue Grass region.

Checks should be drawn in favor of the Bethesda Industrial College and mailed to the Second National Bank of Lexington, Ky. Thanking you in advance for your favor, we are for the race,

BETHESDA INDUSTRIAL COLLEGE.
O. LEONIDAS MURPHY, President.

J. Y. BROWN, Secretary.

Illustration 8: Ad in Lexington Herald Leader by O.L. Murphy seeking funding to open the school. Dated September 7, 1910. By September 28, he was no longer involved with the effort.

Dr. Mary E. Britton

Lexington's first female doctor lived at 545 North Limestone street, just around the corner from the heart of Taylortown. The following pages in this chapter are a reproduction from my first book. As I have done in several chapters, I am reproducing that text in this section but with updated information.

Born April 16, 1855, to Henry and Laura Britton, a couple who were free blacks. Henry Britton, born around 1826, was a freeman and a carpenter, who later became a barber in Berea, Ky. Laura was born in slavery, belonging to the Kentucky Statesman Thomas Marshall who was also her father. She was emancipated at the age of 16.

At the time of Mary's birth, the Britton family lived on Mill Street in the area that today is called Gratz Park. Mr and Mrs. Britton had ten children, Susan, Julia, Joseph, Robert, Mary, Martha, William, Hattie, Lucy, and Thomas. Two of her siblings earned fame and notoriety in their own way. Her brother Tom Britton, born in 1870, was a black jockey. He nearly won the Kentucky Derby in 1892, mounted on a horse called Huron, coming up inches short to Alonzo Clayton, another black jockey. The previous year he would be the winner of the 1891 Kentucky Oaks. After a bad accident, his health declined and he eventually killed himself. This took place in Cincinnati. He had ingested carbolic acid.[26] He was one of two of their siblings to commit suicide. Their sister Hattie, resid-

---

26. Smith, G. L., McDaniel, K. C., Hardin, J. A., & Powell, S. l. (2015). Britton, Thomas M. "Tommy". In *The Kentucky African American Encyclopedia* (p. 65). University Press of Kentucky.

ing in Memphis, shot and killed herself in 1891.[27]

Dr. Britton's sister, Julia Britton Hooks, born in 1852, was a teacher at Berea College. She was the first black faculty member at Berea, teaching instrumental music. After relocating to Memphis, Tennessee, she married Charles Hooks and eventually opened up a music school. Blues legend W.C. Handy was one of her students at the school. She was also the grandmother of NAACP Executive Director, Benjamin J. Hooks.[28] Another sister, Lucy, was married to a black jockey named Monk Overton.[29] Overton won six consecutive races at Washington Park in Chicago in 1907.

Dr. Mary Britton enrolled at Berea College in 1871, where she remained a student until 1874. Berea was the first institution in Kentucky to allow African Americans to attend. Some great and distinguished black men and women are Berea alum such as Carter G. Woodson, the man responsible for what we know today as "Black History Month." In the 1800's, the only available courses of study for women were nursing and teaching. Dr. Britton chose teaching. After her parents passed, one after the other in 1874, she left to seek employment.

In 1876, she was employed as a teacher at the Colored school in Chilesburg, Ky. And later on taught at Colored School Number 3, aka the Patterson Street School.[30]

27. Killed Herself: Hattie Britton Kills Herself With A Pistol. (1891, June 1). *The Kentucky Leader*, p. 4.

28. Smith, G. L., McDaniel, K. C., Hardin, J. A., & Nelson, P. D. (2015). Hooks, Julia Britton. In *The Kentucky African American Encyclopedia* (p. 251). University Press of Kentucky.

29. Burial of Monk Oveton's Wife Will Be In Lexington. (1905, December 21). *The Lexington Leader*, p. 1.

30. Very Creditable: Were The Closing Exercises of the Patterson Street Colored Schools. (1895, June 7). *The Leader*, p. 6.

Dr. Mary Britton was also a journalist. In the same vein as the notable Ida B Wells, at roughly the same time period. She wrote articles against segregation and the Jim Crow Laws of the south. She wrote for several newspapers throughout the country and Lexington such as; The Lexington Leader, The Daily Transcript, Our Women and Children and The American Citizen, to name a few. She is also credited for penning columns for newspapers such as The Cleveland Gazette, Baltimore Ivy, and Indianapolis World. One example of her writings would be an article against the General Assembly's desire to pass a law requiring blacks and whites to ride in separate railway coaches.[31] In the April 19, 1892 edition of the Kentucky Leader, the transcript of a beautiful speech that she gave at the Kentucky General Assembly, protesting against this new law, was printed. Much of what she spoke of deserves documentation. Some of her statements were the following:

>"We are aware that the Assembly has the power to inflict such a law, but is it right? While we have no longer to chill the blood of our friends by talking of branding irons, chains, whips, blood hounds and to the many physical wrongs and abominations of slavery, this foe of American prejudice renders our lives insecure, our homes unhappy, and crush out the very sinew of existence — freedom and citizenship."

>"All are cognizant of the fact that during slavery the possession of a book by a black man was a crime, that is if he made any effort to read it, hence all avenues of intelligence were closed

---

31. Thompson, Rico (2020). Chapter 1 – Dr. Mary Britton. In *Sankofa Lexington* (p. 5). Afrakan World Books n Moor.

against him, and no possible development could in a few years obliterate the growth of centuries.

The Progress since emancipation has been the most amazing recorded in history. We believe, gentlemen, that you feel the state owes you something to a people so long oppressed, degraded and despised, yet ready and willing to make the stride for all that is lofty when given the opportunity.

It is not fair to chain their hands and feet and then tell them to make an even race with people who have had two hundred years the advantage and no obstacles to fight."[32]

This was beautifully spoken, however, I must state that I broke the speech up into smaller sections and each paragraph quoted is not in successive order. Despite her best efforts and that of others, the law soon passed.

At a time where women, in particularly African American women, were relegated to the roles of teachers and domestics, she sought to achieve something greater. Something no black woman in the city had done prior. She enrolled in medical school and by 1902, she was licensed to practice medicine in Lexington, becoming the first black woman to ever do so. The colleges that she attended were the Battle Creek Sanitarium in Battle Creek, MI, and the American Missionary College of Medicine, in Chicago.[33] Dr. Britton specialized in massage therapy and electricity in the treatment of diseases. Her practice was out of her home that she had constructed in 1903, on Limestone Street. Prior to purchasing this property, she

32. A Woman's Appeal To Members of the Kentucky General Assembly. (1892, April 19). *The Kentucky Leader*, p. 3.

33. Smith, G. L., McDaniel, K. C., Hardin, J. A., & Sears, R. D. (2015). Britton, Mary Ellen". In *The Kentucky African American Encyclopedia* (p. 65). University Press of Kentucky.

lived on Lexington Avenue, just off of High Street.[34]

Dr. Britton was also heavily involved in the woman's suffrage movement of the time period. She served as President of the Women's Improvement Club that formed to improve the social status of women. At the Ninth Annual Convention of the Kentucky Negro Education Association, which she was an original member in 1877, she gave a speech, that was later a published work titled "Woman's Suffrage: A Potent Agency in Public Reform."[35]

This founding member of the Colored Orphan Home's tireless work on behalf of the black race was even recognized by the likes of the poet Paul Laurence Dunbar. He penned a poem for her titled "To Miss Mary Britton and I think it's a perfect ending to this chapter:

> "God of the right, arise And
> let thy pow'r prevail; Too
> long thy children mourn In
> labor and travail.
> Oh, speed the happy day!
> When waiting ones may see
> The glory-bringing birth Of
> our real liberty!"

> Grant thou, O gracious God,
> That not in word alone
> Shall freedom's boon be ours,
> While bondage-galled we moan!
> But condescend to us
> In our o'erwhelming need;
> Break down the hind'ring bars,
> And make us free indeed.

---

34. Killed Herself: Hattie Britton Kills Herself With A Pistol. (1891, June 1). *The Kentucky Leader*, p. 4.

35. Thompson, Rico (2020). Chapter 1 – Dr. Mary Britton. In *Sankofa Lexington* (p. 7). Afrakan World Books n Moor.

Give us to lead our cause
More noble souls like hers,
The memory of whose deed
Each feeling bosom stirs;
Whose fearless voice and strong
Rose to defend her race,
Roused Justice from her sleep,
Drove Prejudice from place

Let not the mellow light
Of Learning's brilliant ray
Be quenched, to turn to night
Our newly dawning day.
To that bright, shining star
Which thou didst set in place,
With universal voice
Thus speaks a grateful race:

Not empty words shall be
Our offering to your fame;
The race you strove to serve
Shall consecrate your name
Speak on as fearless still;
Work on as tireless ever;
And your reward shall be
Due meed for your endeavor."[36]

She passed away in 1925, was never married and had no children. She is buried at Cove Haven Cemetery.

36. Dunbar, P. L. (1893). To Miss Mary Britton. In *Oak and Ivy* (pp. 30–31). Press of United Brethren Publishing House.

Illustration 9: 1910 meeting among black physicians and dentists. Dr. Britton is the only female in the picture

Urban Communities West

"We need to create media outlets that help educate our people and our children, and not annihilate their minds."

- Assata Shakur

Chapter 11 – Yellmantown & Forest Hill

Yellmantown, this community was developed in Northwest Lexington in late 1800's. A predominately African American community that was mostly residential, although there were several businesses in the area.

The geographical location has borders that intertwine with other communities such as Forest Hill and Taylortown. In a 1914 newspaper article, the Yellmantown neighborhood was explained as follows:

> "Yellmantown starts at Second and Georgetown and would be bounded in a line run west on Georgetown to Payne Street, south on Payne Street to West Main, west on Main to the Belt Line Railroad to Georgetown Street, up Georgetown St to where it forks with Newtown Pike, then east on Fourth to Blackburn

Avenue, from there to Third Street and then down to Georgetown to Second."[1]

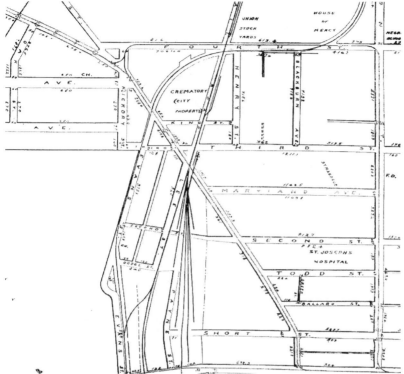

Illustration 1: Map of the Yellmantown Neighborhoods. The borders zig zag a bit, so you will have to follow the direction on the previous page for specific borders. The Street at the bottom is West Main and the northernmost horizontal st is West Fourth

(Slade, J. T. & Lexington & Central Kentucky Title Co. (1912) Lexington & Central Ky. Title Co.'s Map of Lexington, Ky. and vicinity. [Lexington: Lexington & Central Ky. Title Co] [Map] Retrieved from the Library of Congress, https://www.loc.gov/item/79691619/.)

---

1. Herr, J. G. (1914, February 1). The Eight Little Towns in Lexington. *Lexington Herald Leader*, p. 3.

The name came from German immigrant and hemp dealer John George Yellman. Yellman had a hemp bagging factory on the corner of Fourth and Georgetown Street. His home at 539 West Third Street was built around 1860 and the community developed around it.

As with the majority of these black communities within the city, it developed quite a notorious reputation. Hickory Street, at the far end of West Third became known as "Hell's Half Acre," as well as "Shooter's Row." The latter referring to the alley where crap games were a normal occurrence. These games quite often ended in fights and shootouts.

On the extreme end of West Third street, in an alley known as "shooters' row," yesterday afternoon at 5:30 o'clock, George Williams was shot in the thigh by a strange negro, who, during his few days' residence here, has been known as "Dinkey." No one seems to know his real name. "Shooters' row" has won its name by being a rendezvous for crap-shooters, and it was while engaged in tumbling the bones that a dispute arose which resulted in the shooting. "Dinkey" made his escape.

As he ran away a negro named Frank Frazier is alleged to have shot several times after him. Williams was taken to his home and a physician extracted the ball. His condition is not considered serious. Few Sundays pass over Yellmantown without a shooting of some character. The locality probably deserves the name it has so long worn—"Hell's half acre."

Illustration 2: Lexington Herald Leader 21 Sept., 1896

George Broadus

    The article shown on the previous page is one of many examples of what occurred on this block and why it received it's names. One character in particular had a huge reputation in the neighborhood and earned the moniker "Mayor of Yellmantown." George Broadus aka the mayor was always involved in one thing or another in Yellmantown. He had served time in prison for killing a man, and not long after being released, shot a man called Sam Hope in Yellmantown.[2] This shooting was in 1896. He would be arrested a week later but wasn't long before he was back out, up to his usual shenanigans. The mayor would be stabbed in the back on September 30, 1897 on Seventh St by a woman named Sarah Jane Smith.[3] Supposedly, in passing by she spoke to him in a friendly manner and he cursed her out. She in turn, stabbed him. He would survive the stabbing.

    In 1899, he was arrested and fined for beating his wife, then arrested again in January, 1900 for allegedly cutting his sister Mag Broadus' ear off.[4] November of that year, he would meet his demise when inside of a saloon owned by Dave Thomas at the corner of Georgetown and King Street in Yellmantown. The newspaper reported it was a shotgun wound to the head that literally blew his brains all over the saloon.[5] A man called Charles Down-

---

2. Fatal Craps. (1896, January 20). *The Leader*, p. 5.

3. On Seventh Street. (1897, August 1). *The Morning Herald*, p. 5.

4. The Trial of George Broadus, the Cutter, is Postponed. (1900, January 8). *The Daily Leader*, p. 7.

5. His Brains Blown Out. (1900, November 4). *The Morning Herald*, p. 1.

ing was arrested for the shooting. Broadus was buried at the Auxiliary Cemetery on Seventh St. This section in no way was to glorify this individual nor pass judgment upon him, it is my intention to share available information about each of these neighborhoods and some of the characters who called them home.

Forest Hill

The Forest Hill community consists of Whitney and Charles Avenues, which intersect with Hickory Street in Yellmantown, as well as Ash, Michigan, Elm, Oak streets and the areas aligning Georgetown Street up to around the north side of the Orphan Home, present day Glen Arvin Dr.(Black Street then.) Present day Michigan Street was formerly Forest Street, and changed around 1906 due to confusion with another street on an opposite end of town "Forest Ave."[6] These streets on the West side of Georgetown street began developing in the late 1800's as the Forest Hill Company began selling plots on Whitney Ave, Charles Ave and that vicinity. Prior to this, it was a rural area with not much development. Forest Hill began as "Lee's Woods" in the 1700's and was changed sometime in the late 1800's. Lee's Woods was likely named after Hancock and Willis Lee who founded a town in Kentucky's capital city of Frankfort that was called "Leestown." Present day Leestown Road is on the other side of Lexington Cemetery, whose eastern border is Whitney Ave. A part of Yellmantown was also referred to as Lee's Row. At any rate, it must be stated that this is purely speculation on my part, as to the origin of the

6. The Petition. (1906, June 28). *Lexington Leader*, p. 4.

name Lee's Woods. It makes since however simply because of the prevalence of the name Lee in this northwestern portion of Lexington.

A little known fact is one of the city's very first horse race tracks was in the area at this time. Williams' Race Track was built in 1789 in Lee's Woods.[7]

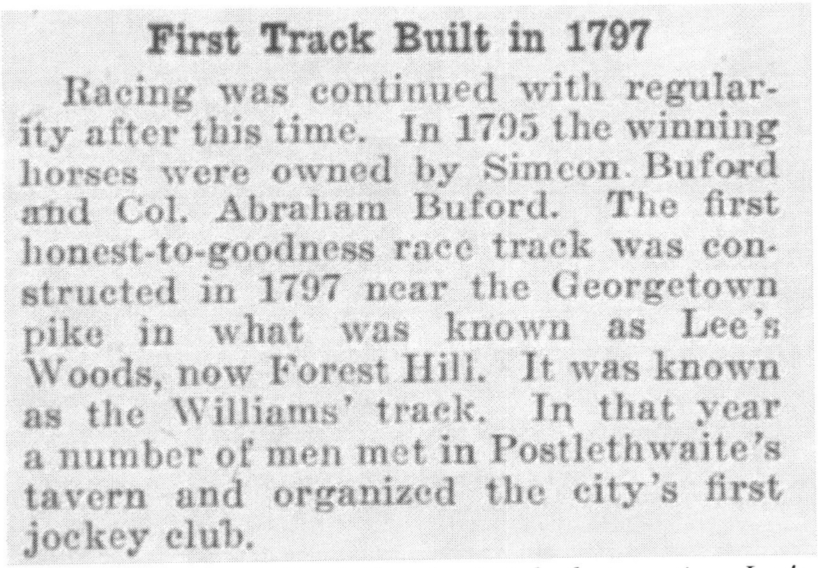

First Track Built in 1797

Racing was continued with regularity after this time. In 1795 the winning horses were owned by Simeon Buford and Col. Abraham Buford. The first honest-to-goodness race track was constructed in 1797 near the Georgetown pike in what was known as Lee's Woods, now Forest Hill. It was known as the Williams' track. In that year a number of men met in Postlethwaite's tavern and organized the city's first jockey club.

Illustration 3: 1928 Herald Leader Article that mentions Lee's Woods

Greenwood Cemetery

As I write this, I presently live in this community and my home was built in 1910. The community continued to grow in the early 20th century. Several grocers, saloons, restaurants and other businesses populated the area. In 1907, the Greenwood Cemetery and Realty Com-

---

7. Hoover, F. K. (1928, February 23). Lexington Has Had Racing for 140 Years. *The Lexington Herald*, p. 33.

pany was formed by a group of black men. One of these men was Jordan Jackson, who was the husband to one of the founders of the Colored Orphan Home, which we will discuss later, Elizabeth Belle Mitchell. Other members of the company were Henry Turner, Edward Chenault, George Russell, William H. Ballard, Charles H. Yancey, John E. Hunter, Samuel Underwood, Henry A. Tandy, Zachariah H. Jones, Marshall T. Clay, Pherril L. Parrish, Robert F. Bell and John B. Caulder.

These men got together, formed this company and on 16 acres at the end of Whitney Avenue, Greenwood cemetery was born, becoming the second black cemetery in Lexington. The African(Colored) Cemetery Number 2 was organized by the Union Benevolent Society Number 2 in 1869. This group of black men formed solely for the purposes of "taking care of the sick, bury the dead and perform other deeds of charity."[8] The 16 acres was at the time, farmland owned by a Mrs. Bradley and was purchased by the newly formed Greenwood organization.

The Articles of Incorporation for the Greenwood Cemetery and Realty Company were filed May 15, 1907 and filed with the Secretary of State the next month on June 28, 1907.[9]

As with the African(Colored) Cemetery on the east side of town, many of Lexington's prominent black citizens were buried here at Greenwood. Lexington's first black female doctor, Dr. Mary Britton, is buried here.[10]

8. "African Cemetery No. 2 (Lexington, KY)," Notable Kentucky African Americans Database, accessed July 10, 2022, https://nkaa.uky.edu/nkaa/items/show/1254.

9. "Greenwood Cemetery / Cove Haven Cemetery," Notable Kentucky African Americans Database, accessed July 10, 2022, https://nkaa.uky.edu/nkaa/items/show/300004510.

10. Thompson, Rico. "Chapter 1 - Dr. Mary E. Britton." *Sankofa Lexington*, Afrakan World Books and Moor, 2020, pp. 4–12.

Educator Green P. Russell, whom the Russell School takes it's name, as well as musician Saunders "Smoke" Richardson, famed twin photographers Marvin and Morgan Smith and a host of others including personal friends of mine and family.

GREENWOOD CEMETERY

NEW BURYING GROUND FOR COLORED PEOPLE OF LEX- INGTON AND VICINITY.

Landscape Gardeners Laying Out Beautiful Sixteen-Acre Tract in Forest Hill Neighborhood, Which Will Soon Be Open.

Illustration 4: The new cemetery announcement in the local papers. (Lexington Herald Leader 19 Apr., 1908)

A black man by the name of Marcellus Clayborn was the cemetery's very first burial, May 3, 1908.[11] He had passed away weeks earlier but his body was kept in

11. Greenwood Cemetery. (1908, May 2). *Lexington Leader*, p. 2.

a vault for the purposes of burial in the yet to open cemetery.

In 1942, "Realty Company" was dropped from the name and the organization was incorporated again as "Greenwood Cemetery."

Fast Forward to 1987, they reorganized one more time as a Kentucky Non Profit under the name Cove Haven Cemetery and this is the name that exists today. Burials still take place here. A number of my childhood friends are buried here as well as some ancestors of mine I never met. Abigail Morton, childhood friend, Walter Gray, childhood friend, my mothers sister, Aunt Robin Turnbough(Dyer), the woman who raised my grandmother, her great aunt Ada Napier(Williams) and a host of others.

Forest Hill Cemetery

If you come up Whitney Avenue, right before you enter Cove Haven, to your left, or if you are traveling up Ash Street, directly in front of you, at the Whitney, Ash intersection, there's a small empty field. At least it appears to be empty. There is no signage but closer to the back, you will notice only three headstones. This space was/is actually Forest Hill Cemetery. If you walk into the area, you'll notice many indentations in the ground, indicating past burials.

Forest Hill Cemetery was a "pauper's cemetery." A pauper's grave is defined as "a grave paid for at public expense because the deceased persons family could not afford one." This is basically the same as what is called a "Potter's Field," where unknown or indigent people are buried. I have even discovered a couple of my family members buried here, during my genealogy research. There is one person in particular whose story I am familiar with. He is buried here. His name is Ed Harris.

Illustration 5: The three headstones in Forest Hill Cemetery. (Photo by me (9/25/2022)

Ed Harris

In January, 1926, three members of a white family of four were found dead with gunshot wounds and another was critically injured. Clarence Bryant and his two small children were the deceased. His wife survived the attack and it was alleged that Ed Harris was the culprit after a black man named George Blanchard informed the police.

According to letters written from the Director of the Kentucky Interracial Commission, James M. Bond to W.E.B. Dubois, Harris and Bryant were partners in an illegal moonshine and whiskey operation. Harris went to the Bryant farm to settle a dispute between the two men and things got heated.[12] He shot and killed Mr. Bryant as well as his children. To leave no witnesses, the wife was shot too and left for dead.

Ed Harris would be apprehended in Scott County, from the information George Blanchard gave the authorities. Harris was sent to the Kentucky State Reformatory to await trial in an undisclosed location to prevent "Mob Violence."

During the trial, the governor of Kentucky ordered 1000 troops to patrol the streets near the courthouse so - that law and order could be carried out.[13] We know that mob violence was frequent in those days. Any black man accused of anything would be tortured, shot or hung, by mobs of angry white men, preventing any potential trial. Quite often there were cases were the mobs would break into jails and "steal" the accused away to be murdered, regardless of innocence or guilt.

The trial lasted all of 16 minutes. Harris was sen-

12. Bond, James, 1863-1929. Facts on the Ed. Harris alias John Henry Jones murder and assault case, ca. February 1926. W. E. B. Du Bois Papers (MS 312). Special Collections and University Archives, University of Massachusetts Amherst Libraries

13. Thousand State Guardian to Patrol Streets for Trial of Harris; Business to be Temporarily Suspended. (1926, January 31). *The Lexington Herald*, p. 1.

tenced to die by hanging on March 3, 1926. It was recorded in the papers that his final words were as follows:

> "I prays all the time...and at last the Lord
> has listened to me and my sin is gone. I want to
> tell the people about it. I aint going to say noth-
> ing about the affair, my crimes but I want to
> tell them, I am not afraid."[14]

According to his own words, Harris had been in
Lexington for 23 years but originally hailed from Georgia. He had gotten himself into trouble in his home state
when driving a carriage which had white children as
passengers. He was involved in an accident with another
motorist, whom he says he "cut." As punishment, he
was given four years in prison for the incident but only
served a month. Afterwards, he left Georgia and was in
Lexington ever since that time.[15]

---

14. Ed Harris Buried Within Half Hour After Hanging. (1926, March 5).
The Lexington Leader, p. 1.

15. Ibid,, p. 1

Illustration 6: Ed Harris hanging outside the Courthouse 1926 (Transylvania University)

ED HARRIS, ALIAS
JOHN HENRY JONES

Illustration 7: Ed Harris

The Colored Orphan Home

The Colored Orphan Home is another business and service that opened up in the Forest Hill Community on Georgetown Street(Georgetown Pike, at the time). The land was between Black Street and Thompson Ave(now Ash Street extended across Georgetown)

December 18, 1865, the state of Kentucky freed over 200,000 of the black men, women and children that were held as chattel property by the state's slave holders. This created a housing crisis and many landowners seized the opportunity to make some cash by selling plots of land to these newly freed citizens. Communities such as the one's we have written about in this book, formed throughout Lexington, and the state as a whole. With the ability to read being illegal during slavery, many citizens were illiterate and void of self sustaining life skills. There was a market and need to teach these life skills and a group of black women came together to create a service to meet those needs.

Lauretta Flynn Byars writes in her 1995 publication the following:

> "Children experienced the economic problems most acutely. Lack of adequate housing, food, clothing and recreational and educational opportunities or the death of one or both parents seemed to signal a future of despair for most children, particularly the orphaned."[16]

---

16. Byars, Lauretta Flynn. "Introduction." *Lexington's Colored Orphan Industrial Home: Building for the Future*, I. B. Bold Publications, Lexington, KY, 1995, p. 12.

These black women led by their appointed president Elizabeth Belle Jackson, formed the Ladies Orphan Home Society in 1892. The Articles of Incorporation were filed in September 1894, and the following names were listed as organizers: E. Belle Jackson, Emma O. Warfield, Ida. W. Bate, Mary B. Hunter, Priscilla Lacey, Dr. Mary Britton, Caddie Clay, Lucy Clay, Mary L. Fletcher, Mary A. Gillis, Marie Hawkins, Jane Saunders, Maria Vaughn, Eliza Washington, and Lizzie P. Wilson.[17]

The home was financed through fund raising, donations and their own pockets at times. Some members would sew various garments and sell them to raise the necessary funds as well.

Besides children, women in need of shelter were also housed at the home, given that a physical examination was conducted, and recommendations from at least six citizens who could vouch for the woman's character.[18] This was to protect the children from potentially shady individuals.

The young girls were taught necessary kitchen skills while the boys were taught shoe making and even some blacksmithing. These are skills that could benefit them later on in life once they step out of the home and into the world on their own.

By 1988, due to declining numbers, the Homes function changed and the Robert H. Williams cultural center was ran out of the building. The building still remains today. For a more thorough reading and detailed history of the Colored Orphan Home, one can obtain the referenced book, "Lexington's Colored Orphan Industrial Home by Laura Flynn Byars. I would highly suggest that.

---

17. Ibid., p. 16

18. Ibid., pp. 27-28

One more personal thing to note, my great grandfather, James Hayes, that I spoke briefly about in the Pralltown chapter, he was an Orphan here in 1910. I found him on the census record.

Schools

There were a few black schools that existed in this community or in the vicinity throughout the years. Three in particular we will discuss in this section. The first one being what was known as the Chandler Normal School. The Chandler Normal School did not begin in Forest Hill nor was that the name initially. The schools inception in 1866, was with the church organized by the Reverend Frederick Braxton, the Independent Baptist Church(Now Main Street Baptist.) Classes were held in a building on Church Street called "Ladies Hall." Much like with the Orphan Home, fundraising by Lexington's black women is how they were able to purchase the facility and offer free classes to the city's black children.

The school took on the name "Howard School," named for the director of the Freedman's Bureau "Oliver Otis Howard and opened with an enrollment of 300 to 500 students. Enrollment increased to over 900 students just two years later and with the assistance of the Freedman's Bureau in 1870, they were able to acquire another building.[19] This was on Corral Street, in the Goodloetown neighborhood. Other black schools of Lexington merged with Howard and before long, enrollment exceeded capacity. The school closed and reopened once or twice be-

19. Thompson, Rico. "Chapter 8 - Rev. Frederick Braxton." *Sankofa Lexington*, Afrakan World Books and Moor, Lexington, KY, 2020, p. 64.

tween 1874 and 1888, but under a new name, the Normal Institute. A "Normal School" was a place where teachers underwent training.

With the school beyond capacity once more, a new space was needed. With funding from a northern philanthropist named Phoebe Chandler, they were able to purchase a new lot and build a new school to meet enrollment needs. This was a four acre lot in Forest Hill between Georgetown Pike and Newtown Pike, also between what was Thompson Ave(Ash Street) and College Street(this part is now Michigan Street.)

This private high school received adequate funding over its lifespan and lasted about four decades. Many of its graduates went on to become prominent members of the community of Lexington and also prominent members of communities in various other cities and states.

Isaac Scott Hathaway, a famous black sculptor from the Davis Bottom section of Lexington graduated in 1890.[20] Another graduate was educator and author Luther Porter Jackson, who was also a colleague of Carter G. Woodson. He graduated in 1910.[21] Jackson has a school named after him in Virginia. Lastly, we can not forget the man who would go on to design Webster Hall, and that is Lexington native Vertner Woodson Tandy.[22] He is recognized as New York State's first black registered architect. Aside from Webster Hall, he designed Madame C.J. Walker's mansion in Harlem, NY and St. Philip's Episco-

---

20. Ibid. pp. 32-38

21. Ibid. pp. 48-54

22. "Howard School / Normal Institute / Chandler Normal School / Webster Hall (Lexington, KY)," Notable Kentucky African Americans Database, accessed July 13, 2022, https://nkaa.uky.edu/nkaa/items/show/2153.

pal Church in Manhattan.

Webster Hall was built in 1914 at 548 Georgetown Street and was used to house the teachers and principals of Chandler.

Chandler Normal School would close down for good in 1923. The building remained standing and by 1960, an auditorium was built onto it.

The Chandler School Building and Webster Hall were both added to the National Registry of Historic Places in 1980. Sadly, in January of this year, 2022, the Chandler building, a church at the time caught fire and is no more. Webster Hall remains today.

Illustration 8: Webster Hall. The Chandler Normal School stood directly behind this building. (Photo by me 9/25/2022)

Another school that served the community was the short lived Forest Hill School. This school opened up in 1907 on College Street. College Street is now the section of Michigan Street that's between Georgetown Rd and Newtown Pike, in the vicinity of the Lincoln Terrace Apartments. At inception, the school operated out of a five room cottage, while awaiting the school board building the new school. Black children from the neighborhoods of Smithtown, Forest Hill, Taylortown, Yellmantown, and Peach Orchard attended the school in which Daniel Isaiah Reid, was principal. Anna B. Jones taught first grade, Mary E. Buckner, was the 2nd and 5th Grade teacher. Third was taught by Lottie Stewart, Mary B. Woodard taught Fourth and Sixth was taught by A.R. Webb. Each of these were taught out of the five rooms which means some grades were forced to share rooms with others. In total, there were 249 students.[23] There was clearly a need for a bigger space to accommodate the enrollment. However, the school board in a roundabout way stated that it was too expensive to educate Lexington's colored children, so Forest Hill would close three years later in 1910. The plans to build a new school remained although it never occurred. Members of the community petitioned the school board to reopen the school in 1911 and the petition was denied. By 1915, the push for the school continued, and the school board began accepting bids for the construction and yet it never came into fruition.[24] These students were then sent to the Russell School. One of the main concerns for the Forest Hill, Peach Orchard and Yellmantown community was that the Russell School was too far away for the children to walk each day and was dangerous due to them having to

---

23. Colored Schools. (1910, April 10). *Lexington Leader*, p. 24.

24. "Forest Hill School (Lexington, KY)," Notable Kentucky African Americans Database, accessed September 25, 2022, https://nkaa.uky.edu/nkaa/items/show/2515.

cross several streets as well as railroad tracks. This was an argument Jordan Jackson, husband to Orphan Home founder Elizabeth Belle Jackson, had argued in 1910.[25] Despite the communities best efforts, no school was ever built.

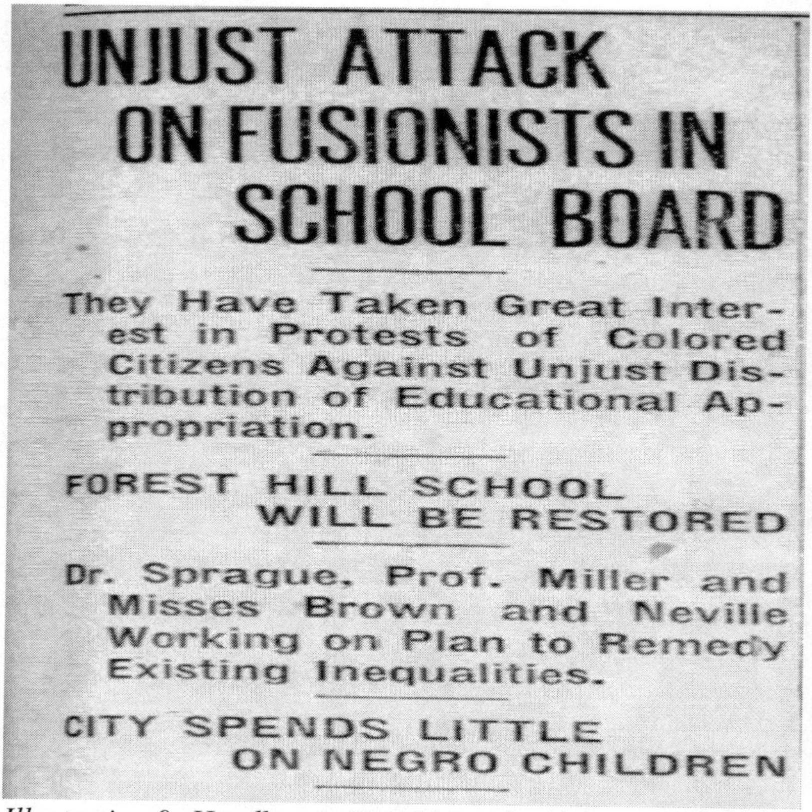

UNJUST ATTACK ON FUSIONISTS IN SCHOOL BOARD

They Have Taken Great Interest in Protests of Colored Citizens Against Unjust Distribution of Educational Appropriation.

FOREST HILL SCHOOL WILL BE RESTORED

Dr. Sprague, Prof. Miller and Misses Brown and Neville Working on Plan to Remedy Existing Inequalities.

CITY SPENDS LITTLE ON NEGRO CHILDREN

Illustration 9: Headline in Herald Leader showing community outcry. 13 Jun., 1911

---

25. School System is Praised. (1910, October 14). *The Lexington Herald*, p. 3.

One final school that we would like to mention in the community is the Booker T Washington school. The Booker T. Washington school was built in 1916 at 498 Georgetown St. The elementary school operated out of this building until moving into it's new location in 1971. The old Booker T. became then known as the Black and Williams Center and that is its present name today.

Illustration 10: Old Booker T. Washington School (Photo by me 9/25/2022)

<u>Laura Carroll Colored Branch Library</u>

This branch of the Lexington Public Library opened up in 1949 at 572 Georgetown Street. Prior to opening, a naming contest was held at the Booker T. Washington School and the name Laura Carroll was selected. A student named Helen Henderson won the contest. Laura Carroll was a teacher at the Chandler Normal School whose library was donated to Booker T. after her death in 1939. Daisy Combs, Genevie Covington and Elizabeth Botts were the librarians.

Two years later, the Lexington Public Library closed this branch and gave no explanation. However, library service via the bookmobile did begin servicing the area shortly thereafter in 1951.[26]

Illustration 11: Laura Carroll Branch Library

---

26. "Laura Carroll Colored Branch Library, Lexington, KY (Fayette County)," Notable Kentucky African Americans Database, accessed September 25, 2022, https://nkaa.uky.edu/nkaa/items/show/2836.

Illustration 12: This is the building thats in the location of the Laura Carroll Colored Library today. (Photo by me 9/25/2022)

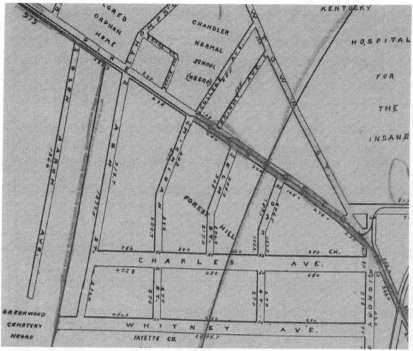

Illustration 13: 1912 map of the Forest Hill section.

Church

The Quinn Chapel African Methodist Episcopal Church, began in 1872 as a mission of the Historic St. Paul's A.M.E. Church, according to one source.[27] Another places the date around 1865.[28] The church held it's 50th Anniversary in 1925, which places the date around 1875.

27. Perrin, W. H. (1882). Chapter X, The Colored People of Lexington, Their Religious Advantages, Colored Churches, Educational Facilities, Secret and Benevolent Organizations, Fairs, ETC. In *History of Fayette County, Kentucky* (p. 472). Southern Historical Press.

28. Quinn Chapel A. M. E. Church. (1999, April 10). *Lexington Herald Leader*, p. 34.

Dates may vary but all agree that Green C. Riley was the church's first pastor and that the congregation began with services in several homes on Lee's Row in Yellman-town. They decided to call their congregation "Quinn," which is in honor of William Paul Quinn, the fourth bish-op of the African Methodist Episcopal church founded by Richard Allen in Philadelphia in 1794.[29]

Around 1878, a church was built near the corner of West Second Street and Evans Street. Today, Evans Street is Lauderman Alley and runs adjacent to Lee Street or what was known as Lee's Row. This land was a dona-tion from Samuel Lee. The church remained here until 1910.[30] A vacant lot next to the church was used as a dumping ground and the railroad was encroaching on the property which made the location unsuitable. A move was made.

They were able to obtain some property lots on Charles Avenue, but with the mismanagement of funds and other discord, there were several setbacks in getting the church built. The result was, for nearly two years, Quinn A.M.E., had no permanent church home. They would hold services in various places such as on Bright Street, in the Forest Hill School Building on College Street and under a tent at the Charles Avenue site.

Finally in the summer of 1913, the church was suc-cessfully completed at 744 Charles Avenue and the church remains in this location today. A new building

29. Staten, C. (2014, June 30). *William Paul Quinn (1788 - 1873)*. BlackPast.org. https://www.blackpast.org/african-american-history/quinn-william-paul-1788-1873/

30. New Quinn Chapel; Being Built By A. M. E. Church In Attractive Location and Assistance is Greatly Needed. (1913, January 17). *Lexington Leader*, p. 4.

was erected in 1930 and it's the present building.

Luther Porter Jackson

One of Forest Hills' great citizens is chronicled in the following pages.

The name Luther Porter Jackson is a household name among the black population of the state of Virginia, but he is a native born Lexingtonian, who grew up in the Forest Hill section.

Edward and Delilah Jackson, two prisoners of Americas war on melanin aka southern slavery, gained their freedom at the conclusion of the civil war. Together they had a total of twelve children. Luther was born ninth in Lexington, Ky, on July 11, 1892.

Like the majority of blacks in Lexington at this time, his early education began at the Chandler Normal School. He graduated in 1910.

Graduating in 1914 with a Bachelors of Arts degree from Nashville's HBCU Fisk University, Jackson was a student in the schools very first African American History Class. From there, he went on to study at the University of Kansas and City College in New York. Jackson obtained a Master's degree in 1922 from Columbia University Teachers College, and finally received his Doctorate in History from the University of Chicago in 1937.[31]

Most known for being an educator and historian, his career as a teacher began in 1913 at Topeka Industrial and Educational Institute in Kansas. There he taught history and music until moving on to Denmark, South Carolina in 1915. In South Carolina he taught at Voorhies In-

31. Thompson, Rico. "Chapter 6 – Luther Porter Jackson ." *Sankofa Lexington*, Afrakan World Books and Moor, Lexington, KY, 2020, p. 49.

dustrial School. He was also Director of the Academic Department. Voorhies Industrial School, today is the HBCU 'Voorhies College' and was the first black college in South Carolina to become accredited by the Southern Association of Colleges and Schools. He remained here teaching until 1918. His first two articles that were published later on in the Journal of Negro History, were researched in this time period while in South Carolina. He was also an editor of this same publication, it being a quarterly journal of African American life and history. It was founded in 1916 by the great historian Carter G. Woodson, personal friend of Jackson. Today, the name of the publication is Journal of African American History. The journal was published by Carter G Woodson's organization "Association for the Study of Negro Life and History," which was founded that same year with the assistance of Jackson and others.[32] He served as the Head of the Virginia chapter and in 1935 at the request of Woodson, was placed in charge of all fund raising activities. This same organization headed by Woodson promoted Negro History Week, which morphed into "Black History Month" today.[33]

Jackson joined the staff of Virginia Normal and Industrial Institute in 1922. This Historically Black College/University today is called Virginia State University. That same year he married Johnella Frazier. She was also a native Kentuckian from Shelbyville and a Fisk Univer-

32. Jones, M. B. (n.d.). *Luther Porter Jackson.* Retrieved January 24, 2023, from https://qa.vsu.edu/files/docs/student-activities/student-handbook.pdf

33. Pruitt, S. (2017, February 2). *The Man Behind Black History Month.* History.com. Retrieved January 24, 2023, from https://www.history.com/news/the-man-behind-black-history-month

sity alum. It was at Fisk in Nashville where they became acquainted. She would become a music teacher at Virginia Normal Institute and was able to pull some strings to get Jackson his position there. This position as history professor and Chairman of Social Sciences he would remain at until his death.[34]

Being a well established Professor of History and working alongside Carter G. Woodson, with the Association, many of his writings were political in nature. His dissertation was published in 1942 as "Free Negro Labor and Property Holding in Virginia, 1830 – 1860." He provided empirical data disproving the notion that Virginia freed blacks were unable to function in society on their own in that time period. He showed the increasing property and land ownership of Virginia's black population even while being at a disadvantage due to the segregation, slavery and the dehumanizing laws of the period. This book is available on Amazon and for free at Archive.org.

In 1944, Virginia Negro Soldiers and Seaman in the Revolutionary War was published, followed by Negro Office Holders in Virginia. This book gave brief biographies of many of Virginia blacks elected to the General Assembly. It's now in the Public Domain and can be found digitized online.

Jackson believed that racial equality could be obtained through politics and voting rights, so with members of the community, the "Petersburg League of Negro Voters" was formed in 1934. In 1935, they drafted a constitution for the organization. The preamble stated:

---

34. Thompson, Rico. "Chapter 6 – Luther Porter Jackson." *Sankofa Lexington*, Afrakan World Books and Moor, Lexington, KY, 2020, p. 50.

"We, Negro Citizens of Petersburg, Virginia in order to promote better citizenship, secure race unity, and take active part in the government of our city, state, and nation, do hereby create an organization to manage, direct, and protect these principles."[35]

Jackson penned a column from 1942 to 1948 for the Norfolk Journal and Guide under the heading "Rights and Duties in a Democracy." It was penned to encourage blacks in Virginia to vote. He wrote an annual report documenting black voting in the state called "The Voting Status of Negros in Virginia." This report would be disseminated throughout the state reaching teachers, newspapers, libraries, government officials and other organizations. An estimated 10,000 to 12,000 copies were distributed by the League.

Jackson's work, time, and energy extended beyond work with the Petersburg League of Negro Voters and the Association for the Study of Negro Life. He also was a member of several other organizations. These organizations included: Petersburg Negro Business Association, Virginia Teachers Association, Southern Regional Council, Southern School for Workers, Southern Conference Education Fund, N.A.A.C.P., and Southern Conference for Human Welfare. He received a plaque "for unselfish and devoted services in enhancing the voting status of Negroes," in 1948 from the N.A.A.C.P.[36]

Jackson was a man of many talents. We've already discussed his work as an author, historian, teacher, journalist, community activist, and member of numerous organizations, somehow he still found time to organize an-

---

35. Ibid,. p. 51

36. Ibid,. p. 51

nual concerts as a musician. A cornet player, he founded the Petersburg Community Choir in 1933. They would perform from 1933 to 1941. This comes as no surprise because he was married to a musician and music teacher, Johnella Jackson. Again, the couple met while students at Fisk University and would eventually marry September 18, 1922. Mrs. Jackson toured with the Fisk Jubilee singers for a couple of years before joining the staff of the Virginia Normal and Industrial Institute(VSU) as a piano instructor. This was a first for the school, the music department didn't come to be until 9 years later.[37]

Luther and Johnella would have four children together, Edward, John T., Laura Frances and Luther Jr.

1950, regrettably, was a year of multiple setbacks for our warrior scholars. Jackson's friend, Carter G. Woodson passed away April 3, 1950. Seventeen days later on April 20, Luther Porter Jackson succumbs to a heart attack. He is buried at the Blandford Cemetery in Petersburg, Va.

In all of the articles that I have viewed in gathering content for this chapter, I've seen nothing mentioning military service, however, I have located a WWI Draft Card belonging to Jackson dated June 15, 1917. Whether he was deployed and actually served in the war, I cannot say but it unmistakably is his card. This draft card can be viewed free of charge at familysearch.org, a free genealogy website organized by the Latter Day Saints.

His legacy and name lives on. He is forever immortalized in books such as this one as well as the numerous middle and high schools in Virginia that are named after him. Much gratitude to him and his family for his tireless work being a great champion of our race.

---

37. Ibid,. p. 52

I'm thankful to be able to dedicate this section to this great man.

Chapter 12 – Peach Orchard, & Charlotte Courts Housing Projects

Peach Orchard was a section in what is now the West Side of Lexington. At the time of formation, this section off of Georgetown Pike was outside the city limits but within Fayette County. The streets that comprised this section were Howard Ave, Black Street, White Street and Clay Street. Black street was on the west side of the Colored Orphan Home. This neglected area sprang up sometime in the late 1800's. Most of the homes in the area were shotgun styled and little small cottages. By the 1920's, it was considered a slum and targeted for Slum Clearance. There is not a lot of information on the formation of Peach Orchard, or where the name originated. We do know much of this section was called Lee's Woods in the 1700's and early 1800's, so it is likely that there may have been a Peach Orchard in the vicinity prior to it becoming a residential community, albeit that is purely speculation on my part. During the trial of one individual the following remark was made about Peach Orchard:

> "At this point in the dialogue prosecutor Morgan suggested that young Frame be dismissed provided he would go back to Peach Orchard where he lives and reform.
>
> "What could I do out there"? Asked the witness.
>
> "Raise peaches," was the response.
>
> When it is known that there is not a peach tree in Peach Orchard, the humor of the advice is readily apparent."[1]

With that said, we can confirm that there weren't any peach orchards in the section, so the name remains a mystery.

The community was home to about two hundred people. The majority of them were black and were employed on nearby farms.[2] While other sections of Lexington had street lights, Peach Orchard was without until citizens voiced their concerns about having to walk the non-paved streets that were without sidewalks in the dark. So lights soon were installed on Howard, Black and White Street. They were tax paying citizens and felt the

---

1. Riley and His Henchman Morgan Rap Their Lifetime Friends Over The Shoulders of Charlie Frame. (1905, November 15). *Lexington Leader*, p. 5.

2. Territory to be Annexed. (1906, March 13). *The Lexington Herald*, p. 10.

city should not be neglecting their neighborhood when it came to improving the streets.[3]

There was also a county school in Peach Orchard for black children. For a short time, Fannie Hathaway White, the sister of famed Davis Bottom sculptor Isaac Hathaway, taught at the school in 1901.[4]

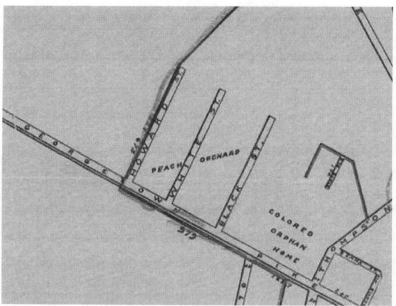

Illustration 1: 1912 Map of Peach Orchard

Chapter 9 of my first book "Sankofa Lexington," was about a formerly enslaved woman who was called "Aunt Charlotte." Charlotte Courts were named after her and in the chapter, I wrote that the projects was built in a

3. Commissioner McCorkle Hopes To Secure Lights For Peach Orchard. (1913, October 2). *Lexington Leader*, p. 12.

4. Schools of The County Open Tuesday. The Assignment of Teachers. (1901, September 3). *The Morning Herald*, p. 6.

"slum area" however, I failed to identify specifically what this slum area was. It was Peach Orchard.

That chapter was relatively small and this book will likely be read by many who are unfamiliar with my first small booklet, so we will reproduce her history here. This next section is taken verbatim from that book. Immediately following her story we will then proceed with the history of the projects itself.

Aunt Charlotte

Throughout history, you may find obscure names of people who have made an impact of some kind, for their names and deeds to even be known to us today. However, many details of their lives will forever remain a mystery. Such is the case of this chapters subject, Aunt Charlotte. She became a household name in Lexington in the year 1833 and because one of Lexington's historically black neighborhoods bore her name, she deserves to be known and thus this chapter is being written.

Charlotte was born in slavery in the state of Virginia. She was brought to Lexington in the late 1700's, however the exact year is unknown. After her owner had passed away, she gained her freedom as well as property. She made her living selling fruit, pies, and other baked goods.

Her name didn't become recorded in history because of her pies, it was the fact that she attended an auction and made the purchase of a white drunkard and vagrant known as "King Solomon." It is said that the two were acquainted with each other while she was enslaved in Virginia. Solomon was originally from there as well.

Much of Solomon's story will be omitted purposely from this work but what's important and connected to Aunt Charlotte will be retained, so lets proceed.

Solomon was arrested quite frequently in Lexington, often found passed out in various places all over town, drunk. After one arrest and court date, the judge sentenced Solomon to serve nine months as a servant. Solomon was auctioned off to serve his sentence. The bidding was between two Transylvania medical students and Aunt Charlotte. Aunt Charlotte eventually won the auction and legally became owner of Solomon. The actual price paid varies according to the source, one says she paid $0.13, another $0.50 and another saying $13. The exact price paid will likely remain unknown but whats for sure is, this event is recorded in history, this black woman purchased this white man in 1833. According to newspaper accounts, a friend asked Charlotte why she bought that "poor white trash," and her reply was:

> "Kase white folks own niggers, and I want to know how a nigger feels to own a white man."[5]

A Cholera outbreak struck Lexington the summer of 1833, and this is where Solomon gained his fame. About 500 people died from the epidemic, and hundreds more fled Lexington. Solomon remained behind to help dig graves for the dead. He, alongside the Rev. London Ferrill, stayed in Lexington while hundreds more fled the city. Charlotte was preparing to leave Lexington as well but when Solomon refused to leave, she remained behind. This event is what made Solomon a hero and how

5. "King Solomon--By Someone Who Knew Him Well." *Lexington Leader*, 30 Aug. 1908, p. 7

we come to know about Aunt Charlotte. As I said previously, I left out most of the details about Solomon because I wanted the focus to be on Aunt Charlotte, there's various web pages with all the details of Solomon's life.

What became of Aunt Charlotte is unknown. One account says she died of cholera soon after the outbreak began, another says she survived this epidemic. Whatever the case, had she not purchased Solomon, gave him his freedom and befriended him, his heroics would've been impossible.[6]

Charlotte Courts Housing Projects

The "S" at the end of Courts that you see above and in the title is not a typo. It may be presumed by people familiar with the neighborhood because natives of this city refer to it simply as Charlotte Court, but the official name includes the "S'" Moving further, we will just use Charlotte Court in the remainder of this text as that's what I am most familiar with.

Charlotte Court was opened in 1941 on 24 acres of land in the "Colored Section" formerly known as Peach Orchard and became Lexington's second housing project. Bluegrass Aspendale was the first and that will be covered in a later chapter.

The Lexington Housing Authority became the local branch of the U.S. Housing Authority when it formed in 1937. It was created by the United States Housing Act that passed in that year. They formed to provide funding to local agencies for affordable housing as well as for Slum Clearance.

---

6. Thompson, Rico . "Chapter 9 – Aunt Charlotte." *Sankofa Lexington,* Afrakan World Books and Moor, 2020, pp. 68-72.

Slum Clearance is defined as "an urban renewal strategy used to transform low income settlements with poor reputation into another type of development or housing." What the Federal Government failed to realize in its desire to clear slums is, they themselves created the socioeconomic problems that lead to an area becoming a slum. Not long into the history of this housing project was it labeled a slum once more. Poverty, drugs, and crime plagued this 206 unit housing project. These same factors plague nearly all poverty stricken and racially segregated communities throughout the country and the world as a whole. Poverty itself creates crime. Many fall victim to alcohol and drugs to escape their everyday realities. Drugs were imported into black communities by the federal Government and many of these poor citizens saw an opportunity to make lots of money and make it fast, thus the drug trade was born. It had always existed but when crack cocaine was unleashed in urban communities in the 1980's, we saw devastation in our neighborhoods unlike anything before. This community was no different. Despite these conditions we come from, this was home and all we knew. There was a sense of family among the residents and a sense of community.

These 206 units grew to about 356 units by the 1960's when additional barrack styled units were built.

In March of 1940, a library was established in the housing project. It was separate from the Lexington Public Library. It was operated by an all black board of directors. Manchester Street Library, another independent branch had given the newly formed library a total of 250 books.[7]

---

7. "Colored Libraries in the Charlotte Court and Aspendale Housing Projects, Lexington, KY (Fayette County)," Notable Kentucky African

Lexington received a federal grant in 1998 for "slum clearance" once more and in 1999, the projects were torn down to make way for single family dwellings in a community that became "The Arbors."

Illustration 2: Charlotte Court 1990's (Courtesy of Melanie Foster)

Illustration 3: Charlotte Court 1990's (Courtesy of Melanie Foster)

Americans Database, accessed September 20, 2022, https://nkaa.uky.edu/nkaa/items/show/2829.

HOUSING PROJECT—Here is the architect's drawing for the 22-building addition to the Charlotte Court Housing Project established by the Lexington Municipal Housing Commission. The buildings will provide space for 150 families in 745 rooms. The estimated cost of the project is $1,685,162. It will be located on Charlotte Court and Georgetown Street.

Illustration 4: Architects drawing of Charlotte Court Housing Projects, 22 building addition (Lexington Herald Leader 26 Jul., 1965)

CHARLOTTE COURT HOUSING PROJECT—Work has started on the construction of 22 buildings which will house 150 units in the new Charlotte Court addition located off Georgetown Street. A part of the city's municipal housing project, 50 units are scheduled to be completed by Jan. 24. Fain and Johnston are the general contractors for the project and the buildings are being designed by Watkins and Burrows.

Illustration 5: Additional Units being built (Lexington Herald Leader (1 Oct., 1965)

Frederick Douglass Park

As with the vast majority of southern cities, Lexington was segregated. The city parks such as Woodland and Duncan park were white only. Lexington's black community needed their own parks and recreation areas.

As early as 1912, there were discussions among the city and Lexington's black leaders to create two parks for the black community. James Alexander Chiles, a local black lawyer, was among those leaders. Beyond his duties as a lawyer, he was very active in the affairs of Lexington's black citizens. Chiles, the 2nd black lawyer in the city of Lexington, believed that two specific areas of the city were perfect for these said parks. In 1912, he suggested that an area in Peach Orchard be acquired for one park and another area on the east side of town, in the Goodloe section, be acquired for the other.

The city acquired 25 acres of unused land from a prominent grocer in Lexington by the name of Elijah Lee Martin. Most sources state that he was African American however, census records show that he was not. He was in fact a white man. It is necessary to clear this up because if you look this information up on a search engine, every source states "prominent African American grocer." When you look at the Property Value Administrator site of Fayette County, Ky, you will see that Elijah L. Martin and wife Anna L. Martin sold the property to the city of Lexington on April 17, 1915. On the 1940 Census record, you will find him and wife Anna living at 468 N. Limestone, near Duncan Park, and their race is listed as white.

After the land acquisition, Frederick Douglass park opened to the public on July 4, 1916. There was an estimated 5000 people who were in attendance. There

TWO SITES FOR COLORED PARKS

Peach Orchard on Georgetown Pike and Dr. Goodloe Property on East Third Street Proposed as Desirable Locations.

J. ALEXANDER CHILES OFFERS SUGGESTION

Editor LEXINGTON LEADER:

The selection of suitable sites for parks for colored people of the city is of vital importance to our people; therefore I sincerely hope that due consideration will be given us before final determination of the question. We simply want a "square deal." Will not you and other good citizens help us to obtain that object?

Now, the place and location suggested by Mr. Barron is in no way proper for such a park as would meet the approval of the best people of either race. A few may desire it, but not because of what good result may come to my race nor to the city, but doubtless for speculative ideas.

In my judgment the sites for parks should be where some fresh air and some outdoor exercise can be obtained. Then, too, the parks should not be in the same locality. We voted with other good citizens for the bond issue that was to give the colored people two parks, and since its adoption I have been observing different localities, and it seems to me that the following sites possess advantages of great importance:

First, the whole of Peach Orchard on the Georgetown pike next to the Colored Orphan Home property. From appearance it contains about five acres. This could be the "West End Park" or "Peach Orchard Park."

Second, the Dr. David Goodloe property on East Third street. This, I am told, contains also about five acres. This could be the "East End Park" or "Goodloe Park."

Both of these places have some good trees. They also have certain improvements thereon which may be used to good advantage. Both front on good streets, and if they can be purchased not at speculative but reasonable prices, and thereafter properly beautified, I feel confident that the people of this city will be proud of them.

Therefore I hope that the Park Commission or whoever be the party or parties to select and purchase sites for parks for us will first duly consider our wishes and let us have some say as to location. Yours for the best and highest interest of all.

J. ALEXANDER CHILES.

Illustration 6: Illustration 6: Lexington Herald Leader article from James Alexander Chiles, offering his suggestions for the two negro parks. Both sites were eventually chosen. (20 Dec., 1912)

was a parade, live music, as well as speakers. This park would be a central piece of African American life in Lexington for over a century. Douglass Park, named after notable abolitionist, author, activist and former slave, Frederick Douglass, would become the premier place for family reunions, summer festivals, concerts, sporting events and everyday recreation.

Illustration 6: Entrance to the Park (Photo by Me, 9/26/2022)

In the 1930's, a "street shower" was installed in the park, which provided the neighborhood children an opportunity to enjoy summer fun. A pool would be built later. Over the years, there would be tennis courts, basketball courts, baseball fields, a golf club, volleyball court, and a playground. Various baseball leagues operated by Parks and Rec would have it's games on the baseball fields in the park. I myself, at the age of 11, played for the PAL Royals in 1994. All of our games were held at the park. I wasn't that good at the sport of baseball, it was just something to do after school, and several of my friends in the neighborhood were on the team as well. Nonetheless, its a great memory that I have and one that I reflect upon every time I visit or think of this historic African American park. Enough about me.

Illustration 7: This is me in my baseball uniform at Douglass Park (1994)

Dirt Bowl

There has been much debate between Kentucky's two major cities, Lexington and Louisville, about where the Dirt Bowl originated first. Some suggest it began in Lexington in 1962, some say in 1967, others suggest it started in Louisville in 1968.[8] Dirt Bowl organizer Herb Washington states in 1975:

> "This league is modeled after the Dust Bowl in Louisville.......they've got some kind of league in Louisville with guys like Artis Gilmore and a lot of ex college players."[9]

Was this alluding to it originating in Louisville or that some elements were borrowed from the states largest city's tournament/league? We may not be able to pinpoint specifically but what we do know is both cities have enjoyed the annual festivities surrounding one of the nation's top summer basketball tournaments since at least the 1960's. Some of Kentucky's top basketball players have participated in this tournament. The University of Kentucky's Jack Givens, Melvin Turpin, James Lee, Erik Daniels among others, laced up their sneakers on the basketball court at Douglass Park. Spectators over the years have included the likes of the New York Knicks Point Guard Walt Frazier, who led the Knicks to two NBA Championships in 1970 and 1973, as well as Ken-

---

8. Smith, G. L., McDaniel, K. C., Hardin, J. A., & Adams, L. (2015). Dirt Bowl. In *The Kentucky African American Encyclopedia* (1st ed., p. 144). essay, University Press of Kentucky.

9. Johnson, M. (1975, August 13). Dirt Bowl Offers Basketball at it's Best. *Lexington Herald Leader*, p. 13.

tucky's own and 1975 NBA Champion, Butch Beard. College coaches would also attend, always scouting for new talent. In 1978, the coach of Western Kentucky, Clem Haskins was in attendance as well as coaches from several other NCAA schools including Mississippi State, Mississippi Valley, Albany State and a few others.[10]

Walt Frazier, Butch Beard To Appear at Local Dirt Bowl

Profession basketball players Butch Beard and Walt Frazier will appear today at the Dirt Bowl Basketball Tourney at Douglass Park.

Tourney director Herb Washington said he expects 3,000 people to attend the five-game slate beginning at 2:30 p.m.

Illustration 8: Headline in Lexington Herald Leader (03 Jul., 1977)

Herb Washington was one of the early organizers of the event and the complex would become named after him. In 2007, the center court was named Ethan Jenkins Center Court, after the 26 year old man died from a heart

---

10. Fitzmaurice, D. G. (1978, June 18). College Scouts Scramble For Dirt Bowl Seats. *Lexington Herald Leader*, p. 34.

condition during one of the games.

Illustration 9: Photo by me (September 26, 2022)

The Dirt Bowl and a replica of Douglass Park was even featured in EA Sports 2007 Playstation and Xbox video game titled NBA Street: Homecourt.

One last piece of history in regards to the Dirt

Bowl we would like to share is that, Kentucky's first black female official, cut her teeth officiating games in this tournament. Brenda Lee Garner Hughes was a postal employee who also worked for Parks and Recreation. This is where she learned to officiate basketball and February 2, 1973, she was the first black woman to officiate the Kentucky High School Athletic Association Girl's State Basketball Tournament, better known as the "Sweet Sixteen."

Lexington's First Black Police Officers

Several people spoken of in this book are included in various chapters, as they were significant enough in one way or another in Lexington's black community as a whole and not just one specific neighborhood. Such is the case of the man who became Lexington's first black police officer in 1918. This man being R.F. Bell or Robert Bell. Bell was one of the owners of the short lived Gem Theater, that story is to come much later in the book.

Bell along with attorney James Alexander Chiles, were among the city's black leaders who put pressure on Lexington for the creation of Douglass Park.

After the parks opening in 1916, there was a need for patrols throughout the park to maintain law and order. Bell was hired by the Lexington Police Department for ten weeks in the summer of 1918, to patrol the park grounds.[11]   He wasn't alone, Jane Christy[12], another influential member of Lexington's black community, was to patrol alongside him.[13]

R.F. Bell sat on various boards and was president of a number of black organizations within his lifetime. He passed away at his home at 274 East Fifth Street on September 28, 1931 and was interred at the Greenwood Cemetery.(Cove Haven)

---

11.   In a 1922 Lexington Herald Leader it states that Bell was an officer for several years and not the ten weeks various other sources are reporting. It is likely suggesting that this was a role he was elected to annually for the summer months.

Leader, L. H. (1922, June 17). To Push Work on West Sixth. *Lexington Herald Leader*, p. 8.

12.   This same newspaper article refers to her as Jennie Christie.

Ibid., p. 8

13.   Jones, C. (n.d.). *Lexington Police Dept. recognizing first black police officers who served in the city*. https://www.wkyt.com. Retrieved September 27, 2022, from https://www.wkyt.com/2021/02/24/lexington-police-dept-recognizing-first-black-police-officers-who-served-in-the-city/

Illustration 10: Robert F. Bell

Washington Terrace

Washington Terrace was a subdivision directly across the street from Peach Orchard and Douglas Park, on the opposite side of Georgetown Street. The principal street in the subdivision is Roosevelt Blvd. Named so after one of the Presidents of The United States, Theodore Roosevelt, whose quote "show me the man paying on a home and I will show you a man worthwhile," was used to advertise the new development that sprang up around 1925. Ads went out that year looking for "colored" contractors to build the homes.[14] These homes were marketed to "high class colored people." In other words, they only wanted the black working class and did not want to sell to "poor" individuals.

> "We are offering to a few forward looking colored men and women an opportunity that was never offered them before, namely a restricted lot, where no one can erect a shack beside your home."
>
> "We haven't sold to any cheap colored people, simply because the atmosphere don't suit them, we have sold to practically all the professions that colored people make their livelihood from."[15]

---

14. "Colored Notes." *The Lexington Herald*, 12 Sept. 1925, p. 6.

15. "Roosevelt Said." *The Lexington Leader*, 25 May 1926, p. 15.

Lincoln Park
Addition & Douglass Heights

Situated directly behind Washington Terrace is a subdivision that is a bit older. This one began developing after 1910 and consists of the streets Florence Ave., Booker Ave(now Breathitt Ave.,) and Chiles Ave. These streets were accessed from Douglass Ave., and Walter Ave(now Price Road.)

Douglass Heights was established around the same time as Lincoln Park. The one street in this subdivision is Douglass Ave.

Urban Communities South

"The most common way people give up their power is by thinking they don't have any."

- Alice Walker

Chapter 13 – Pralltown

This predominantly African American community gets it's name from the former enslaver and lawyer, John Prall, who purchased 5 acres of land at the southern edge of Lexington, alongside Limestone Street in 1868. The street on his property became known as Prall Street. There were two other white enslavers who owned property in the community and sold lots to and rented to African Americans.

Frederick Montmollin, Jr, also purchased five acres. Adjacent to Prall Street, the street on his property became known as Montmollin Street. The spelling was later changed to Montmullin and that's what remains today. I have a story to share from my ancestry that occurred on this street later in this chapter.

The final landowner within the community was Willard Davis. Davis owned several slaves, was a lawyer, and also the namesake of another African American community not too far from Pralltown called Davis Bottom or Davistown. The street in his section became Colfax Street.[1] Sellers Alley was a back alley, running next to the Kentucky Central Railroad, which was the western border of the little community. The Alley was added much later but connected the three major streets in the neighborhood together. It's of note that there was a black carpenter named James "Jim" Sellers, who was one of the early black property owners in the section, and it's possible that Sellers Alley received it's name from him. But, that has not been verified. He passed away in 1898 and according to his death record, his address was 60 Prall Street. Collectively, this entire community took on the name Pralltown.

---

1. Jones, R. F. (n.d.). The Development of Pralltown, 1868. In *History of the Pralltown Community, Lexington, Kentucky* (p. 1).

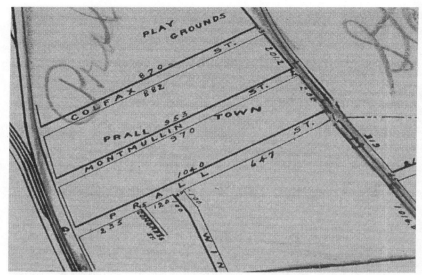

Illustration 1: 1912 Map of Pralltown. Westernmost is the Railroad and Sellers Alley. The eastern border is Limestone Street.

Sitting at the edge of Lexington, alongside Limestone Street, these flood prone lowlands were slowly developed over the course of several years. By 1880, this section had approximately three hundred and fifty residents with nearly 300 being black and about 50 residents being white.[2]

The Shotgun styled homes were the dominant architectural style in the majority of these black communities, Pralltown was no exception. The shotgun homes were T or L shaped, single story dwellings that lined the three street community.

---

2 . Jones, R. F. (n.d.). Further Development of Pralltown, 1876-1940s. In *History of the Pralltown Community, Lexington, Kentucky* (p. 4).

Illustration 2: The only remaining shotgun house in the com-munity, at 179 Prall Street(Photo taken by me in 2020)

Nearly all of the communities discussed in this book had schools, but Pralltown is an exception. Children attended the city schools for black children.

The neighborhood was mostly residential. Over the years, there were various stores and a couple of saloons in the community. Most of the residents however, worked outside of the community, many of them being farm hands. Nathan Biggs, an African American was one of the first lot owners in the community and he operated a grocery store.[3] Basil Black was another, and on the 1870 Census, his occupation is listed as fence maker. He also bought and sold property in various sections

---

3. Jones, R. F. (n.d.). The Seven Early Lot Owners in 1868. In *History of the Pralltown Community, Lexington, Kentucky* (p. 3).

throughout Lexington during the late 1800's.

In a KET interview, lifelong resident William Bingham stated that men from the community would often jump the passing trains for meat and coal. The coal coming from the Eastern part of the state was used to heat the homes. It was a matter of survival, so these men would get into the train cars, throw the necessities down and the residents would take what was needed.[4] Pralltown was a tight knit community where everybody shared with one another.

Prall Street Christian Church

A small frame church house was erected at 131 Prall Street, in 1926 and became known as Prall Street Christian Church, founded by Rev. T. R. Everett. This church was an extension of the East Second Street Christian Church, in which Everett was an Elder. The price tag to build the church was $1500.[5]

In the 1950's, a new congregation purchased the property from East Second Christian Church and began holding services within. This new church took on the name Prall Street Church of Christ. This congregation was organized by Theodore Wallace and his family. They began holding service inside his home in 1956. This home, is literally next door to me. As I type these words, I can see this house on Whitney Avenue, outside my window. It's a vacate, abandoned property today. As the congregation grew, more space was needed and that's when

---

4. KETVideos . "Pralltown | Kentucky Life | KET." *YouTube*, YouTube, 9 Oct. 2019, www.youtube.com/watch?v=iiNtOdVayCA.

5. Prall Street Church. (1926, August 19). *The Lexington Leader*, p. 8.

the Pralltown property was acquired. The Church of Christ remained in this location until they moved to a new location in 1998, on Russell Cave Road, and the name was changed to New Birth Church of Christ.[6] This building as of today, no longer exists.

Illustration 3: Pralltown Church (Lexington Herald-Leader Aug.19, 1926)

Lou Johnson

Pralltown has had a few interesting characters over it's years. From the most famous man to dress in drag in Lexington, James Herndon aka Sweet Evening Breeze, to local blues musician and club owner T.D. Young. Even at one time, the famed Harlem Drug King-pin Frank Lucas, before his notoriety in New York City, moved to Lexington as a teen and lived briefly in the community at 169 ½ Colfax Street.[7] He stayed with Miss

6. *Prall Street Church of Christ*. New Birth CC. (n.d.). Retrieved January 16, 2023, from https://www.newbirthchurchofchrist.com/histroy

7. *Frank Lucas Interviewed By Korey Rowe*. (2015). *YouTube*. Retrieved January 16, 2023, from https://www.youtube.com/watch?

"M" or Mary Emma Harris, who had a bootleg alcohol operation in the 1940's. This is the same Frank Lucas played by Denzel Washington in the film American Gangster.

The most famous person to come from the Pralltown community was former Lexington Hustler and Major League Baseball Player Lou Johnson. Louis Brown Johnson aka "Sweet Lou" was born in 1934 in Lexington, Ky. He had a professional baseball career that lasted 17 years. Eight of the 17 seasons were in the Major League. Johnson's claim to fame came in 1965, Game 7 of the World Series as a member of the Los Angeles Dodgers. He hit the game winning home run to give the Dodgers its 4th National Championship. Prior to his 1965 debut as a Dodger, Sweet Lou was signed by the New York Yankees in 1953. Played for the Yankees minor league team until 1960 when he was picked up by the Cubs, then traded to the Angels a year later. Johnson played only one game in California before going to the International League with Toronto. From Toronto, the Braves acquired his services. From Milwaukee in 1962, he was traded to the Detroit Tigers, where he played 2 years for their minor league team. After the stint with Detroit, he landed a deal with the Dodgers and it was here that he gained his notoriety, hitting the game winning home run mentioned above. In this championship game he had 8 hits, 2 of which were home runs. Johnson retired from baseball in 1970 but remained with the organization in the teams community relations department, a total of 40 years with the organization. Sweet Lou Johnson passed away

---

v=q8mYqmzz1_o&t=751s.

in Los Angeles, California on September 30, 2020.[8]

He was 86. The neighborhood park is named Lou Johnson Park and one of the streets was renamed in honor of Sweet Lou, the Pralltown Legend, "Lou Johnson Way."

Reuben Givens

The paternal family of actress Robin Givens also hail from Pralltown. Givens as we know, is the former wife of the Heavyweight Champion Boxer Mike Tyson. Her father is Reuben Givens, who is the nephew of the aforementioned Lou Johnson and brother of former University of Kentucky and NBA player Jack "Goose" Givens. Reuben Givens made a little local history himself becoming Lafayette High Schools first African American basketball player. Prior to attending Lafayette, he was a star basketball player at the all black Douglass High School. Due to integration and Douglass' Highs closure, he attended Lafayette, graduating in 1964. That same year, he married Robin's mother Ruth Newby. His family was among the first families to call Pralltown home in the 1860's.[9]

8. Press, Associated. "'Sweet' Lou Johnson, Who Hit Winning Homer for Los Angeles Dodgers in '65 World Series, Dies." *ESPN*, ESPN Internet Ventures, 2 Oct. 2020, www.espn.com/mlb/story/_/id/30025247/sweet--lou-johnson-hit-winning-homer-los-angeles-dodgers-65-world-series-dies.

9. "Givens, Reuben and Ruth Newby Givens Roper," Notable Kentucky African Americans Database, accessed May 29, 2021, https://nkaa.uky.edu/nkaa/items/show/1655.

James William Hayes

As a native Lexingtonian, I myself have ancestral ties to many of these communities I am writing about in this book. For that reason, I like to include a little bit of my own family history in the chapters where it applies. Such is the case with Pralltown. My great grandfather, whose name was James William Hayes lived in Pralltown for a number of years at a home located at 187 Montmullen Drive. In April of 1952, James, who passed away before I was born, got into an argument with a roommate living in the same house. Hayes opened fire and the man, Kane Compton, lay dead in the street, right outside of their residence in Pralltown. Hayes claimed self defense and was found guilty of manslaughter later that year. He was sentenced to 10 years in Prison.

I had no personal knowledge of him prior to doing some genealogy research and discovering this killing in the newspaper. I was able to connect it to my family because my fathers father' name is also James Hayes and when he married my Grandmother in the 1950's, his residence was 187 Montmullen, the same address as the elder Hayes. His son, my dads father, was a military man, in the Air Force and Army. Prior to joining the service, he was a Golden Gloves boxing champion in the 1950's, a track star and singer in a local group called "The Bronze Balladiers." He moved to Dallas, Tx in the 1970's and that's where he lived until his death in 2006.

HE SINGS, TOO—James J.
Hayes, bowling - alley pinboy,
hopes to be knocking 'em down
instead of setting 'em up in the
Golden Gloves tourney. He's
leader-manager of the Bronze
Ballodiers, a male quartet, and
is Negro track champion of
Lexington.

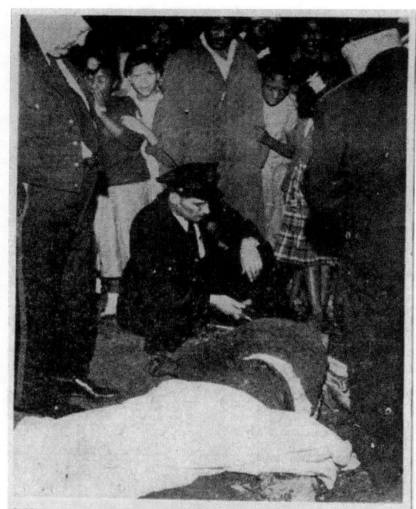

VICTIM OF GUNFIRE—City Patrolman H. T. McClure is shown examining the body of Kane Compton, Negro, 64, of 187 Montmollin street, who was killed Sunday night at his residence. James William Hayes, Negro, 54, of the same address, was charged with murder in connection with the shooting. An examining trial for Hayes will be held at 10 a.m. May 6 before County Judge William E. Nichols. Police said Hayes fired five bullets from a .38 caliber revolver. Compton was hit four times, Deputy Coroner James Chasteen reported.

Illustration 5: Newspaper article about the murder my great grandfather committed in 1952 (Lexington Herald Leader, 28 Apr., 1952)

Signal Depot Worker Tells About Killing

A Lexington Signal Depot employee who told a jury that after being slapped and threatened "I reached and grabbed my gun and started shooting" was on trial yesterday in Fayette Circuit Court on a charge of murder.

The case—in which James William Hayes, Negro, 54, of 187 Montmullin street, is charged with slaying Kane Compton, Negro, April 27—was ready for closing arguments when Judge Joseph J. Bradley adjourned court until 9 a. m. today.

Hayes, who testified he had been employed at the Lexington Signal Depot for 10 years, declared he fired in self-defense after a sporadic, but noisy, argument with Compton, a roomer in the house.

The defendant said the argument began when Compton objected to Hayes turning over two pictures in Compton's room to Mrs. Katie Marshall, wife of a Methodist district superintendent. Hayes said the pictures belong to Mrs. Marshall and had been left at the house before Compton rented the room.

"He was on the front porch and opened the screen door and slapped me hard," Hayes testified. "Then he reached his hand in his pocket and I reached and grabbed my gun and started shooting."

Hayes testified he fired five times, but didn't know how many times he hit Compton. Under cross-examination he testified he had placed the pistol on the table in case of trouble with Compton.

Principal testimony against Hayes was given by Compton's common-law wife, Hester, a blind woman, who told of hearing the argument and the shots.

Illustration 6: An account of what occurred that evening (Lexington Herald Leader 21 Oct., 1952)

Illustration 7: 1950 Golden Gloves Champions. (from left to right): Hilliard Fann, Coach George Edwards, Jimmy Burns, Garland Dishman, William Talbott, Joe Ed Dawson, James J. Hayes, Dempsey Hale, W.H. Davis. (January 25, 1950) In the very center of the photo, the short guy with the dark pants and light shirt, that is my Grandfather James Jerome Hayes. He lived in Pralltown at the time of this photo.

Unfortunately, I never had the pleasure to meet my grandfather James Jerome Hayes or my great grandfather, James William Hayes. The elder, as stated passed before my birth and the younger, moved to Texas prior to my birth.

I do have a story however. One afternoon in 2013 or 2014, at a bus stop, I met an elderly lady named Gladys or Grace. We began casually conversing and when she told me she was in her 80's, I replied that my grandmother was the same age. After asking who my grandmother was, I told her and she knew her. She asked was James Hayes my grandfather. I replied that he was but I didn't know him personally. She took one look at me and said "yes you look just like him. He used to sing really well and was in a singing group, can you sing?" I told her I wasn't blessed with that skill. We parted ways but I never forgot that interaction. Fast forward to about one year ago, 2020, I found an article in the newspaper. It was a picture of my granddad, and in the caption, it stated exactly what she told me, that he was a singer.

Other than my father, I do not personally know anyone from this line and Great Grandfather Hayes' parentage remains a bit of a mystery for me. I have been unsuccessful in finding anything about this family beyond him. The only thing I've discovered is, the home he lived in at 187 Montmullen, was owned by Frank and Laura Warren. On the 1950 census, Frank was deceased. Laura, James W., his wife Mary E. and my granddad James Jr., were listed on the record as being its occupants. Laura Warren is listed as James Sr's aunt. At this time, I'm unsure if shes a blood aunt or if its by another means. At any rate, when she passed away, the home became his. On his military records, she is also listed as his next of kin, an indication that his parents have long been deceased or estranged. I found on the 1910 Census record a 13 year old African American orphan living in the Colored Orphan Home and his name was James Hayes. The age matches up with my great grandfather so it's highly probable that this is him.

Nonetheless, he was paroled after 5 years, and married his third wife, Lottie Coleman, just a couple of years prior to his death in the 1970's. Before that, my great grandmother Mary Jewett, was his wife. She passed in 1939 and he then married Mary E. Mitchell. She also passed away making him a widow times two.

Urban Renewel

Urban Renewal is defined as "the rehabilitation of city areas by renovating or replacing dilapidated buildings with new housing, public buildings, parks, roadways, industrial areas, etc., often in accordance with comprehensive plans." A comprehensive plan was exactly what was put in place for the majority of Lexington's black communities. In 1924, Pralltown became a target of the city's plan for renewal. The City of Lexington's Board of Health described the shotgun homes that dominated the black communities as having "outlasted their usefulness." Further stating:

> "Houses hastily built for Negroes who rushed to the city after the Civil War; Negro tenant houses and houses for servants built on the rear of deep lots; depressed neighborhoods where both white and colored families of low standards of living tend to congregate; houses that bring a meager rental because of lack of repair and lack of sanitation."[10]

Before the neighborhood fell into a decline, it reached its zenith around 1900. By then, the community grew to about 389 African American residents and 170 whites. Many of the whites were immigrants from places such as Canada, Ireland and Italy.[11] There was a sense of

10. Board of Health, City of Lexington, Kentucky, Report of Housing Survey of the City of Lexington (Lexington, Ky: City of Lexington 1924), 10

11. Jones, R. F. (n.d.). Further Development of Pralltown, 1876-1940s. In

pride within the community and this was attractive to home seekers and prospective tenants. There was so much neighborhood pride, that the community began organizing an annual Pralltown Day celebration in the 1960's, and it continues til this day. This celebration brings residents and former residents together for a day of laughter, camaraderie and fun. People from all over the country, who once called Pralltown home, come back on this day.

> "It's a sense of pride that our grandparents and parents instilled in us.....they always said, this is y'alls neighborhood. These kind of things you don't want to let go. Pralltown is a part of who we are."[12]

This quote comes from a former resident in a 1998 article about the community. But overtime, residents began to feel the heat from city officials and the encroaching University of Kentucky, who had eyes on the land. They felt as though these entities were conspiring to push them out. And the evidence of such is sufficient.

Some property owners, largely white ones whose only concern was their rent payments, failed at upkeep of their property and many homes fell into a state of dilapidation. The city also purposely neglected its duties with the upkeep of the community, as is customary in poor black communities and what happened to nearly every community we have written about thus far in this book. Other residents simply could not afford the maintenance

---

History of the Pralltown Community, Lexington, Kentucky (p. 5).

12. Becker, L. (1998, July 2). Pralltown plan allows two year leases of homes before buying. *Lexington Herald-Leader*, p. 4.

of the buildings.

Pralltown was deemed a slum and became one of the city's target areas for elimination. The original plan to eliminate Pralltown was scraped in the 1950's after protest from the residents and failure to come up with a sufficient relocation plan for said residents. In the 1970's, the Prall Place Apartments were built to improve the neighborhood and provide affordable housing for the residents.[13]

Urban Renewal razed a bunch of residences in the 1960's and 1970's. Some community members even believe that the organization razed many of the good homes and kept bad ones, to further justify the necessity of its removal program. In 1940, there were 229 homes, but by the 1990's, there were only 62.[14] Homes came down but none came up.

Pralltown's neighbor, the ever growing University of Kentucky purchased much of what was left of the community in the 1960's, beginning with 44 lots. The initial plan was to expand it's facilities on the land but they later decided to expand them in another area, so they used their property in Pralltown for student and faculty parking, much to the dissatisfaction of the neighborhood.[15] This created a lot of traffic for the typically quiet community and the majority of the students and faculty, had no regard for the neighborhood. To them, it was just

13. Appler, Douglas R., and Julie Riesenweber. "Urban Renewal through the Lens of Unsuccessful Projects: The Pralltown Neighborhood of Lexington, Kentucky." Journal of Planning History 19.3 (2020): 164-186.

14. Becker, L. (1998, August 30). Fighting for a Living History. *Lexington Herald-Leader*, p. 21.

15. Heston, V. (1974, February 17). Pralltowns Attributes Unequal to Challenge of Environment. *Lexington Herald-Leader*, p. 5.

a place to park. The section was clogged with cars by people who did not live in the area. The added traffic, also created fear that one of the neighborhood children could be hit.

Nearly all of the area homes are now used for student housing including the last remaining shotgun house pictured earlier in the chapter. Pralltown remains in name and in the hearts of it's residents, but it is no longer a historic community whatsoever and that is unfortunate. It is also why I am writing these pages in this book, bringing the forgotten past to a new generation, who may have no knowledge of these places.

Chapter 14 – Adamstown

"The most interesting development in the real estate world this week is the announcement by Patrick Devereux that he has practically completed plans for the complete elimination of Adamstown and Winslow Street as a colored section," reads an article from the Lexington Herald Leader dated August 2, 1914.

This quote being a reference to the former black community that once existed where Memorial Coliseum currently sits. This chapter will serve as a memorial in its own right, a memorial for the people who built and lived in the community. This is our history.

Adamstown's existence began when Barbourville, Ky native and white land-owner George Adams sold plots of land to African Americans in 1872. The community was established on 22 acres between what was then Adams Street, which is now the Memorial Coliseum parking lot and The Avenue of Champions. Martin Luther King Blvd and Rose Street were the other borders. The Avenue of Champions at the time was called Winslow Street and then later Euclid Avenue before becoming what it is today. Situated directly across from Stoll Field where the University of Kentucky Football team had its games prior to the construction of Kroger Field in 1973, many residents of Adamstown would sit on top of their homes to watch the games. Black people were not allowed to attend UK at the time so this was a necessity if they wanted leisure time watching the game. UK and the Southeastern Conference as a whole did not have a black football player to play in a SEC game until Nate Northington entered the contest against Ole Miss on September 30, 1967. Greg Page was another black player on the UK football around this time but he was injured in practice before playing any games. Page would succumb to this injury 6 weeks later on September 29, 1967, one day before Northington's SEC barrier breaking game mentioned above. It was reported that Nate had a rough time dealing with the loss of his roommate and teammate. Shortly thereafter, he would leave UK for Western Kentucky. Both are Kentuckians, Page nor Northington were residents of Adamstown. Being on the team prior to Kroger Field's inception, having played at Stoll Field, I felt it was necessary to include them in this chapter. For more on this story, Nate Northington published a book called "Still Running: The Autobiography of Nate Northington."

As with the majority of homes in black communities at this time, the homes built here were of the shotgun style. The width of the homes are usually one rooms length and elongated from front to back. When you enter the front door of the home, you enter the living room. From the living room, a door leads to a bedroom and then another door to the kitchen as there are no hallways. This of course not being absolute but a basic description of a shotgun home. The homes in Adamstown were wooden structures of this model.

By the 1880's, about sixty-six families called Adamstown home. The community had no school of it's own, the children attended the Colored schools within the city. Many of the residents were employed by near-by University of Kentucky, or at that time State College. Some parts of the neighborhood were without paved streets, running water and many of the homes were in poor condition. It's understandable that many of these homes were uninhabitable, however, the city made no attempts to truly clean up the area. It was known that most of the residents did not have the resources to do so, nor did the white property owners truly care as long as the rents were paid. The city stated numerous times their plans to improve the conditions but they were simply filibustering. It was deemed a slum and a perfect oppor-tunity for the University to encroach and erase the com-munity from existence. Only recently has there been an emergence of attention to what was this historically black community that has been lost.

Just one month before Patrick Devereux's plan, the city Housing Inspector surveyed the community and of the forty houses inspected on Adams Street, none had water. There were two water hydrants in the area and one was a few blocks away. He stated it was his duty to install a water main on the street and begin the necessary improvements.[1] But of course, this did not happen. The University of Kentucky had other plans.

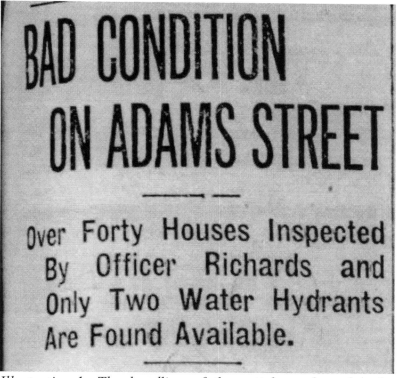

Illustration 1: The headline of the article spoken of on the previous page, see footnote 1. (Lexington Herald Leader 12 Jul., 1914)

Church

Before we get to the University and Lexington's gentrifying plans, lets delve into a brief history of the church and other elements of the community.

Church is the mainstay of nearly all historic black

---

1. Bad Condition on Adams Street. (1914, July 12). *Lexington Herald Leader*, p. 5.

communities. As you've read this book, you probably noticed the trend that churches are the only thing remaining from these communities. Not long after Adamstown's inception, there were two churches that were organized in the community. One being Rose Street which arose in 1884. The Reverend Alfred Britten became the first pastor of the church. Macedonia Baptist Church emerged in the area in 1891 at 124 East Winslow Avenue. Four years later, the two churches would merge to become one and the name was changed to Consolidated Baptist Church. They remained in this location until moving to South Upper Street in 1923 after State College, UK, bought the building. 80 years later in 2003, the church moved once again to it's present location on Russell Cave Road in North Lexington.

Illustration 2: Consolidated Baptist Church on Winslow Ave(Euclid), intersecting with Limestone. 1920s (UK Special Collections)

Ujamaa

One of the biggest things that we can learn from our ancestors of yesteryear is the concept of Cooperative Economics, or what we know in Swahili as Ujamaa. Ujamaa literally means "extended family," and is the fourth principle in the African American tradition of Kwanzaa founded by Maulena Karenga and others in 1966. The community is the extended family and this principle is vital, especially among poorer people who are on the bottom of the economic ladder. In the days following emancipation, many of our people were uneducated and illiterate. Yet with literacy rates low among these newly freed Africans, they had the understanding of pulling resources together to create things and businesses the community needed. One such example of the residents of Adamstown coming together for their own benefit and putting Ujamaa into action was the creation of their own grocery store. Nothing special about this within itself but 100 residents came together to make it happen. Sometime in 1895, these residents invested $2 each into this community grocery store and the profits were split equally among the investors. $2 in 1895 is the equivalent of $65.14 today. Making the total investment $6,514 with today's dollar value. What became of this grocery store is unknown to me at the time of this writing. This section was written to show an example of how we can collectively build the things we desire, within our communities. However, whatever failures our ancestors experienced in those days, can serve as lessons for us today, to ensure the longevity and prosperity of our endeavors.

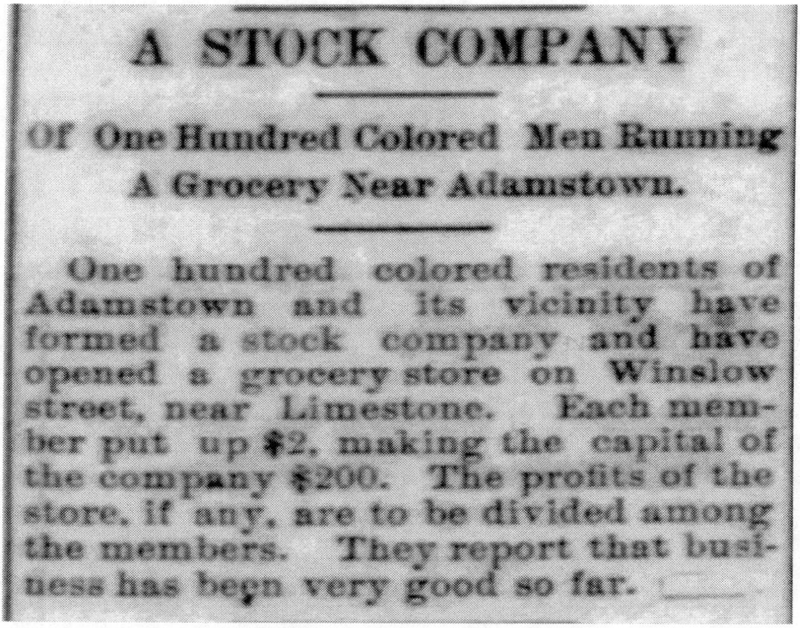

A STOCK COMPANY

Of One Hundred Colored Men Running A Grocery Near Adamstown.

One hundred colored residents of Adamstown and its vicinity have formed a stock company and have opened a grocery store on Winslow street, near Limestone. Each member put up $2, making the capital of the company $200. The profits of the store, if any, are to be divided among the members. They report that business has been very good so far.

Illustration 3: Blurb in local paper about the endeavor. (Lexington Herald Leader 12 Jun., 1895)

We began this chapter with a quote in the Newspaper that Patrick Devereux completed his plans for the elimination of Adamstown. This was in 1914. Devereux was a white business man from Winchester, Ky, who purchased the majority of the homes in Adamstown,

> "And is now perfecting the plans for the transformation of the entire section bounded by College View Avenue, Limestone Street, the State University campus(UK), and Rose Street into a high class residence district, with modern public improvements and restrictions."[2]

---

2. Aims at Colored Part of Winslow and Adamstown. (1914, August 2). *Lexington Herald Leader*, p. 7.

This was the next part of the referenced quote. State University's sitting President at the time, advised Devereux to get into Real Estate for the purpose of removing the community stating:

> "The Adamstown colony occupied lands which, if properly improved, would be of value to the university, and that It was possible that funds would be available either for the purchase of the Adamstown tract by the state for university purposes or by the members of the faculty for the construction of homes."[3]

The University had made earlier attempts to acquire this land but were unsuccessful. Getting Devereux to buy into the plan was a win for the University of Kentucky. Progress to some is Devastation to others. And with the following words, the plan of elimination was enacted:

> "It was announced Saturday that all of the tracts of any value for improvement into a residence district have passed under Mr. Devereux's control to dispose of as he saw fit."[4]

That last sentence tells it all, "...under Mr. Devereux's control to dispose of as he saw fit." But what about the families that called Adamstown home? What was to become of them? The original plan was to relocate the homes to a new location, a six acre tract with "good streets and sidewalks," to establish "a new colored

---

3   Ibid., pp.7

4. Ibid., pp.7

community under much better conditions."[5]

Removal of residents began as early as the next month when a vacating order was ordered for a number of tenants. They were given a notice to vacate their homes within six days or the health department would "abate the nuisance."[6] With those few tenants forced to move in less than a week, Devereux's plan to move the homes in the neighborhood never came into fruition because Adamstown was still in "slum clearance" removal plans 20 years later in 1934.[7] Slowly but surely residents were forced out of the community with no where to go. One Adamstown resident remarked in 1947 " we were forced to move from Adamstown and there was no sub-stitute."[8]

Less than 5% of the residents in the community owned their homes, so they were left basically to fend for themselves in regards to finding housing. The city nor university helped in the relocation process as was promised. Many eventually settled in the recently emerged housing projects on the east end and George-town St.

By 1950, the University opened up Memorial Coli-seum on what was formerly Adamstown. I personally never knew the community existed at all until I attended a presentation about the community at the Central Li-

---

5. Ibid., pp.7

6. Vacating Order to be Carried Out. (1914, September 5). *Lexington Herald Leader*, p. 3.

7. Slum Districts Are Inspected. (1934, September 14). *Lexington Herald Leader* , p. 2.

8. New Auditorium Still in Lead in Poll of Lexington's Needs. (1947, March 25). *Lexington Herald Leader*, p. 8.

brary in 2015.

Illustration 4: Historical marker that the University unveiled in 2019 behind memorial coliseum, the former site of Adamstown. taken by me in 2020.

Illustration 5: 1916 image from Stoll Field of a University football game. In the background, Adamstown can be seen. We were not allowed to attend games so residents would climb to their rooftops to watch the games. (University of Kentucky Collections)

Illustration 6: Adamstown Street. Unknown date (University of Kentucky Collection)

Illustration 7: Adamstown Neighborhood, 1943. (University of Kentucky Special Collections)

Illustration 8: Adamstown Neighborhood, 1943. (University of Kentucky Special Collections)

Illustration 9: Adamstown Neighborhood, 1943. (University of Kentucky Special Collections.)

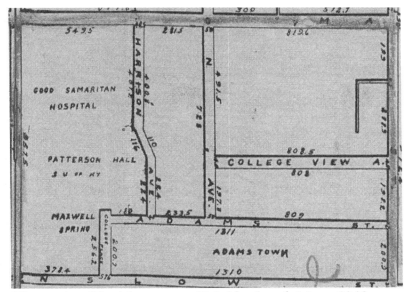

Illustration 10: Adamstown Neighborhood Map, 1912

Chapter 15- Davis Bottom and The South End

"I am going to model busts of negros and put them where people can see them," remarked a young man born and raised in the community known as Davis Bottom. This comment was made during a visit to a museum and the young man was disappointed with the lack of busts of negro men. This young man was none other than the famed black sculptor Isaac Scott Hathaway. Before we share his story, let's take a look at the community in which he was brought up.

Located in Southwest Lexington and established around 1865, this community Davis Bottom, sometimes called Davistown, was named after white land speculator and former slave owner, Willard Davis. He was a Fayette

County attorney and later would become a civil rights advocate and anti slavery proponent, even though he himself at one time admitted to being a slave owner for the majority of his life:

> "I was all my life the owner of a few slaves inherited, and I know that no man rejoiced more over their emancipation than I did."[1]

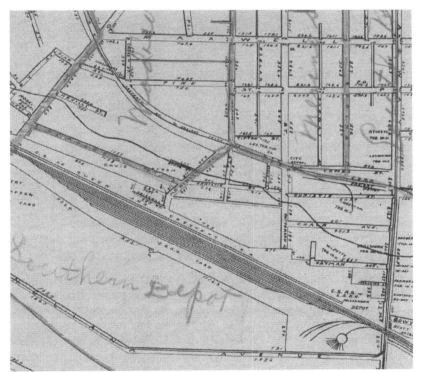

Illustration 1: Davis Bottom.

1. *The Davis Bottom History Preservation Project: William Willard Davis* .(n.d.). Retrieved February 12, 2023, from https://arch.as.uky.edu/sites/default/files/6%20William%20Willard%20Davis%20Biography.pdf

In 1865, Davis purchased 43 lots on what was then Brisbin Street. Those lots were subdivided and then sold to the first families that would call this newly formed community home. Twenty five of those lots were bought by Rudolph DeRoode, a land speculator and music teacher from Holland. He resold his property in the community to black buyers and the principal street, Brisbin, was changed to bear his name and became DeRoode Street.

Twelve Cottages

—AT—

PRIVATE SALE

—TO—

COLORED PEOPLE

WEEKLY RENT PAYMENTS WILL PAY FOR A HOME.

I offer for sale, at low prices

TWELVE COTTAGES

On BRISBIN STREET, Between Patterson and Merino Streets.

Terms—Fifty dollars cash, balance in weekly payments, same as rent. This is your chance to buy a home, for the usual rent payments.

FIRST COME, FIRST SERVED . For additional information call to see me at the Milward Company's Piano Store, 305 West Main street. . ..

R. DeROODE

Illustration 2: Advertisement for the sale of twelve cottages by Rudolf DeRoode on Brisben Street (Lexington Herald Leader June 7, 1911)

The majority of the homes were shotgun and t-plans. The communities borders included Broadway to the east, Maxwell Street to the north, High Street to the west and the southern border was the railroad. Based on the 1912 map, the streets that made up the neighborhood included: DeRoode, Spring, Pine, Dunaway, Hayman, Christie, Blackburn, Combs, Merino, Lower (Patterson), Chair, McKinley, Tipton, Magazine, Poplar and Byas. There was also an alley that was unnamed for a number of years, but in 1927, it was called "Nig Alley."[2] At the time of this writing, I am uncertain of where specifically the name originated, but at first glance, I'm sure you are thinking the same thing I am. NIGGER ALLEY! Using the Davis Bottom map on a previous page, Nig Alley is the unnamed street just to the south of Christie Street, and it connects to Patterson and McKinley. Kentucky has a history of naming places, creeks and streets using what some would call racial epithets. A few examples would be "Nigger Fork," in Magoffin County, "Little Nigger Creek" in Knox County, my mothers birthplace, "Nigger Hollow" in Martin County, "Nigger Creek" and "Nigger Town Hill Road," in Rockcastle County, to name a few.[3] So, if Nig Alley got its name from "Nigger", it comes as no surprise but again, I am uncertain of the origin of the name of the street.

Davis Bottom was home to approximately 387 people by 1880. The majority of them were black, 266, but Davis Bottom was also home to many European immi-

---

2. Resolution No. 377, Naming Certain Unnamed Alleys in The City of Lexington. (1927, December 17). *The Lexington Herald*, p. 9.

3. Kentucky Faces Tradition Of Offensive Road Names. (1996, November 11). *The New York Times*, p. 13.

grants. That same year, these immigrants numbered around 121.[4] This community grew slowly in comparison to other communities, likely due to the heavy flooding in this bottomland any time there was rain. Davis Bottom was built in a valley.

> "The conditions in Davis Bottom are al-most as bad. In many of the houses, the water stands several inches deep in the living room, and everything that would float has been car-ried away. In some of the lower streets, only the tips of the fence pickets are visible above the surface of the water."[5]

> "Many of the colored residences in the city bottoms were hard hit Sunday by the flood. Davis Bottom, Goodloetown and Eddy Street are the well-known flood areas. The watermark on houses in Davis Bottom in places registered 24 inches."[6]

By 1900, there were 941 residents in Davis Bottom. 584 were black and 356 were white. Some streets in the community were completely segregated, such as Byas, Poplar and Tipton, which were all black, while Chair, Magazine and Hayman Streets, housed all white resi-dents. Most of the streets however, were integrated or

---

4. Dollins, H. M. (2011). In *East End and Davis Bottom: A study of the demographic and landscape changes of two neighborhoods in Lexington, Kentucky* (p. 59).

5. Fourth Street Floats, Results of Heavy Rain. (1907, January 18). *The Lexington Leader*, p. 1.

6. Colored Notes. (1922, September 6). *The Lexington Herald*, p. 13.

predominantly black[7]

Although collectively, the entire community is known as Davis Bottom, the northern part of the neighborhood actually was called Davistown. And in this section is where the majority of the businesses were. There were several grocery stores throughout the years. Some black owned and some white. Historian Dr. Doris Y. Wilkinson lists several of them in the 1939 Directory of African American businesses. These include Mrs Olga E Jones store at 555 Merino, John H. Smith's at 582 Patterson, and Robert B. Williams at 619 DeRoode.

Other businesses listed in this directory include John Hawkins Funeral Home at 632 West Pine Street, Harley Kings Bakery, 526 Pine Street, James G. Byars Barbershop, 715 Byas. Lunchrooms and restaurants were owned by Benjamin Harvey, 520 Patterson, William Hughes, 539 DeRoode, Howard Robinson, 503 Patterson, and Nellie Wallace, 435 Patterson.[8]

School

Like nearly all of the early black schools in Lexington, post civil war, what became known as the Patterson Street School, has roots in the community churches. Specifically, the Historic Pleasant Green Baptist Church in 1874, when classes were held in the basement. Almost a decade later in 1883, enrollment reached 108 students

---

7. Dollins, H. M. (2011). In *East End and Davis Bottom: A study of the demographic and l andscape changes of two neighborhoods in Lexington, Kentucky* (pp. 61-62)

8. Wilkinson, D. Y. (1989). *A Directory of Afro-American Businesses in Lexington in 1939*. Dept. of Sociology, University of Kentucky.

and a need for a new schoolhouse was born.[9] The same year, the school committee acquired a lot near the church for $900 and the Patterson Street School, a two story brick structure with seven rooms was built on the site[10] First grade thru seventh were taught within its walls. Dr. Mary E Britton, Lexington's first black female doctor taught at this school for a number of years before switching professions and attending medical school. Fannie Hathaway White, sister of famed sculptor Isaac Scott Hathaway, also taught at this school for many years.

The school was built near a railroad and class was often disrupted any time a train would pass. The building would shake and the teachers would halt instructing until the train passed. This school served the community from 1883 until 1934 when it was closed, razed, and a new school was built that year.[11] Twenty homes were also razed to make room for the school.

This school would become known as George Washington Carver Elementary. There were suggestions to name it after former First African Baptist Church pastor and former slave London Ferrill, who gained notoriety during Lexington's cholera epidemic of 1833.[12]

When the school opened in 1935, Fannie Hathaway White was it's first principal. It had an auditorium, ten classrooms, a library and a cafeteria. Nine teachers

9. *Carver community center.* Kentucky Archaeological Survey. (2020, April 15). Retrieved March 17, 2023, from https://www.kentuckyarchaeologicalsurvey.org/carver-community-center/

10. Fahey, P. (1972, November 5). A Bit of History Dies With Closing of The Schools. *Lexington Herald-Leader*, p. 5.

11. Ibid,. p. 5

12. Name Suggested For New Patterson School. (1934, January 31). *The Lexington Leader*, p. 1.

were also employed at Carver at inception.[13] Carver would close its doors in 1972 when the city schools were integrated. The building remains standing today and serves as a community center since the 1970's.

Churches

There were two black churches that served the Davis Bottom community at one time or another. The first to be mentioned is a short-lived African Methodist congregation by the name of Frazier Chapel A.M.E. Their church was located at 577 Patterson Street and was pastored by Nettie M. Ingram. It appears that there was never any official church building but rather they held services out of a home at this address. In 1929, this address was listed as a 3 bedroom for rent. Frazier Chapel had weekly advertisements about their services at this address all throughout the 1930's. The last mention was in 1940. Rev. Nettie M. Ingram, moved around quite a bit in the 1940's and this could be the reason the church no longer was mentioned. She had moved to New Mexico and to West Virginia. She passed away in 1952 and her obituary states she was a member of St Paul A.M.E.

The second church was located at 573 Mckinley Street. This church was called the St. James Pentecostal Church. It existed since the mid 1910's up until the 1980's. It is unknown to me at this time who organized this church. One can reason that it was formed from members of Ruth Murphy's Pentecostal Power organization that you read about in the Taylortown chapter.

---

13. Public Schools Will Open Soon, New Buildings are Ready. (1935, August 25). *The Lexington Herald*, p. 2.

Isaac Scott Hathaway

Lexington, Kentucky, our little city known as the "Horse Capital of The World" can lay claim to one of the greatest African American Sculptors to ever make history. This sculptor is the brilliant Isaac Scott Hathaway who was born here April 4, 1872 to Rev. Robert Elijah Hathaway and Rachel Scott Hathaway. They had three other children, Fannie and Eva Hathaway. Their first born Jenny died between 1870 and 74. Raised primarily by their father after their mother Rachel's death when Isaac was about two, the Hathaway's were one of the first families to live in the Davis Bottom neighborhood. Their dwelling stood at 208 West Pine Street. His father Robert Elijah, along with his step-father Isham Jackson filed a deed for this property on December 26, 1865. This was a small shotgun home where Isaac and his siblings were born. The family built a much larger two story home next door, in which the extended family resided. Both of these homes stood until 1983 when they were razed.[14]

Robert Elijah was born in slavery, owned by state Senator Garrett Davis of Bourbon County, Kentucky. He escaped after a fight with the younger Garrett Davis and upon the threat of being flogged for it. After his escape at the age of 22, he joined the Union Army, enlisting as a private in Company B of the 100th Regiment Infantry, Kentucky at Large, United States Colored Troops. The date was June 6, 1864[15] After his time in the military, he met his soon to be wife Rachel and they bore the four children mentioned above.

---

14. Giles, Yvonne. 2011 Interview, "The Davis Bottom History Preservation Project," KAS/KHC.

15. Ibid

The young Isaac Scott's passion for art began around age nine when his father took him to a museum. In search of African American art at the museum, young Isaac strayed away from the group. When asked "What were you looking for?" by his father, Isaac responded "I was looking for the statue of Frederick Douglas." To which the elder Hathaway responded "You won't find that here." Isaac's disappointment lead him to state "I am going to model busts of negros and put them where people can see them."[16] Isaac would do that very thing. And do it very well.

Isaac began his studies at Chandler Junior College in Lexington, Ky in 1890. Shortly thereafter, Isaac would take classes in Art at Boston's New England Conservatory of Music. He attended multiple universities and colleges in his lifetime. These schools include: Pittsburgh Normal College, Cincinnati Art Academy, New York State College of Ceramics, and The Ceramic College at the State University of Kansas. It was in Boston that his first bust was sculpted. The sculpture was of Bishop Richard Allen, who was an early black leader and the founder of the African Methodist Episcopal Church.

After his studies at various colleges throughout the country, he returned home to Lexington and taught high school. He taught a cast modeling class for 5 years at Keene High school in Jessamine County from 1897 to 1902 and also taught at an elementary school.[17] His first art studio was opened in Lexington at 766 West Pine Street. At this studio he made plaster parts of human anatomy for schools and the medical industry. His work

16. Thompson, Rico (2020). Chapter 4 - Isaac Scott Hathaway. In *Sankofa Lexington* (p. 33). Afrakan World Books n Moor, LLC.

17. Ibid., p. 33

began to gain recognition across the country. In 1904, he was commissioned to create a bust and a death mask of former Russian ambassador Cassius Marcellus Clay and one of Colonel W.C.P. Breckenridge in 1905. In the year 1907, Hathaway took his talents to Washington D.C., and it was here that he would create a company to distribute sculptural products on a national scale. In particularly sculptures of African Americans. The company established was called "National Afro Art Company." The name was later changed to "Isaac Hathaway Art Company." The slogan for his company was:

> "What the white man does is information, but what the negro does is inspiration to our boys and girls . Put Negro busts in your homes, schools, and churches."[18]

He believed that "the art of a people not only conveys their mental, spiritual, and civic growth to posterity, but convinces their contemporaries that they can best portray in crystallization, their feelings, aspirations, and desires."[19]

At his studio in DC, located at 1234 U Street, he created masks and busts of many prominent African American figures. A couple of these figures were: Monroe Work; an African American Sociologist and founder of the Department of Records and Research at the Tuskegee Institute, as well as the notable historian and author of the now classic book, The Mis-Education of the Negro,

---

18. Ibid., p. 34

19. Otfinoski, S. (2011). Hathaway, Isaac Scott, The Dean of Negro Ceramists(ca. 1874-1967), ceramist, sculptor, illustrator, educator. In *African Americans in the visual arts* (p. 93). Facts on File.

Carter G. Woodson. The esteemed historian was familiar with Isaac's work and saw the importance of it, Woodson remarked to Isaac "I'll keep what the negroes say and do, you keep what they look like."[20]

From his studio, Isaac created twelve inch busts of many great black historical figures. Mentioned above, Richard Allen was one of the subjects of his work, as well as: Paul Lawrence Dunbar, Booker T Washington, W.E.B Dubois, and Frederick Douglas. In Isaac's own words, he found inspiration for the bust of Frederick Douglas from a lion at the zoo. It was more than likely the lion's mane and the hair of Douglas:

> "I modeled Douglass under trying and peculiar circumstances. In Washington, D. C., beset with rent and food problems, I had worked in vain for three days trying to produce even a semblance of a likeness when suddenly God led me to the Washington Zoo. I say God led me because when I am working at a problem of any kind whether that problem is in clay or finance I pray for guidance; then go as far as I can with the means I have at hand, and invariably something turns up a solution. So I know God led me out to the zoo that day I was trying to model Douglass. The minute I walked in the zoo, a lion stood up as if to say, Take note!! I noticed and cried, 'There he is! My model, at last I have you.'"[21]

These busts were made of plaster, but he also

---

20. Isaac Scott Hathaway: Artist and Teacher. (1958). *Negro History Bulletin, 21*(4), p. 79 http://www.jstor.org/stable/44213169

21. Perry, R. L. (n.d.). *Isaac Hathaway, Sculptor.* The University of North Carolina at Chapel Hill. Retrieved from https://dc.lib.unc.edu/cgi-bin/showfile.exe?CISOROOT=/03709&CISOPTR=896&filename=869.pdf

sculpted many in bronze. His company sold these pieces for $1 to $1.50 a piece. In 1914, he was hired by the curator of the Division of Physical Anthropology at the Smithsonian Institution's National Museum of Natural History to prepare the anthropological exhibit for the 1915 world's fair.

By 1915, he was an Arkansas resident after leaving Washington, D.C. It was here in Pine Bluff that he finished the bust of Frederick Douglas he had started while in D.C. He taught Ceramics at the Branch Normal College, which is now The University of Pine Bluff. He opened the Ceramics Department at the university. Simultaneously, he taught at a local high school. He also met his third wife, Pine Bluff native Umer George Porter, and they were married in 1926. An artist in her own right, she created a bust of her husband that is displayed at the University of Arkansas Pine Bluff.[22] Together Isaac and his wife would leave Pine Bluff for Alabama in 1937 and establish the Ceramics Department at the Tuskegee Institute established by Booker T. Washington. Isaac and George Washington Carver, both teachers at Tuskegee at the same time, would develop a friendship. Carver would be the subject of a couple of Isaac's pieces, a bust bearing his likeness and a coin. Hathaway stayed at Tuskegee until 1947.

"I do not believe there is a sculptor in the United States who can excel you in producing a likeness." These are the words of Father Bruno Drescher of Chicago, to Isaac, after requesting and receiving 100 sculptures of Catholic Saint Martin De Pores. This took place in the

---

22. Register, Heather. "Hathaway, Isaac Scott." *Encyclopedia of Arkansas*, 29 July 2011, https://encyclopediaofarkansas.net/entries/isaac-scott-hathaway-5973/.

year 1938.[23]

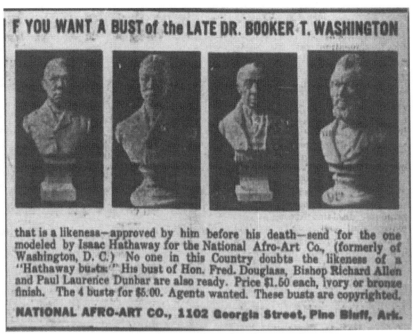

F YOU WANT A BUST of the LATE DR. BOOKER T. WASHINGTON

that is a likeness—approved by him before his death—send for the one modeled by Isaac Hathaway for the National Afro-Art Co., (formerly of Washington, D. C.) No one in this Country doubts the likeness of a "Hathaway busts." His bust of Hon. Fred. Douglass, Bishop Richard Allen and Paul Laurence Dunbar are also ready. Price $1.50 each, ivory or bronze finish. The 4 busts for $5.00. Agents wanted. These busts are copyrighted.

NATIONAL AFRO-ART CO., 1102 Georgia Street, Pine Bluff, Ark.

Illustration 3: Advertisement for the busts of prominent negro men by the National Afro Art Company (The New York Age, May 11, 1916, page 3)

In 1945, he designed a half dollar coin with the face of Booker T. Washington at the request of the Fine Arts Commission of the United States Mint, then commissioned again five years later to design another coin. This time it combined Booker T. Washington and George Washington Carver. These coins were produced from 1946 to 1951 and from 1951 to 1954, respectively. After his ten years at Tuskegee, he remained in the state of Alabama, establishing a ceramics class at Auburn University. At this time, Auburn was called Alabama Polytechnic Institute and was a segregated, all white school. Auburn

---

23. Ibid.

would integrate 16 years later, so to have a black teacher at that time speaks to the quality of work Isaac produced. In 1948, he became director of Ceramics at Alabama State College in Montgomery, Alabama, a position he held until he retired in 1963.[24]

Isaac was married on three occasions. He met and married his first wife Etta Pamplin in 1912. She died giving birth to their son Elsmer during the first year of marriage. Elsmer passed away in 1941 at 29. He was married a second time to Mary A. Edmonds, in 1915 in Washington, D.C.[25] This ended in divorce.

In March of 1967, four years after retiring, Isaac passed away in Montgomery, Alabama.

Valley of Neglect

Around the 1920's, Lexington had adopted the policy of what is known as "redevelopment by attrition." To sum it up, this means allowing certain neighborhoods, in particularly black ones, to deteriorate and allow businesses and industry to encroach upon the community, for the sake of lowering property value and increasing the justifications to get rid of the community. Pralltown, Davis Bottom, Adamstown, and other historically black communities would succumb to this policy.

The 1920's brought much industry to the community. In the process, many of the homes were razed to

24. *Sculpting a better Auburn: Isaac Scott Hathaway.* Auburn Alumni Association. (2021, June 24). Retrieved from https://www.alumni.auburn.edu/isaac-scott-hathaway-sculpting-a-better-auburn/

25. Marriage Licenses. (1915, October 25). *The Evening Star,* p. 8.

make way for several tobacco warehouses, and scrap-yards. From 1900 to 1930, the community's population decreased by 20%, from 941 residents to 756. The number of households had a decrease of 38% from 1920 to 1930.[26]

From the 1950's onward, there were talks by city officials to get rid of the neighborhood altogether. The homes fell into disrepair, due to a combination of neglectful landlords, neglectful tenants and of course an intentionally neglectful city government. In 1950, city engineer Tom Robinson proposed that a new city dump be located in Davis Bottom, annexing DeRoode, Nig Alley, Neville, Lower and Merino streets. This the residents rightfully protested and these plans were ultimately scrapped.[27]

Over the next thirty years, the homes became even more dilapidated. This section along with it's neighbor, just across the High Street viaduct, Irishtown, collectively became known as the poorest section of Lexington and earned the nickname "Valley of Neglect."

The city made plans to extend Newtown Pike as far back as the 1950's and in doing so, it would call for the complete removal of Davis Bottom. Much like the city dump proposal, this was met with many protests from the residents who feared being removed and having nowhere else to live. Although most in the community lived in squalor and in homes that likely needed to be condemned, this was all that they could afford, so the fear of removal was warranted. However, the Newtown extension plan resurfaced time and time again, causing the

---

26. Dollins, H. M. (2011). In *East End and Davis Bottom: A study of the demographic and landscape changes of two neighborhoods in Lexington, Kentucky* (pp. 69).

27. Protest Filed Against Davis Bottom Dump. (1950, July 19). *The Lexington Herald*, p. 2.

city to neglect efforts to clean up the community, as it was said to be wasted dollars if the Newtown Pike proposal went forward. Not only did the city neglect the upkeep of the homes, the landlords did as well. Some from a lack of care, others for the unknown factor as to the future of the community.[28]

Fast forward to around 2008, and the residents fears came into fruition. By then, all of the area homes were razed and the Newtown Extension project was under way. This road extended from West Main, where Newtown originally ended, all the way to South Limestone. This new street was named "Oliver Lewis Way," after the black jockey and first Kentucky Derby winner in 1875. Some residents moved to other sections of the city while some were put up in temporary housing near DeRoode Street. They were permitted to live rent free for several years until permanent housing could be completed. Davis Bottom was officially no more.

Pleasant Green Hill

Pleasant Green Hill, adjacent to Davis Bottom, was another section of Lexington, inhabited predominately by poor black residents. Portions of Pine, Patterson, and Poplar, were within this neighborhood, and portions of these streets were also in Davis Bottom. Brown Street, Merino and Spring Street also made up the community. Sometimes this whole area is lumped into Davis Bottom although it's a separate neighborhood altogether. Much like the latter, housing was in substandard conditions,

---

28. Woestendiek, J. (1980, December 19). Valley of Neglect. *The Lexington Leader*, p. 58.

and the residents and community also suffered at the hands of "Urban Renewal," and "Slum Clearance."

In the 1970's Spring Street, from Main to Maxwell was eradicated to make room for the New Lexington Civic Center parking lot. In the process, countless poor residents from the 31 homes were forced to move without any relocation plan or assistance with funding. The Lexington Center Corporation bought all of the homes from what they claim were absentee landlords and forced the residents out. Eviction notices were given and despite this, many remained while demolition was in progress.

"The wrecking crews hop-scotched from lot to lot down Spring Street, working around houses which are still occupied-- some legally, some not so legally."

"At least five of the houses scheduled for demolition are still occupied. Minter said that the contractors had been asked to turn the heavy equipment on them last, which means sometime in the next 30 days."[29]

The Lexington Center Corp. claimed that they had no money to allocate to relocation efforts, therefore these residents were forced out with nothing. Brown Street, also was completely removed for this project. What was Brown is now called Lexington Center Drive.

Those last few Spring Street tenants that remained while demolition was in progress, looked on from their

---

29. Gatz, C. (1975, November 21). Lawsuit Filed... *The Lexington Herald*, p. 10.

porches and windows in despair, knowing they were next and not knowing what their next move would be.

It is of note that one Lexington Historian of the 1800's states that this section of Spring Street, prior to the arrival of white men in the 1700's, was an Indian Mound.

"Early in this century, a large circular earthen mound, about six feet in height, occupied a part of what is now called Spring street, between Hill(High Street) and Maxwell. It was located between the property of Dr. Bell and the rear outbuildings of Mr. P. Yeiser. In course of time it was leveled, and was found to consist of layers of earth of three different colors. In the center was discovered an earthen vessel of curious form and a quantity of half-burnt wood. The mound is supposed to have served the purpose of a sacrificial altar."[30]

Pleasant Green Baptist Church

For nearly a century, there has been much debate between two churches about which one is the oldest. Both, Pleasant Green Baptist and the First African Baptist make the claim that their church began with Peter Durrett, or as he was affectionately called "Old Captain."

What both congregations do agree on is in 1790, a black congregation by the name of African Baptist Church was organized by Captain. Pleasant Green states that the name was changed from African Baptist Church

---

30. Ranck, G. W. (1872). Chapter 1 - Ancient Lexington. In *History of Lexington, Kentucky: Its early annals and recent progress* (p. 2). Clarke.

to Pleasant Green Baptist Church in 1829.[31] They also use Perrin's History of Fayette County, published n 1882, to justify their claim as being the oldest black baptist church west of the Allegheny Mountains. On their website it states "Perrins History" lists Pleasant Green as, "The First Church Among People of Color in Lexington." But the book does not state that at all. In the book, William Henry Perrin states that, "It(Pleasant Green) was probably one of the earliest church organizations of the colored people in this city."[32] His usage of the word "probably" when referring to Pleasant Green being the earliest is not stating that it was with certainty. It's speculative at best.

Their claim is that the church Durrett founded is their church and he was their first pastor. However, there is one huge problem with the source that they use to justify their claim. Perrin himself states that the history of the church's beginnings are obscure and the only information available was from an old woman over one hundred years old and her account was "too incoherent to throw much light on the subject." He referred to the history she gave as "vague tradition."

Using the same source, Perrin writes that the First Baptist Church(Colored) is believed to have been organized about 1801, and Peter Durrett was it's first pastor.[33] He gave no dates for Pleasant Green, for the record. Then furthermore, he suggests that the two congregations were

---

31. *Pleasant Green Missionary Baptist Church - About Us*. Pleasant Green Missionary Baptist Church . (n.d.). Retrieved March 21, 2023, from http://www.hpgmbc.com/about-us/

32. Perrin, W. H. (1882). Chapter X. The Colored People of Lexington-- Their Religious Advantages—Colored Churches—Educational Facilities-- Secret and Benevolent Organizations—Fairs, Etc. In *History of Fayette County, Kentucky* (p. 470) Southern Historical Press.

33. Ibid., p. 471

one and likely split at some point in their history. With that said, we know that Pleasant Green's first church building was not built until 1822. Their website has the slogan: "Serving since 1790, ...Same Site since 1822."

According to a lawsuit filed in 1833 by the Trustees of the African Baptist Church, a deed to this property(Pleasant Green's current location) was obtained illegally in 1821 by a group who were expelled from Captain's church upon charges of immorality.[34] This group led by Harry Quills and Barry Admon misrepresented themselves to Dr. Ridgely, from whom the property was purchased in 1819. The doctor held onto the deed until it was paid in full in 1821 and the aforementioned men pretended to be trustees in order to obtain said deed. The Disposition, typed in full in the book "One Grain of the Salt," also mentions that Quills, Admon, and others assumed the name of Pleasant Green African Church.

There are a couple of other noteworthy things to mention in regards to this confusion between the two churches. "Old Captain" passed away in 1823 and by all accounts was succeeded in his church by the Reverend London Ferrill. Pleasant Green's history on their own website states that after Old Captain died in 1823, "Reverends January and Brent served faithfully," until the year 1855.[35] There is no mention of London Ferrill on their website. The title of his biography published in 1854, mentions the First African Baptist, not Pleasant

---

34. McIntyre, L. H. (1986). Dispositions. In *One grain of the salt: The first African baptist church west of the Allegheny Mountains* (p. 80). L.H. McIntyre.

35. *Pleasant Green Missionary Baptist Church - About Us*. Pleasant Green Missionary Baptist Church . (n.d.). Retrieved March 21, 2023, from http://www.hpgmbc.com/about-us/

Green. It's called "Biography of London Ferrill, Pastor of the First Baptist Church of Colored Persons, Lexington, KY." Not only that, the source that Pleasant Green used to make their claim, Perrin's work, states the following in regards to their early pastors:

> "Among the preachers of this church, after "Old Father Captain," Revs. Mundy, Loudoun[sic] Ferrill, Orlando Payne, Dick Price, George Brent, Jr., George W. Dupee, Robert Clark, M.M. Bell, E.M. Mamon, H.P. Jacopy.[sic]"[36]

On their own website, of these, only George Brent, George Dupee, Bell and H.P. Jacobs are mentioned. Again, no mention of London Ferrill. Clearly, Perrin has confused the two churches if they don't even acknowledge Ferrill as one of their pastors, when every other source states he succeeded Old Captain.

You also see the name Orlando Payne as an early pastor of Pleasant Green. This is significant because there was a letter written in 1822 by Harry Quills where they had reached some sort of agreement with African Baptist to use the property obtained from Dr. Ridgely, and in this letter, it states that they chose "Lander Payne" as their pastor in 1822. Lander Payne is not associated with First African Baptist, only Pleasant Green and even their source, Perrin, says so. Captain is still alive at this time. Keep in mind, Perrin received his information from an elderly member of the church. And it's clear to everyone reading this that Orlando Payne and Lander Payne are

---

36. Perrin, W. H. (1882). Chapter X. The Colored People of Lexington--Their Religious Advantages—Colored Churches--Educational Facilities--Secret and Benevolent Organizations--Fairs, Etc. In *History of Fayette County, Kentucky* (p. 471). Southern Historical Press.

one and the same. The letter, signed by Harry Quills on behalf of the congregation that became known as Pleasant Green and signed by Rolley Blue, who represented the African Church, is presented in full below.

> "Whereas disputes have arisen between great parties of the African Baptist Church in Lexington, Called Captain's Church, which has terminated in a division of said Church, and which appears to be irreconcilable, each party claiming privileges in the meeting house, and to the property of said Church, and whereas propositions have been made to divide the property or funds of the church, so as to be satisfactory to each contending party, and thereby to remove all ill will among them, we the undersigned have taken in behalf of the parties to which we severally belong in said division to make the following arrangements.
>
> That is to say, Rolla Blue engages in behalf of the Church now in possession and occupying of the meeting house which is now under the care of **CAPTAIN** and **LONDON FERRILL** as their ministers and pastors, and the said Harry Quills for the other party, now claiming **LINDER PAYNE** as their present minister and Pastor."[37]

Before we move further with the remainder of the letter, we have to keep in mind, this was an agreement signed by Harry Quills, representing the church that became known as Pleasant Green and Rolley Blue, representing the African Church. As you can clearly see, Captain was still alive at the time of this split and clearly, he was pastoring the African Church and not the splinter

37. H. Quills Paper, Fayette County Circuit Court Case File #760. Division of Archives and records Management, Commonwealth of Kentucky.

group. Linder Payne was their pastor, according to Harry Quills himself. Why would Pleasant Green exclude mention of Orlando or Lander Payne in their history? That damages their claim of being the "one and only church of Old Captain," as claimed on their website. Now, more of the letter.

> "The said Harry Quills agrees on his part as representative of said church, as aforesaid, to give up all claim and interest in, and to the Meeting House as aforesaid, and the lot on which stands on Mulberry Street extended, with all the appertainences[sic] thereunto belonging, together with his claim on said church for forty one dollars and fifty cents, for money paid for said church some time past, for the following consideration:"

It's important to stop here and offer an explanation. Harry Quills, on behalf of the newly formed church agrees to give up their claim to the meeting house as stated in the agreement. The first part of the letter suggests that the meeting house, was under the care of Captain Durrett and London Ferrill. So what is the meeting house? The meeting house was an old cotton factory on a piece of land situated on Hill Street(now High street) and Mulberry Street(now Limestone). This property was purchased in 1815 and deeded to the trustees of the African Church, who were Rolla Blue, William Gist, James Polluck and Solomon Walker.[38] As the congregation continued to grow, a new property was sought out and purchased. Let's analyze the remainder of the letter.

---

38. McIntyre, L. H. (1986). The First Co-Pastor, London Ferrill. In *One grain of the salt: The first African baptist church west of the Allegheny Mountains* (p. 12). L.H. McIntyre.

"That is to say, the said Rolla Blue agrees on his part for the above consideration; he will convey or cause to be conveyed to the said Harry Quills and the party he represents on their order, the lot which said church bought of Fredrick Ridgely, near the Quarry, called Patterson's Stone Quarry, containing 50 ft in the front on the street and about one hundred and fifty feet back."

This letter was dated November 29, 1822 and was witnessed by Sam Ayres.

We have indicated previously that this property was purchased in 1819 and there is a court case where the Trustees of the African Church claim that Harry Quills and another misrepresented themselves as trustees in order to obtain the deed. This property is the site of present day Pleasant Green. It should be clear from the letter, that Rolla Blue was a representative of Captain's church and by this agreement, he with the permission of Captain and Ferrill, allowed the land to be used by Quills and the new church. Now we understand why their website says "same site since 1822." There were several lawsuits between African Church and members of Pleasant Green over the property in question, however, in this book, we only wanted to lay out the basis of the argument and reasoning we reached the conclusions that we have. For a complete breakdown of this situation, you can read and see the deeds and dispositions in the book "One Grain of the Salt." This can be cross-referenced using Pleasant Green's own history book called "Essence of a Saga."

It's also clear from analyzing the information on both sides, that the genesis of First African Baptist and Pleasant Green are with the original African Baptist

Church, organized by Captain. Captain was an old man around 90 by the time he passed away in 1823. By all accounts, he and London Ferrill co-pastored the church until Captain's death, and it was he, Ferrill, who expelled the members that went on to create Pleasant Green Baptist Church,

At any rate, Pleasant Green Baptist Church is historic in it's own right. It is said that the name was chosen in 1829 to help slaves identify it's location, as the church was situated on what was called "Pleasant Green Hill."[39]

Again, the first church building was built in 1822 on property on the corner of Maxwell Street and Patterson Street, once owned by Dr. Ridgely, a white surgeon. The property was deeded to enslaved men who were "Trustees of the African Baptist Church." According to the lawsuit of 1833, their first pastor at this location was Lander Payne, although their' website suggests it was Reverend January. Information in One Grain of the Salt suggests that Rev. January did not come to the city of Lexington until after the cholera epidemic of 1833.[40] That would mean that Rev. Payne pastored the church for about ten years or someone unnamed succeeded him sometime before the arrival of Rev. January.

In 1872, under the pastorate of Rev. William M. Bell, a new wood frame church building was erected on the site.[41] This building, unlike the present structure,

39. Burdette, D. (2000, August 30). Pleasant Green: Church Took Whole New Direction. *Lexington Herald-Leader*, p. 49.

40. McIntyre, L. H. (1986). Preface. In *One grain of the salt: The first African baptist church west of the Allegheny Mountains* (p. x). L.H. McIntyre.

41. *Historic Pleasant Green Baptist Church*. Kentucky Women in the Civil Rights Era Site Wide Activity RSS. (n.d.). Retrieved March 25, 2023, from http://www.kywcrh.org/voices/churches/historic-pleasant-green-baptist-

faced Patterson Street, whereas the current church, built in 1931 under Rev. E.T. Offutt, faces Maxwell Street.

R.C.O. Benjamin, the martyred newspaper editor, even pastored at this church for a short while in 1898.[42]

While the claim of being the first black baptist church west of the Allegheny Mountains based on my unbiased findings, is incorrect, Pleasant Green can say they had one of the oldest black schools in Lexington. Daniel Seales, who we wrote about in the same chapter as Benjamin, had a school in Lexington as far back as the 1840's, so Pleasant Green certainly is not the first. But, we can say it was one of the only schools that began as an independent school but grew to become one of the city schools, Patterson Street School, which morphed into George Washington Carver Elementary.

George W. Dupee

One of the most interesting characters to be at the head of the Historic Pleasant Green Baptist Church, would be the Reverend George Dupee. Rev. Dupee was born a slave in Gallatin County, Kentucky, in the year 1826. His parents were Cuthbert and Rachael Dupee and the family belonged to a baptist preacher by the name of Joseph Taylor, who moved the family to Franklin county in George's infancy. As a young man, he alongside his father, worked in a rope and bagging factory, then on the Versailles courthouse in 1841.[43]

church

42. Quarles Gives His Side. (1898, March 3). *The Daily Leader*, p. 2.

43. Simmons, W. J. (1887). CXXVI. Rev. George Washington Dupee. In *Men of Mark; Eminent, Progressive and Rising by William J. Simmons* (p.

*Illustration 4: George Washington Dupee
(Public Domain)*

In the year 1842, he was converted to the baptist denomination and gained the desire to preach. Two years later, he learned the alphabet and began learning to read the bible. Finally in 1851, he was ordained as a minister of said faith.

He is recognized as being the first pastor of the First African Baptist church of Georgetown, Kentucky, in 1851, not to be confused with the First African Baptist of Lexington.[44] In 1853, he organized a church in Woodford County, at the "Old Big Spring," and another church in Paris, Ky, a couple of years later. The same year that he helped organize the Paris church, 1855, he accepted the call to pastor at Pleasant Green. Here he served as the head until 1864.

Keep in mind that all of the above occurred while

847).

44. Ibid., p. 854

he was still being held in bondage. That all changed in the year 1856, when his congregation at Pleasant Green were faced with the dilemma that their enslaved pastor was on the auction block in Lexington and was to be sold. They appealed to the white baptists, who fronted them the funds to purchase his freedom. This they did for a total of $850.[45] They re-payed the white baptists in full with weekly payments. Rev. George Dupee was now a free man and able to move about as he pleased.

In 1864, he declined the call to remain pastor at Pleasant Green, moved to Covington, Ky and organized a church there, then moved to Paducah and accepted the pastorate at the Second Baptist Church, Colored. This church later would be renamed the Washington Street Baptist Church. This was a move, he began to regret initially due to some of the immoral and lawless things he would witness by the members of the church. He would state:

> "If I could have gotten the Pleasant Green church after I had gone to Paducah, I would not have stayed in Paducah very long. The Union Army and the devil had the place, and I didn't see any place for God and myself But as I burnt the bridge behind me, I had to fight it out or surrender. The civil, religious people were gone to other places, and strangers that didn't know "Joseph" had come in from everywhere, it seemed, but from where God had been."[46]

---

45. *Pleasant Green Missionary Baptist Church - About Us*. Pleasant Green Missionary Baptist Church. (n.d.). Retrieved March 21, 2023, from http://www.hpgmbc.com/about-us/

46. Simmons, W. J. (1887). CXXVI. Rev. George Washington Dupee. In *Men of Mark; Eminent, Progressive and Rising by William J. Simmons* (p. 847).

William Simmons, author of the book "Men of Mark," writes the following of Dupee:

> "When he began the work, men would smoke cigars in the church, drink whiskey and curse when they were spoken to. They would curse at him fearfully when he spoke to them, so he prepared himself a hickory stick, about two inches thick and three feet long, and took it in the pulpit with him and showed it to the men and told them what he would do with it. Well, they believed him and let him alone."

This is where he earned the nickname "Pappy Dupee." Despite the initial doubts and hardships he encountered at Washington Street, he remained pastor of the church for 39 years, until he passed away in 1897.[47]

While still pastor at Washington Street, he founded a religious newspaper called the Baptist Herald, which ran from 1873-1878.

Dupee in his career pastored at over twelve churches, married more than 13,000 couples, and preached at over 12,000 funerals. An illustrious career and life he had in the service of his fellow black brothers and sisters.

Historic South Hill

Although this community called South Hill can not be considered a black community, it was home to several members of Lexington's free black middle class and

---

47. History. Washington Street Baptist Church. (n.d.). Retrieved March 29, 2023, from https://washingtonstreetbaptist.org/index.php/history/

it's impossible to write this book and not include a section for them.

The Historic South Hill community is bounded by South Limestone Street, South Broadway, Oliver Lewis Way(between S. Broadway and S. Lime), High Street, and S. Martin Luther King Blvd. Keep in mind these listed streets are today's borders, obviously MLK Blvd. and Oliver Lewis Way, didn't exist in the 1800's.

Prior to emancipation, free blacks lived alongside whites in this section of Lexington. Samuel Oldham and his wife Daphney, were two of these free blacks. Born in slavery, Oldham was able to purchase his freedom and that of his wife and child by the 1830's. In doing so, he erected a two story, seven room home located at 245 South Limestone Street(then Mulberry Street) in 1835.[48] He would only live here a short time because in 1839, he sold the property. This home still stands today.

Along with his barbershop, he operated a "fancy store" where he sold various items such as colognes, wigs, children's toys and other items. Not only that, there was also a "bathhouse" that he operated, all of these out of the same location, which was No. 18 Main Street.

48. VisitLEX. (2021, February 24). *Free Black Entrepreneurs - A Neighborhood for Free Black Entrepreneurs*. VisitLEX. Retrieved April 7, 2023, from https://www.visitlex.com/guides/post/free-black-entrepreneurs-a-neighborhood-for-free-black-entrepreneurs/

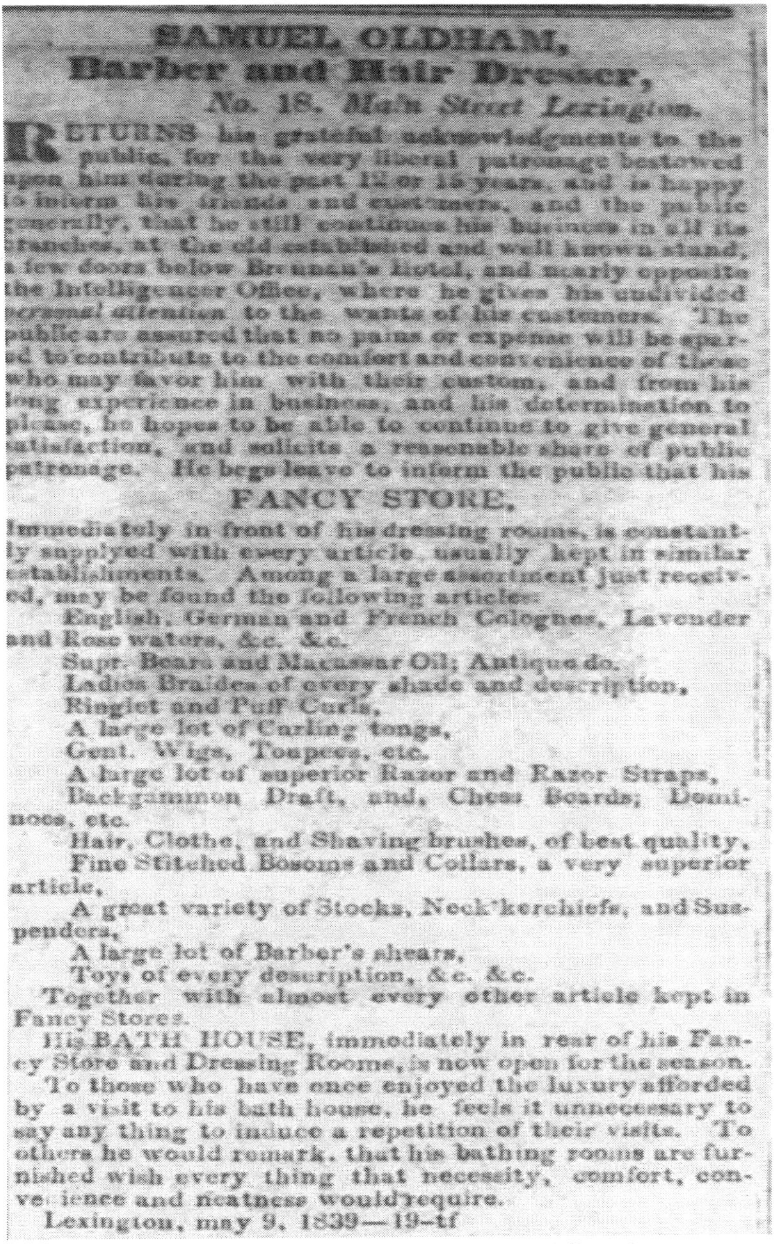

SAMUEL OLDHAM,
Barber and Hair Dresser,
No. 18. Main Street Lexington.

RETURNS his grateful acknowledgments to the public, for the very liberal patronage bestowed upon him during the past 12 or 15 years, and is happy to inform his friends and customers, and the public generally, that he still continues his business in all its branches, at the old established and well known stand, a few doors below Brennan's hotel, and nearly opposite the Intelligencer Office, where he gives his undivided *personal attention* to the wants of his customers. The public are assured that no pains or expense will be spared to contribute to the comfort and convenience of those who may favor him with their custom, and from his long experience in business, and his determination to please, he hopes to be able to continue to give general satisfaction, and solicits a reasonable share of public patronage. He begs leave to inform the public that his

FANCY STORE,

Immediately in front of his dressing rooms, is constantly supplyed with every article usually kept in similar establishments. Among a large assortment just received, may be found the following articles:

English, German and French Colognes, Lavender and Rose waters, &c. &c.
Supr. Bears and Macassar Oil; Antique do.
Ladies Braides of every shade and description,
Ringlet and Puff Curls,
A large lot of Curling tongs,
Gent. Wigs, Toupees, etc.
A large lot of superior Razor and Razor Straps,
Backgammon Draft, and, Chess Boards; Dominoes, etc.
Hair, Clothe, and Shaving brushes, of best quality,
Fine Stitched Bosoms and Collars, a very superior article,
A great variety of Stocks, Neck'kerchiefs, and Suspenders,
A large lot of Barber's shears,
Toys of every description, &c. &c.

Together with almost every other article kept in Fancy Stores.

His BATH HOUSE, immediately in rear of his Fancy Store and Dressing Rooms, is now open for the season. To those who have once enjoyed the luxury afforded by a visit to his bath house, he feels it unnecessary to say any thing to induce a repetition of their visits. To others he would remark, that his bathing rooms are furnished wish every thing that necessity, comfort, convenience and neatness would require.

Lexington, may 9, 1839—19-tf

Illustration 5: 1839 Advert of Samuel Oldham's services (Kentucky Gazette, May 9, 1839 - pg. 3)

Valuable City Property for Sale.

THE subscriber will offer at public sale on Friday, the 17th of May, TWO DESIRABLE RESIDENCES, adjoining the property of Richard Higgins, Esq., situated on Mulberry Street; in a delightful part of the city. The first is a Brick House, nearly new, having been built in 1835, with seven large well finished rooms, and an ell of brick running back 35 or 36 feet. The lot upon which it is situated is 51 ft. front, running back 150 ft. An alley nine feet wide, runs from the front to the rear of the lot, leading to the stable and cow house. All necessary buildings, in addition to those above mentioned are upon the premises, such as Smoke-house, Dairy, &c. The lot is enclosed with a good plank fence, and there is a fine WELL of never failing water within 12 feet of the Kitchen Door. This is one of the most delightful and convenient family residences of the city. It is now occupied by Samuel Oldham.

The second is a FRAME HOUSE and LOT adjoining the above. The lot is 40 by 150 feet, enclosed with a plank fence, and is a handsome residence for a small family.

The above property will be shown to persons wishing to purchase at any time between this and the day of sale by Samuel Oldham.

The terms of sale will be liberal, and will be made known on the day of sale.

JACOB ASHTON,
MADISON C. JOHNSON.

Lexington, may, 9, 1839—19-td.

Illustration 6: Advert for the sale of his home (Kentucky Gazette May 9, 1839 - pg. 3)

Rolley Blue, sometimes spelled "Rolla," was another free black who purchased property in South Hill. The freed blacksmith and land speculator purchased a home at 346 S. Upper Street in 1829. This home he rented to other free blacks.[49] Rolley Blue was also one of the trustees to whom was on the original deed of the Pleasant Green Church.

James Turner is another former slave who purchased his freedom. He and his wife Arena, lived in a duplex located 331 S. Mill Street. This home remains today. Turner was the second pastor of the Historic St. Paul A.M.E. Church on Upper Street.[50]

Henry King, a founding member of the Union Benevolent Society No. 2, which organized the African Cemetery, lived with his wife Betty at their home at 340 S. Mill St.[51]

Michael Clarke, a formerly enslaved black man, built a home for he and his wife at 344 S. Upper Street in 1818. He purchased the freedom of his wife Hannah and their child in 1804.[52]

Billy Tucker, a downtown confectionery shop owner lived at 521 S. Upper Street, with his wife Hannah. It's reported that they had obtained considerable wealth.[53]

Following the civil war, several black families continued to live and thrive in the South Hill Community. One such person was businessman and inventor Robert Gray, who had a home built at 517 S. Mill St., in 1889. His inventions were a "water pumping apparatus," and a

49. Ibid

50. Davis, M. (2011, September 25). Walking Tour Spotlights Black History. *Lexington Herald Leader*, p. T14.

51. Ibid

52. Ibid

53. Ku, M. (2002, February 23). South Hill Neighborhood District. *Lexington Herald-Leader*, p. 25.

"hay press."[54][55] This lot where he built his home was purchased from his sister in law, his wife's sister Fannie Ellis Scott. She had a home built next door at 513 S. Mill Street, in 1889. Gray also owned the all black Pekin Theater that was short-lived, as well as a hotel for African Americans on Spring Street called "The Terrace Inn."[56]

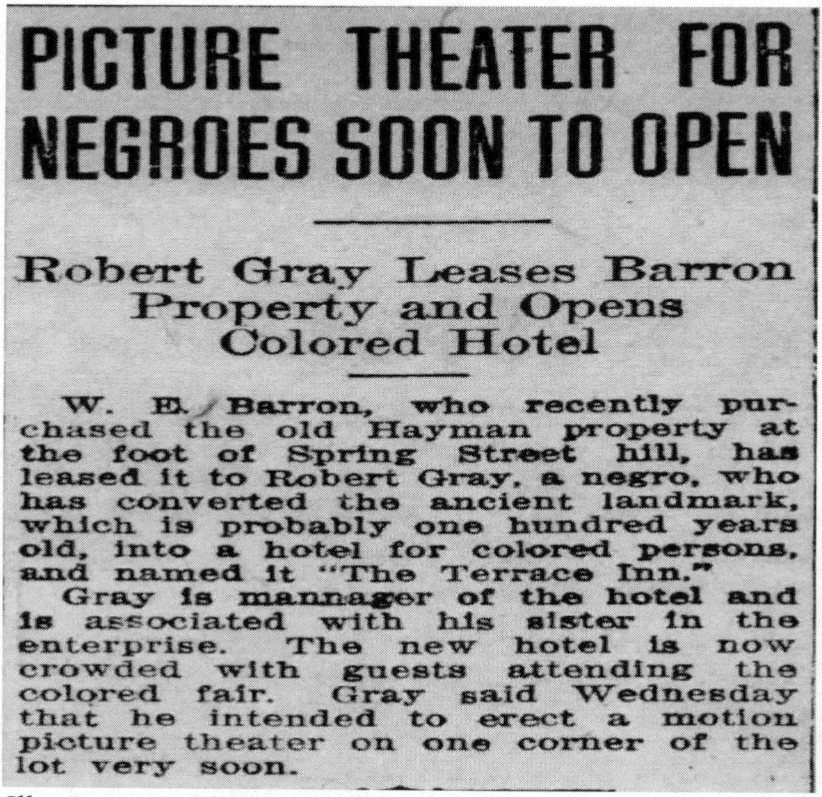

PICTURE THEATER FOR NEGROES SOON TO OPEN

Robert Gray Leases Barron Property and Opens Colored Hotel

W. E. Barron, who recently purchased the old Hayman property at the foot of Spring Street hill, has leased it to Robert Gray, a negro, who has converted the ancient landmark, which is probably one hundred years old, into a hotel for colored persons, and named it "The Terrace Inn."

Gray is manager of the hotel and is associated with his sister in the enterprise. The new hotel is now crowded with guests attending the colored fair. Gray said Wednesday that he intended to erect a motion picture theater on one corner of the lot very soon.

Illustration 7: The Lexington Herald (Sept. 11, 1913)

54. Mastin, B. L. (1993, October 17). Cottage Was Built To Be A Buffer. *Lexington Herald-Leader*, p. 73.

55. Lexington Inventor Robert Gray Procures a Patent on New Pump Apparatus. (1903, May 11). *The Lexington Leader*, p. 6.

56. Picture Theater For Negroes Soon To Open. (1913, September 11). *The Lexington Herald*, p. 8.

LEXINGTON INVENTOR

Robert Gray Procures a Patent on New Pump Apparatus.

Robert Gray, a well known colored tinner and contractor of this city has perfected a pumping apparatus called a conveyor. He has been granted a patent on it and expects to realize a handsome sum from it.

The apparatus is on the order of the bucket pump invented some years ago, but has the conveyor funnel shaped instead of oblong. It areates the water and carries more of it. It has been pronounced by those familiar with the workings of pump apparatus a success in every way. It not only pumps but purifies the water. It is believed that the inventor will find his newly patented apparatus a success from the start.

Gray is one of the best known colored men in the city. He is a business man of marked ability and an inventor of great ingenuity. He enjoys the confidence and respect of representative citizens of both races.

Illustration 8: The Lexington Leader (May 11, 1903)

Thomas J. Wilson, who at one time was the President of Lexington's Annual Colored Fair, built his home at 336 S. Mill Street in 1880. The Colored Fair began in 1869 and was said to be the first for African Americans in the state. People from all over the country would come to Lexington year after year to attend. His home today is on the National Registry of Historic Places.

One Street in particular in the South Hill community was home to predominantly African Americans. This street is called "Mack's Alley," sometimes called "Red Macks Alley," or "Herndon Place." This section however wasn't for affluent African Americans. It was an area of high crime, from disorderly houses to robbery and murder. News reporters of the day sarcastically referred to the area as a "classic park-like Oasis of the city."[57] Mack's Alley sits between South Mill Street and South Upper and intersects with West Maxwell Street. Just casually browsing the newspapers of old on the newspaper database, newspapers.com, can give you an idea of what sorts of lawless things took place on this street.

All in all, the South Hill district was on the original 1781 plat of the city of Lexington and earned it's name due to it being upon a hill overlooking downtown Lexington and the Town Branch that once flowed openly through Lexington.

---

57. Police Court, Couple That Wouldn't Work in Double Harness. (1905, November 2). *The Lexington Leader*, p. 2.

Speigle Heights

The final community we would like to discuss to conclude this chapter would be the community known as Speigle Heights, or sometimes Speigle Hill. You could make the case that this is actually West Lexington, but due to it's proximity to the Davis Bottom community and Irishtown, we felt it necessary to include it here.

Just over the West High Street/Versailles Road viaduct, a stones throw away from Irishtown, sits this secluded predominantly African American community. It is said that the community's beginnings are in 1913, with a man by the name of "Ad Cox," who stood in the back of a wagon auctioning off parcels of land.[58] Ad Cox is actually a man by the name of B.F. Adcock of Winchester, Ky. "Ad Cox" was written in the cited source. The original name of the community is also said to be Adcock's Addition, however one can find the names "Speigle Heights," and "Speigle's Hill," as early as the late 1890's. Deeds dating back as far as 1887, show a woman named Ella C. Speagle, selling property in this section. Clearly the name Speagle Hill or Heights comes from her. Spellings of the name vary from Spiegel, to Speagle and Speigle.

The streets that make up the community include Robertson, Jane, Speigle, Coolidge, Rich Alley, Ferguson, Joel, Martin and Anderson Streets. Robertson intersects with Versailles Road and is the only way in and out of the section. Robertson and Jane are the only streets listed on the 1912 Slade map of Lexington. At this time, deed records show that before there was an "Adcock's

---

58. Davis, M. (2006, June 25). Neighborhoods Reunion Will Have Activities For All Ages. *Lexington Herald-Leader*, p. 19.

Addition," this was known as Robinson's Addition.   Adcock even conveyed a piece of property on Robertson Street to my 2nd Great Grand-Uncle Philip W. Jewett Jr., on January 30, 1915.

Speigle Heights or Hill was a low-income community. The houses ranged from shotgun styled to small cottages. The majority of the residents were home owners. There was not any sewage or sidewalks until the 1960's. Some of the original structures remain, as well as some homes that have been built in recent years.

Church

There was and remains one church in the Speigle Hill neighborhood, which is the Antioch Missionary Baptist Church. This church was founded in 1922 by Rev. Sidney Woodard. In the beginning, services were held out of the home of Will Yates. Then a lot on Jane Street was acquired in 1924 and services were held under a tent. Around 1926, the church building was built upon the site. The current church located at 437 Ferguson Street, was built in 1975.

In 1996, over two hundred members left the Antioch Church and established a church of their own. This church, located on Georgetown Street, would be called Imani Baptist.[59]

---

59. Campen, T. V. (1999, January 16). Antioch Baptist Church. *Lexington Herald-Leader*, p. 30.

Urban Communities East

"We have power in our youth, and we must have the courage to change old ideas and practices so that we may direct their power toward good ends."

- Mary McLeod Bethune

Chapter 16 – Goodloetown

A bottom land area on the East End of Lexington once considered uninhabitable and used for mule stalls, became the largest African American community in the city following the civil war. Bottom land areas are low lying, flood prone tracts of land. These areas were mostly sold to and developed by African Americans, immigrants and poor whites.

Back Street, or what later became Deweese St, was the easternmost developed part of Lexington prior to the civil war.. The area landowners began dividing the land east of Back Street and by 1855, the construction of many buildings began. Two of these landowners were Winn Gunn and David S. Goodloe. Gunn purchased fourteen acres along what was Winchester Road, now Third Street, and Goodloe owned much of Lincoln Street(Race St,) Warnock and Constitution, which is now Second Street. Their respective areas became known as Gunntown and Goodloetown. By 1887, these two communities merged with Bradley Street Bottoms and collectively became Goodloetown.[1]

The neighborhood was primarily residential but a number of businesses did operate in the area. The Negro Hotel or "East End Hotel," which was located at 234 Race St, opened in 1902 and was owned by Tom & Maggie Irvin. This building still stands today. Over the years, there has been exterior alterations, so the building does-n't have the same look as it did when it was operating.

Illustration 1: The East End Hotel at 224 Race Street. Called The Negro Hotel on 1901 Sanborn Map

1. "Goodlowtown, Goodloetown, or Goodloe (Lexington, KY)," Notable Kentucky African Americans Database, accessed September 27, 2020, https://nkaa.uky.edu/nkaa/items/show/322.

Saloons, and grocery stores were the majority of businesses in the community. One such grocery store was located at the intersection of Third St and Race St, at 500 East Third Street. In, 1901, the Sanborn Map lists this location as a grocery store but by 1907, it was listed as a saloon. In the 1920's, it was once again a grocery store, a Kroger. Attached but a separate address, 502 East Third, the adjacent business was home to the People's Drug Company. People's only remained at this location for a few years because by 1932, Consolidated Drug store was in this location. The grocery chain remained in this building until well after World War II. A variety of businesses were here over the next several decades. By the 1990's, we came to love a store here called East End Variety shop, which given it's name, sold a variety of things from clothing to gold teeth. The building suffered much neglect throughout the years and by August 2015, it collapsed.[2] This came as a surprise to no one. The structure looked as if it would fall over at any moment for years.

Other area grocers were Timothy Foley's store at 296 East Third and Ernest Tingle's at 21 Goodloe St. A very peculiar man that you will read about in the next section also had a grocery store in Goodloetown, where he also lived, for a short period of time.

---

2. A Sad Ending: The Corner Store at East Third and Race Streets, Lexington, Kentucky. (2017, October 11). Retrieved September 27, 2020, from http://www.gardenstogables.com/a-sad-ending-the-corner-store-at-east-third-and-race-streets-lexington-kentucky/

Illustration 2: East End Variety aka "Pickles" This photo was taken the moment it collapsed by Melanie Foster. Used with permission.

Churches/Interesting Religious Leaders

One of the most interesting churches that existed in this community was the Power Society, founded by Roxy Ann Turner. The Power Society, better known as the Star of Bethlehem Church, had congregations in several areas of Lexington including Cadentown, Brucetown, Smithtown, Warrentown, Adamstown and congregations in other Central Kentucky towns such as Nicholasville, Harrodsburg and Winchester. The principal location was in Goodloetown at 542 Constitution Street, the corner of Warnock and Constitution.[3] Roxey, herself stated the other congregations were only bands and had no official building:

> "They is only one chu'ch, the one I preaches in here when I'm at home. The others is only bands, and haven't got no chu'ch buildin', but they holds their meetins' and has the power of the Sperrit[sic] come down on them just as it do in the chu'ch here."[4]

The main congregation had a membership of about 120 but with all of the other bands in Kentucky, membership grew upwards of 1000 members.

Pastor Roxy Turner, her husband James, and their son Rolly, lived in a home located at 183 Race St, the location of present day Phillip's Memorial C.M.E. Church.

3. "Turner, Roxy," Notable Kentucky African Americans Database, accessed September 27, 2020, http://nkaa.uky.edu/nkaa/items/show/2815.

4. Roxy: Head of a Strange Kentucky Sect is an Ebony Prietess. (1900, December 23). *St. Louis Dispatch*, p. 43.

Little is known of her early life but it is believed that she was born in slavery, in Kentucky, about 1856. Sister Roxy stood a towering 6'2" and weighed approximately 365lbs.

She began her ministry out of her home and the homes of neighbors around 1890, before acquiring the building on Constitution Street. Those that knew her remarked about how intelligent and eloquent she spoke for a woman who was uneducated. This intelligence is what drew people to her.[5] She stated that she did not know how to read but received the power to read after she "saw the face of the Lawd[sic] and got the power from the Most High."[6] According to her, this power was received after praying on her knees for 24 hours straight. The next morning she states she picked up the bible and was able to read it.[7]

With faithful reverence to God, Roxy, then Kentucky's only licensed female preacher, taught her growing congregation that there were seven powers a person could obtain, she already possessing six of them.

The 1st power is the power of the Holy Ghost. The way to receive this is with hours and hours of prayer. The 2nd power was the ability to heal and cure self and others of any illnesses. The 3rd power is the ability to overcome sin. With the 4th power obtained, one could easily resist temptation. Withstanding any physical hardships was the 5th obtainable power. The 6th power enabled the be-

---

5. Roxey Turner: Founder of the Famous Power Church is Dead. (1901, February 26). *Lexington Leader*, p. 8.

6. Roxy: Head of a Strange Kentucky Sect is an Ebony Priestess. (1900, December 23). *St. Louis Dispatch*, p. 43.

7. The Seven Powers. (1896, October 24). *The Inquirer(Lancaster, PA)*, p. 3.

liever to avoid danger and prevent accidents. And lastly number 7 was the ability to communicate with the dead.[8]

Roxy Turner died in 1901 of the Spanish Flu and is buried in the African Cemetery No. 2.

Illustration 3: Drawing of Roxy Turner from the Hartford Herald 10/18/1896

Another interesting and religious Goodloetown resident was a black man who was known on the streets of Lexington by the monikers "The Barefoot Jesus," and the "Bronze Christ." This individual often preached at the Power Church in Smithtown. This church was a splinter group from Roxy's church and headed by O.L. Murphy. He however, did not have a specific church home, he preached on the streets or anywhere he was invited, such as Murphy's church.

Rev. Claiborne Martin, 519 Goodloe Street[9], was a

8. Ibid,. p. 3

9. Bronze Christ Weds. (1912, June 20). *The Lexington Herald*, p. 16.

tall preacher originally from Virginia, that made his way to Lexington in June, 1903. He gave his age as 34, making his birth year approximately 1869.[10]

He would be seen wearing a long coat or robe and he wore his hair and beard long, in imitation of what some perceive to be the image of Jesus. Martin earned the nickname "Barefoot Jesus" or "Barefoot Prophet," because in winter, spring, summer, or fall, Martin did not wear shoes. Often seen with bleeding feet and sores upon them, he believed that wearing shoes and hats were against the laws of nature and God. He was instructed by the divine to go without those items and preached against wearing them. There was even a white woman arrested for lunacy in 1904, who was said to be imitating Martin. Samantha Johnson was this individual. She also claimed that God instructed her to go without shoes in the winter. However, she never did so until she saw Martin on the streets of Lexington doing such.[11] Speaking of copying another, prior to his stop in Lexington, Martin was residing in Cincinnati, Ohio. He was arrested in 1901 alongside another negro street preacher named Peter Cassidy. The men were held for obstructing the streets during their preaching. Cassidy, was known in those parts for donning his long hair, believing he is an incarnation of Jesus and also walking barefoot regardless of weather.[12]

Martin traveled all over Kentucky barefoot, claim-

10. Clayborn Martin. (1903, June 24). *Lexington Leader*, p. 4.

11. Sent to Asylum. (1904, November 11). *Lexington Leader*, p. 1.

12. Sang At Station: Street Preachers Placed Under Arrest. (1901, September 13). *The Cincinnati Post*, p. 6.

ing to be a divine healer and preaching his set of beliefs to all that would listen. He was run out of Danville, KY, in 1904. In 1905, he was in Owingsville, KY but this time, wearing shoes.[13] He returned to Lexington in 1907, wearing shoes and a hat, stating that his seven year penance is over and the Lord now allows him to wear shoes.[14]

In the 1920's and 30's, you will find him in various places across the country, again preaching while barefoot in the cold. Martin passed away in 1937, while in New York.[15]

Illustration 4: Rev. Clayborn Martin (Morristown Gazette Mail, January 28, 1926)

---

13. Wears Shoes First Time in 25 Years. (1905, December 12). *Evening World Herald(Omaha, NE)*, p. 12.

14. Seven Year Penance. (1907, January 30). *Lexington Leader*, p. 10.

15. Reid, D. I. (1937, July 26). Colored Notes. *The Lexington Herald*, p. 2.

Illustration 5: The Bronze Christ. Caption reads: Shoes and hats have no place in the religion of Rev. Clayborn Martin, picturesque evangelist of a new cult. This picture shows him braving icy winds with his head and feet as bare as he goes about the streets of Washington with his tambourine and satchel. (Burlington Daily News, Burlington, VT December 20, 1926)

Other churches in the neighborhood included Greater Liberty Baptist Church, which began around 1882. Several members of Main Street Baptist Church left and formed their own church. It began as Lansomboro Baptist Church and they held worship service in an old engine house located on South Limestone Street. The name of this new congregation was later changed to Liberty Baptist and finally Greater Liberty Baptist.[16] They would secure a new location on Corral Street in 1883 and then 515 Goodloe Street, before acquiring the former church home of the Chestnut Christian Church in 1925, their present day location.[17] As a child in the 1990's, my household attended this church.

Phillip's Memorial C.M.E. is located 421 Corral St, intersecting with Race St. It was founded in 1900. The First African Baptist was also in this community on Deweese and Short Street.

Schools

The Goodloetown section historically was home to some of Lexington's earliest schools for African Americans. One of the first originates in the days of slavery around 1839, when a black woman Susan Jane Washington was given a school by Judge Graves. It was called the Washington School and was located on Second Street.

16. Parrish, C. H. (1915). History of Main Street Baptist Church, Lexington, Ky. In *Golden Jubilee of the General Association of Colored Baptists in Kentucky ; the story of 50 Years' work from 1865-1915, including many photos and sketches, comp. from unpublished manuscripts and other sources* (p. 245). Mayes Printing Co.

17. "Greater Liberty Baptist Church," *Tour the Historic Bluegrass*, accessed December 31, 2022, https://tourthehistoricbluegrass.com/items/show/27.

Although for free blacks in the area, enslaved children were also allowed to attend as long as they were permitted by their "owner." The students in bondage could learn to read but were barred from being allowed to write, out of fear that they may write themselves passes.[18] Mrs. Washington also taught school in Woodford County, which is where her husband Marshall Washington was enslaved. In December, 1869, while in Woodford County, the teachers monthly report stated that she had 55 students, 28 males and 27 females.[19] How was one teacher able to teach so many students all by herself? We can not time travel back in time to witness how it was done but, it was done. On this same report, three were over the age of sixteen, thirty-four were advanced readers, fourteen were taking geography, eighteen taking arithmetic and twenty were in writing. This indicates that not all of the students were learning the same things at the same time. An amazing feat for one woman to accomplish on her own. Only three of these individuals were free before the civil war, so she was essentially teaching 52 students who were slaves just a few years prior. Most I'm sure were illiterate or barely literate.

Susan Jane Washington was of Native American, European(white) and African(black) ancestry.[20] The 1870

18. Negroes Growing With Lexington: Susan Jane Washington. (1920, December 26). *The Lexington Herald*, p. 34.

19. The National Archives in Washington, DC; Washington, DC; *Records of the Field Offices For the State of Kentucky, Bureau of Refugees, Freedmen, and Abandoned Lands, 1865-1872*; NARA Series Number: *M1904*; NARA Reel Number: *52*; NARA Record Group Number: *105*; NARA Record Group Name: *Records of the Bureau of Refugees, Freedmen, and Abandoned Lands, 1861 - 1880*; Collection Title: *United States Freedmen's Bureau, Records of the Superintendent of Education and of the Division of Education 1865-1872*

20. Negroes Growing With Lexington: Susan Jane Washington. (1920, De-

census, shows her and husband and children as residents of Versailles, Ky, but by the 1880 census, they were back in Lexington and living at 109 Constitution Street.[2122] Her occupation still listed as a school teacher but a city directory of 1898 shows her now living on Ohio Street, this time as a nurse.[23] And then 1910 census shows her living at 682 Winnie Street near Pralltown.[24] Each of these properties the family owned. By this time, she was 88 years old. There are numerous deed records showing Susan Jane Washington buying and selling property throughout Lexington. She would live four more years, passing away October 21, 1914 and buried at the African Cemetery No. 2 on Seventh Street.

The next school to operate in the area was the Daniel Hand School. Daniel Hand was a white philanthropist who created a fund to educate free blacks throughout the south. The Hand School originally began in a building on Fourth Street, later occupied by St. Andrews Episcopal Church, before moving to Race and Corral Street, the present day location of the Philips C.M.E. Church. This was a grade school, that operated for many years before combining with the Chandler Normal School on Georgetown Street.[25]

Several years later in 1907, and in this same loca-

cember 26). *The Lexington Herald*, p. 34

21. Year: *1870*; Census Place: *Versailles, Woodford, Kentucky*; Roll: *M593_504*; Page: *524B*

22. Year: *1880*; Census Place: *Lexington, Fayette, Kentucky*; Roll: *413*; Page: *338A*; Enumeration District: *066*

23. Ancestry.com. *U.S., City Directories, 1822-1995* [database online]. Lehi, UT, USA: Ancestry.com Operations, Inc., 2011.

24. Year: *1910*; Census Place: *Lexington Ward 6, Fayette, Kentucky*; Roll: *T624_474*; Page: *9B*; Enumeration District: *0033*; FHL microfilm: *1374487*

25. Chandler Normal Reopens Sept. 29. (1921, September 18). *The Lexington Leader*, p. 26.

tion, inside the Phillips Memorial Church, the Canadian and Ohio Industrial School opened. Children were taught several industrial skills such as cooking, millinery, and sewing while boys were taught how to utilize hand tools. Tuesday and Friday nights, adults were also taught these skills.[26]

Just a few blocks away, that same year, the Negro Women's Christian Temperance Union leased the Old Good Samaritan Hospital building on Short Street in order to establish a black industrial school. The plan was to open up a nursery for black women who were domestics. A broom factory, chair factory, and shoe making department were also said to be added. However, there was little mention, if any of this endeavor after the initial article.[27] Three years later in 1910, the Rev. O.L. Murphy attempted to establish an industrial school in this same location.

In 1883, the Colored Normal School No. 2 opened up on Constitution Street. With about one hundred students at the school's inception, grades 1-8 were taught. By 1903, a new building was constructed and 12 additional classrooms were added along with a principals office. During the construction of the new building, students were being taught at Phillip's Memorial Methodist Church. A few more classrooms would be added on in the 1930's and an auditorium and cafeteria. Then, a new addition of ten more classrooms followed in the 1950's. By the time all additional rooms were added, the student

---

26. Colored Notes: Colored Industrial School. (1907, February 19). *Lexington Leader*, p. 2.

27. Industry Will Be Practiced At School. (1907, August 31). *The Lexington Leader*, p. 8.

occupancy was about 900 students. The school would serve area African Americans until it closed it's doors in 1972, due to Lexington desegregating it's school system. Today, the Constitution apartments are in it's former location. John B. Caulder, who taught at the Jonestown school in 1902, served as Constitution's Principal for 40 years.

Charles Young Park & Community Center

With all of the city park's being segregated, the city of Lexington purchased a 4 acre lot on Midland Avenue to build a park for the Goodloetown neighborhood. Being the second parcel of land the city acquired for this purpose, Charles Young Park was established in 1930 and by 1935, the community center was built.

The park was named after Colonel Charles Young of Mayslick, Kentucky. A former slave, he went on to become the first African American with military rank after being the third black man to graduate from the U.S. Military Academy West Point in 1889. With encouragement from his father, Young would take the entrance exam to the Academy in 1886. He scored the 2nd highest but was not admitted at the time. He would receive admission only after the chosen candidate before him dropped out. After a long and successful military career, with a myriad of promotions, Young would retire medically and receive rank of Colonel in 1917. While on a trip to Lagos, Nigeria, Young fell ill and passed away January 8, 1922.[28]

---

28. "Young, Charles D.," Notable Kentucky African Americans Database, accessed October 26, 2022, https://nkaa.uky.edu/nkaa/items/show/897.

Various events were held at the community center over the years. From classes to concerts, to basketball games to talent shows. The center was a great place for neighborhood recreation. The recreation room contained a "colored library," with Mrs. Henrietta Jackson serving as the librarian. This library had no connection to the city's public libraries, but was managed by a women's organization called "the Junior's League."

Charles Young Center would close it's doors in 2008. With the East End suffering from "revitalization" and gentrification, the city had plans to demolish the center to build a new road, something completely unnecessary may I add. The community, spearheaded by Quinton Roberts and others fought to keep this important building in the neighborhood. By 2016, the building was placed on the National Registry of Historic Places, thus saving it from being demolished, making it one of the few remaining landmarks of East End.

Deweese Street

The westernmost part of Goodloetown would be Deweese Street. Although I mentioned a few businesses in the early part of this chapter, I purposely left out Deweese St. as it's deserving of it's own section in this book. In the early 1900's the name was Back Street. This served as the black business district of Lexington. A variety of clubs, restaurants, and many other businesses such as John Polk's Doctors office and Mammoth Life Insurance, were located on this street.

Dr. John Polk had his medical practice at 166 Deweese Street. By 1921, he had moved his practice to 148

Deweese. This building still stands and is now home to Lexington's Urban League. Alongside Dr. J.R. Dalton, he practiced medicine and operated a pharmacy out of this location until his health began to decline. The Kentucky Clinic located on Elm Tree Lane Third Street is named after the two doctors. (Polk/Dalton Clinic.)

Directly across the street, in a building still standing today, Mammoth Life Insurance Company sold policies to area African Americans at affordable rates. This company originated out of Louisville in 1915 but grew to have locations in 8 states. They would merge with Atlanta Life in 1992 and the Kentucky chapters closed it's doors.

"Deweese" is the common spelling of the street today but it actually was misspelled. The correct spelling is "Dewees." The street was named after Farmer Dewees of Midway, Ky. In 1907, an "E" was added to the name and it just stuck. There were plans to change the spelling to the correct form in 1919 but that never occurred.[29]

Deweese Street used to intersect with Third Street but with the addition of Elm Tree Lane, it's only a side street today. My former address from 2016-2018 was 169 Deweese Street and the end of the street is the parking lot for this apartment complex.

Deweese St. was affectionately called "do as you please street." Again it became the black business district and there was a variety of things to do. You could literally "do as you please." Several nightclubs opened up on the street such as Club Hurricane and The Derby.

29. Davis, M. (2022, May 12). *Discover Lexington's east end history on a walking tour wasn't bad.* TP Mechanical. Retrieved July 7, 2022, from https://tpmechanical.com/2013/04/30/discover-lexingtons-east-end-history-on-a-walking-tour/

In the 1939 Afro American Business Directory, it lists various restaurants and lunch rooms being on Deweese and owned by the following: Hillious N. Carter, 187 Deweese, The Derby Sandwich Shop, 182 Deweese, Albert J. Harb, 199 Deweese, Bertha Livers, 227 Deweese, Robert Miller, 188 Deweese, Susie Q. Reed, 177 Deweese, and William Wilson, 181 Deweese. As you can see, there was a variety of places to eat on this block. Today, there's not a single restaurant in the area.[30]

Two barbershops were on the block in 1939, Crystal Barbershop, 197 Deweese and Sterling Barbershop, 186 Deweese and many clothing shops, tailors, a drugstore owned by William Ballard, 176 Deweese, a retail shop owned by William Gentry, 225 Deweese, and so much more.

By the 1960's, the district saw much decline as integration emerged and dismantled many of the businesses. It appears that anywhere we look, black businesses suffered when we integrated.

Theaters

Before the "Nation's Finest Colored Theater," the Lyric opened it's doors in 1948 on Deweese St, several black theaters opened up in the area and downtown Lexington. The Frolic Theater, an African American owned and operated theater, was opened on September 28, 1907. "The Only Exclusive Colored Theater in the South," was managed by Webster Thompson and Peter Walker. The

---

30. Wilkinson, D. Y. (1989). Restaurants and Lunchrooms. In *A directory of afro-american businesses in Lexington in 1939* (pp. 9–11). Dept. of Sociology, University of Kentucky.

location of the Frolic was on Water St, close to Mill St. I believe that's in the vicinity of where Fifth Third Bank downtown is today. It would close its doors 3 years later in 1910.

The Pekin Theater, located at 415 West Main Street opened in September 1909. The present location of the Victorian Square Shoppes. It was owned by Robert Gray and C.B. Combs but managed by Charles J. Parker. It barely lasted a year before closing in November of 1910 The same year the Frolic and Pekin closed, Lexington would see another African American Theater emerge.

The Gem Theater opened November 1910. John Clark and Chester Brady were two Cincinnati business-men who owned the theater. They offered motion pic-tures, vaudeville performances as well as music from lo-cal acts. The Gem Theater was right across the street from where the Pekin was on Main Street. It changed owner-ship several times before closing its doors in 1916. The Lincoln Theater opened in the same building that former-ly housed the Pekin. This 250 seat theater was opened May 1911 and was opened by the Collins brothers of Ohio. It closed a few months later in December but was purchased by the owner of the Gem Theater, R.F. Bell. Bell would open another Gem Theater in Winchester, Ky in 1912. After selling the Gem to Willis Burden in 1914, it would close for good in 1916.[31]

The Lincoln would open up again 11 years later on Deweese Street. But again, it was a failed venture that didn't survive a year. This theater reopened once more as the Dixie Theater in 1927 but closed yet again sometime

---

31. Waller, G. A. (1995). Another Audience. In *Main street amusements: Movies and commercial entertainment in a Southern City, 1896-1930* (pp. 170–179). Smithsonian Institution Press.

prior to 1929. The newspaper reported of a burglary at the theater and the equipment was stolen. It stated that the equipment hadn't been used for quite sometime. Records show that the Lincoln nor Dixie were black owned but the target audience was black people.

January 1921 saw the emergence of yet another short lived black theater, "The Star." J.H Bibbs, managed this theater that was situation on Wilson Street and Short, just a few blocks away from Deweese on Lexington's East End in Goodloetown.[32] It closed its doors sometime the same year.

Not until the opening of the Lyric did another black operated theater exist in Lexington. The Lyric held performances by Count Basie, Ray Charles, B.B. King and others. Vaudeville acts, fashion shows and pageants were some of the other events held here. With desegregation picking up steam around the country, the Lyric saw its business declining. By 1963, the Lyric had closed.[33] This building remained boarded up and abandoned until 2009 when it was renovated and reopened.

GEM THEATER OPENS.
(By Wayman Hill).
The Gem Theater, the new colored vaudeville and moving picture house, formally opened its doors Monday evening and the actors played to capacity houses at both performances. That the management has made good its promise that the Gem should be one of the most attractive picture houses in the city is apparent.

Illustration 6: Gem Theater article in Lexington newspaper (Lexington Herald Leader, 30 Nov, 1910)

32. *Ibid, pp. 241*

33. "Early African American Theaters in Lexington, KY," Notable Kentucky African Americans Database, accessed October 26, 2022, https://nkaa.uky.edu/nkaa/items/show/41.

COLORED PEOPLE

Take Notice

Come where you are welcome and meet your friends. The Frolic Theater offers splendid pictures, excellent singing and fine music. The leaders of the colored population endorse it. Open nightly at 7 o'clock. Saturdays and Sundays from 2 o'clock until 10:30. Pictures changed Sunday, Wednesday and Friday. Come tonight and enjoy a good laugh.

Illustration 7: An Advertisement for the Frolic Theater in the Lexington Leader, November 30, 1907

Visit the Star Theater, the new colored playhouse, corner East Short and Wilson. Vaudeville, all colored actors. High class amusement and pictures. Two big shows, 7 and 9:15 p. m. Good management. Excellent order and accommodations.—Adv.

Illustration 8: Ad for the Star Theater (Lexington Herald Leader 06 Apr., 1921)

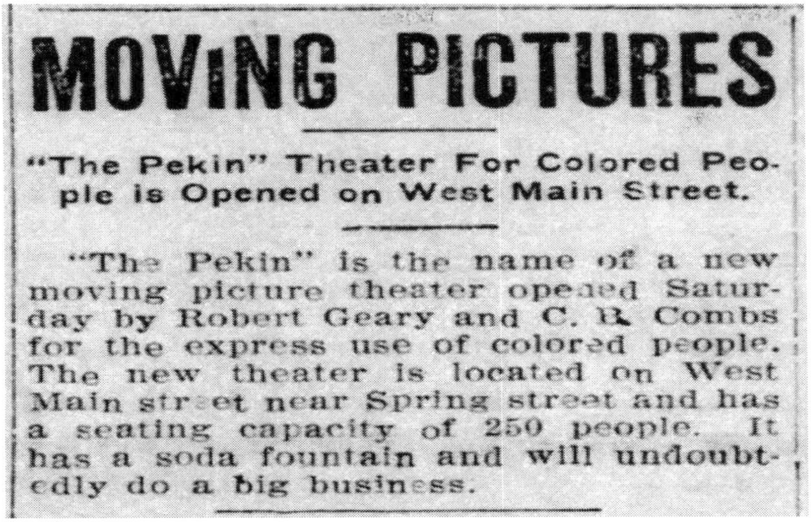

MOVING PICTURES

"The Pekin" Theater For Colored People is Opened on West Main Street.

"The Pekin" is the name of a new moving picture theater opened Saturday by Robert Geary and C. B. Combs for the express use of colored people. The new theater is located on West Main street near Spring street and has a seating capacity of 250 people. It has a soda fountain and will undoubtedly do a big business.

Illustration 9: Pekin Theater announcement in Lexington Newspaper (Lexington Herald Leader, 12, Sept., 1909)

Bradley St & Chicago Bottoms

Bradley Street Bottoms, also called Chicago Bottoms was located between Deweese St and Walnut Street, or what is now Martin Luther King Boulevard. Streets in Bradley Bottoms consisted of Wickliffe St, Noble St, Bradley St, Barkley, Constitution, Spruce and Clark St.

The name Chicago Bottoms comes from Lexington Horsemen, who frequented saloons in Chicago called the Long Branch and the Coney Island. Two saloons in the Bradley neighborhood would take on these names and eventually, the name of the entire neighborhood became "Chicago Bottoms," or just "Chicago."[34]

A number of Saloons and "Disorderly houses," or brothels, were in the neighborhood, as well as a Grocery

34. Jay, J. (1940, April 30). Four Bits. *The Lexington Leader*, p. 1.

store. Many of the neighborhood homes fell into disrepair and in the 1940's, the City of Lexington razed them.

Most of the residents were moved to the new Blue-
Grass-Aspendale Housing Project that opened on the
East End in 1938.

This community was known for violence and high
crime, so it's a bit of irony that the County Jail would
build a new facility right in the middle of the neighborhood, on Clark Street. This occurred in the fall of 1976.
The county jail remained in this location until a new facility was built in the early 2000's on Old Frankfort Pike.

*Illustration 10: A home on Bradley Street that was razed in
the 1940s. (Lexington Herald Leader Nov. 2 1941)*

Street Is Mud Hole, Houses Roofless, Homes Have no Water Connection and Filth Is Much in Evidence

Within a stone's throw of the postoffice and the new hotel building, three blocks from downtown, is a large mud puddle commonly known as Bradley street. The general investigating committee on housing conditions visited this spot on a tour of inspection Friday morning and found that here in the heart of the city people live in far worse conditions than in many New York tenements; that they were sheltered by houses likely to fall down at any minute; that there was no water; that all families on one street have to carry water from the last house at the end of the street, and as a consequence never get enough water to clean themselves or their houses; that when it rains, beds (sometimes there is only one in a house) have to be moved from one spot to another to avoid being rained on since there are large holes in the roofs.

There are no sidewalks, not even a street, just one large mud bed lined by rows of shacks. Every house has a bevy of ill-clad unkept children and at least one dog, very often mangy.

Both black and white people live in this district. Bradley street is just off Clark and the first side street off Walnut, two blocks north from the postoffice.

Illustration 11: Article that gives a visual of the Chicago neighborhood, Bradley Street (Lexington Herald-Leader Nov. 1, 1919)

EAST LEXINGTON.

The east end of Lexington, north of Main street, has not received the attention from the city that its size and importance demands. Time out of mind the East End citizens have been victims of inadequate sewerage, swamps and overflows. "Chicago" was a swamp for many years, known as Bradley Bottom, endangering the health of the neighboring citizens. It was only after years of effort that the city was induced to take hold of the matter and drain the place. It is not thoroughly done yet, but it is better than it was.

Up near the race track the water, in stormy times, crosses Race street and pours through some of the lots of property owners like a deluge. The Jeager lot was thus overflowed and a damage suit was threatened unless some plan was adopted by the city for carrying off the water. Mr. Scott, Chairman of the Joint Improvement Committee, took a common sense view of the situation and recommended a sewer to be built to relieve Mr. Jaeger, which will connect with the Ohio street sewer, which will pour through "Chicago" and which will increase the flood at the corner of Walnut and Main street, where Mr. John has experienced so much trouble.

The sewer is to be built to escape a damage suit at one end and may, possibly result in a damage suit at the other. The truth of the matter is that the sewerage at the northeast end of the city is very defective and inefficient and some day this will be discovered at the end of a lawsuit.

Illustration 12: Lexington Herald Leader Article May 29, 1897. It is explaining the drainage problems on this bottomland.

Julia Amanda Perry

In the remainder of this chapter, we would like to introduce the readers to two individuals who lived in the Goodloetown Community. This first section is a reproduction from my first publication.

Growing up on Lexington's East Side, how was it possible that I could go the majority of my life and know very little black history in my own city? I mean we do have black history month in February and all. So whats the purpose of black history month when all we hear about year after year is Martin Luther King, Harriet Tubman, Rosa Parks, Frederick Douglas and maybe a black inventor or two like Garrett Morgan? What about C.R. Patterson, a black man who built an automobile before Henry Ford? How come I was a thirty something year old man when I learned of him and thousands of other black history makers?

What about Julia Amanda Perry, an iconic world famous black composer? How could I be raised just a few blocks away from her childhood home and hear her name for the first time only recently? Maybe I would've appreciated classical music more had I knew she existed? Instead, I used to think it was just "white people's music."

216 Eastern Ave is the address of her childhood home. Today, it's the New Birth Worship Center. On the 1930 census record of her family, that part of Eastern Ave was called Vertner Ave. She was six years old by that time and lived across the street from Jazz musician Les McCann, making it two amazing future musicians to reside on Eastern Ave.

The fourth of five girls, she was born March 25,

1924 to Abraham and America Perry. The Perry household was a very musically inclined one. Abraham Perry, a physician by trade, was also an amateur pianist. He once went on tour with Tenor and Composer Roland Hayes. Two of her sisters studied violin. Julia's music education began when she was six. She was taught violin before moving on to piano two years later.

The family moved to Akron, OH., sometime in her childhood. The 1940 census record has them living on Scott Street in Akron.

After high school, she attended Westminster Choir College in Princeton, New Jersey, receiving both a Bachelor's and Master's degree in music by 1948. After graduation from Westminster, she continued her studies at Jilliard School of Music in New York. There, she studied conducting. Studying music year round, she spent the summers in Tanglewood, Massachusetts at Berkshire Music Center. Choral singing and composition were the subjects of study at Berkshire.[35]

Around this time she received a Guggenheim Fellowship. The Guggenheim Fellowship are grants given to students "who have already demonstrated exceptional capacity for productive scholarship or exceptional creative ability in the arts."[36] Traveling to Paris, France in 1952, she studied under Natalie Boulanger. Not long after this, she received her second Guggenheim Fellowship and traveled to Italy to study under Luigi Dallapiccola.

35. Sutherland, C. (2013, January 23). *Julia Amanda Perry (1924-1979)*. BlackPast.org. https://www.blackpast.org/african-american-histo-ry/perry-julia-amanda-1924-1979/

36. *About Us*. John Simon Guggenheim Memorial Foundation. (2022, April 6). Retrieved October 26, 2022, from https://www.gf.org/about-us/

While in Italy in 1956 and 1957, during the summer months, she studied in Siena at the Accademia Musicale Chigiana. The Accademia Chigiana was an international institute for advanced musical studies, founded in 1932 by Count Guido Chigi Saracini. She traveled Europe, studying until 1959, when she returned to the United States, even having the United States Information Service sponsor her on a couple tours of Europe in 1951.

1951 was the same year she composed her Stabat Mater and gained notoriety for it. It was a composition for contralto and string orchestras. The Stabat Mater is a 13th century Christian hymn that portrayed the Virgin Mary's suffering during the crucifixion of Jesus Christ. The piece was her dedication to her mother, America Perry.

Homage to Vivaldi, Homunculus C.F., and The Cask of Amontillado are among her best compositions. Early compositions such as "I'm a Poor Lil Orphan Girl" and "Free at Last" blended Negro Spirituals and neoclassical music. Her composing style was explained best by Eileen Southern:

> "Her basically neoclassical style was distinctive for an intense lyricism and penchant for contrapuntal textures. She wrote in all the forms: symphonies, operas, concertos, band works, chamber ensembles, piano pieces, and songs."[37]

Tom Eblem, a writer and journalist for the Lexing-

---

37. Southern, E. (2006). Singers, Instrumentalists, and Composers. In *The music of Black Americans: A history* (p. 551). W. W. Norton & Company.

ton Herald Leader, penned a column about Perry on February 16, 2016 in the Herald where he writes:

> "Perry's catalog of nearly 80 composi-
> tions is incredibly eclectic. It includes pieces for
> a variety of solo instruments, many kinds of
> small ensembles, chamber orchestra and full
> orchestra, many vocal performance platforms
> and even marching band."

Most of Amanda Perry's work unfortunately was not recorded but my personal favorite recorded piece is called "Study for Orchestra," which was performed in 1965 by the New York Philharmonic. It is available on YouTube. Homunculus C.F., is also available on Youtube. It was recorded by the Manhattan Percussion Ensemble. The piece was an experimental piece that Perry described as "Pantonal" because it used all available tones, none being major or minor.

It was stated earlier that she lived and studied for several years in Europe, upon her return to the United States, she took up teaching. She landed a gig in Florida, teaching at Florida Agricultural and Mechanical College, or today Florida A&M University, and at Atlanta College.

Poor health on top of being female, an African American female at that, possibly were contributing factors to her popularity not being what it should have been, given her body of work. She was writing compositions, touring and recording at a time when women were still struggling to be respected in a white male dominated society, so to accomplish as much as she did in her short life was phenomenal.

Perry had a setback in 1971 when she suffered a stroke. This caused her to lose the use of the right side of her body. Determined not to allow her disability to prevent her from doing what she loved, she learned how to use her left hand to write and continued composing. Two of the compositions she penned after the stroke were Five Quixotic Songs in 1976 and Bicentennial Reflections in 1977. The latter was for tenor solo and the former for bass baritone.

Perry would pass away in 1979 in Akron, Ohio.

The Lynching of James Pearsall

The next sketch is of a young man who was hung in Lexington in 1906, for a crime he went to his death stating that he did not commit. This crime occurred in the Goodloetown neighborhood.

I have been unsuccessful in my attempt to learn more of James Pearsall's upbringing, but we do have his father listed as Gabe Pearsall. According to the newspaper account, young James was named after his fathers master Jim McCann.[38] This indicates that the young Pearsall is the son of a slave. It was also stated that Gabe Pearsall was ran out of the country after attempting to slay the parents of his "master" Jim McCann, while they slept in bed. McCann was murdered himself by a man called Seymour Barrington, in St Louis, Missouri, a few years prior.

At the time of this alleged crime, James Pearsall was living with his sister Hattie Hill, her husband Charles and likely a brother by the name of Howard Pearsall, at 554 Goodloe Street.[39] Howard Pearsall passed

---

38. July 6 The Date, . (1906, June 4). *Lexington Leader*, p. 1.

39. Pendergast, P. (2017). Findings and Observation. In *The Life and*

away from Pneumonia in January 1906, and this was his listed address on his death certificate and in a Lexington Leader blurb.[40] Him being 23 years of age, 5 years older than James at this time indicates that he was likely his older brother. Newspaper reports that he also had another sister named Priscilla McCann and it was his sisters who reared him since birth.[41] This is possibly due to their father fleeing the country after his alleged attempted murder. His mother is unknown.

The events that led up to his "legal" lynching began with a few attempts at an alleged burglary, each of which occurred within a few blocks of his own residence. The first one occurred on Nelson Avenue at the residence of Charles Pilan. It was said that Pearsall broke the window to gain entry but was scared away due to a noise coming from inside the home. The alleged burglar then fled and attempted to burglarize another home, this one on East Third Street and was the residence of R.L. Jones. Jones had left the home for work, leaving his wife behind who reportedly was beaten by the assailant upon entering their home. The third and final home Pearsall allegedly entered was the abode of Mr. & Mrs. Charles Wagoner on Warnock Street. The papers report that he scaled a fence and entered the home through the rear door. The occupants were in bed and were aroused from the sounds of an intruder. Mr. Wagoner was then shot and severely wounded. The newspaper account went on

---

Lynching of James Pearsall (p. 5)

40. Vital Statistics. (1906, January 19). *Lexington Leader*, p. 6.

41. Law Extracts Extreme Penalty for the Awful Crime of James Pearsall. (1906, July 6). *The Lexington Herald*, p. 9.

further to say that he dragged Mrs Wagoner to another room, locked the door, then beat and raped her.[42]

After the assault, Pearsall was captured along the Cheasapeake and Ohio railroad. He allegedly gave a confession and admitted guilt. We have to use allegedly here because in these times, little evidence was actually needed to convict a black man for pretty much anything he was accused of. Being black and being accused was usually enough for a guilty verdict from a jury of 12 men and women who looked nothing like the accused, and likely harbored secret racist feelings themselves. We have heard this story time and time again, so the possibility of that being the case here is extremely high. If he did admit guilt, its possible that he did so under duress, coercion, or threat.

James Pearsall was found guilty and was sentenced to be hung on June 6, 1906. He remained in jail for seventeen months awaiting his execution. At the time of the alleged crime, Pearsall was 16 years old, he died at 18.

The newspapers give an account of his final moments of life. Ten minutes were given for religious services in which a black pastor preached a sermon and prayed for the accused. After that service concluded the following interaction was recorded:

> At the conclusion of the prayer, the minister turning to Pearsall said: "If you want to make a statement now is the time for you to make it. Have you any statement to make?"
>
> "Yes Sir," replied the negro.
>
> "Then you can make it now and if you want to make any confession of your guilt, make

---

42. Law Extracts Extreme Penalty for the Awful Crime of James Pearsall. (1906, July 6). *The Lexington Herald*, p. 9.

Chapter 16 – Goodloetown

it now and don't you tell a lie boy, for you are going to see your God in a few minutes."

Firmly and clearly Pearsall said, "I want to thank Mr. Wallace and all the others at the jail for treating me so nice. I want to thank the death watches for being so good to me. I have been in jail seventeen months and I never had any words with any of them. They all treated me nice and I am going home now and I want to meet you all in heaven. I am going home. I'm innocent."

That statement of Pearsall concluded the services. He then walked over to the trap door, turned his face to the East and looked up at the colored people gaping out of the windows of the houses to the West of the scaffold while the officers strapped his feet, tied his hands and adjusted the noose to his neck....[43]

I have neglected to record the remainder of the article in this book to spare the reader the gruesome details. What I have presented is sufficient enough to understand what happened to this young man. If one desires those details, I would suggest reading the cited article in full.

James Pearsall, some sources state that he was a jockey. Some sources state that he was a driver and his death record states that he was a laborer. Whatever his occupation may have been, this young man lost his life and its a strong possibility that he told the truth. During his incarceration, he maintained his declaration of innocence and continued to profess such up until the moment he was hung. Pearsall and his brother Howard, are both buried at the African Cemetery Number 2.

---

43. Dies on the Gallows for His Awful Crime. (1906, July 7). *The Lexington Herald*, p. 4.

JAMES PEARSALL.

Chapter 17 – Kinkeadtown

Kinkeadtown is a community that actually existed during my lifetime. However, I was young when it was demolished, so I have no personal memory of it ever being several blocks away from the neighborhood that I grew up in. As an Ashland Elementary School student, I can remember taking field trips to a place called the Living Arts and Science Center. Little did I know this was just a block away from the Kinkeadtown section and that this center was the former home of the neighborhoods' namesake George Blackburn Kinkead.

As you have read throughout this text, the majority of these communities bore the names of the white landowner who subdivided the land into lots and sold to

African Americans, Kinkeadtown was another number on the list of these said communities.

George B. Kinkead, was a white lawyer who came from a family of slave holders. He however, developed an anti-slavery stance and in the 1840's, had freed all of the people he himself held as slaves.

Those 50 and over from Lexington may have memories of Kinkeadtown, but for those my age, 40 and younger, they may not know. So, where exactly was Kinkeadtown?

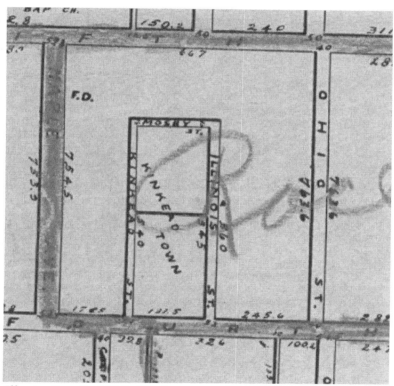

Illustration 1: 1912 Slade map of Lexington. Showing the location of Kinkeadtown.

This community consisted of Kinkead Street, Mosby Street and Illinois Street. Illinois was formerly called Price Street. This section was located between Fourth and Fifth, Maple and Ohio Streets.

Its origin story starts with George B. Kinkead, who alongside Dr. Warren Frazer, purchased a 11.23 acre tract of land from William Brand.[1] This occurred in 1864. This land was split equally among them and Kinkead resold his portion to African Americans. An 1871 birds eye view map shows 13 homes in the neighborhood with three on East Fourth Street, five on Kinkead Street and five on Illinois/Price, however the map doesn't show a street on Illinois/Price but the homes are clearly there.

Illustration 2: 1871 Birds eye view map showing the placement of homes in the developing Kinkeadtown.

---

1. O'Malley, N. (1996). Chapter 2, Kinkeadtown in Historical Context. In *Kinkeadtown: Archaeological Investigation of an African-American neighborhood in Lexington, Kentucky* (p. 13).

Hummons Family

One of the first families to call Kinkeadtown home was the Hummons family. John Hummons and his wife Iantha, purchased a home on East Fourth Street and two of his sons Frank and William, each had a home next door to one another. The 1870 census record incorrectly lists their last name as "Hummings," but it suggests that John worked on area farms while sons Frank and William were both carriage drivers. Hummons Avenue, which presently exists in the area that once was Kinkeadtown, clearly bears the name of this black family. Family lore states that the Hummons family were from Scott County, Kentucky and that there existed a small community there known as Hummonsville, in which the family lived prior to relocating to Kinkeadtown.[2]

Henry Tandy

Another household of note would be the home of Henry Tandy. You may recognize the name Tandy from an earlier chapter in which we stated that Vertner Woodson Tandy became New York City's first black architect. Henry Tandy, who owned a home at 421 Illinois Street, was his father. Henry Tandy, alongside his partner Albert Byrd owned a construction company and are recognized as being the company that laid the foundation for various Lexington buildings such as the Fayette County Courthouse in 1898, Morton Junior High School on Main Street in 1909, First National Bank Building in 1894, Miller Hall at the University of Kentucky and various

---

2. Ibid., p. 25

other buildings throughout the city. In 1900, Tandy was one of the richest black men in the state of Kentucky. So how did he get his start in construction?[3] Henry Tandy was born in slavery and this is really a rags to riches story if there ever was one.

Illustration 3: Henry Tandy

3. *Henry Tandy*. The Blue Grass Trust for Historic Preservation. (n.d.). Retrieved December 4, 2022, from https://www.bluegrasstrust.org/henry-tandy

Progress To Some, Devastation To Others

Tandy's beginnings were in Estill County, Kentucky, in slavery. Freedman savings bank record for Tandy dated March 21, 1870, has his mother's name listed as Bertie. His father was unknown. Due to his light complexion, we can reason that either one or both of his parents were mulatto or he is a product of the white master subjecting his female "property" to his own sexual desires against their will. This was very common in those days. Frederick Douglas writes about his own father and how the master was often the father of his own slave:

> "I say nothing of father, for he is shrouded in a mystery, I have never been able to penetrate. Slavery does away with fathers, as it does away with families. Slavery has no use for either fathers or families, and its laws do not recognize their existence in the social arrangements of the plantation. When they do exist, they are not the outgrowths of slavery, but are antagonistic to that system. The order of civilization is reversed here. The name of the child is not expected to be that of its father, and his condition does not necessarily affect that of the child. He may be the slave of Mr. Tilgman; and his child, when born, may be the slave of Mr. Gross. He may be a freeman; and yet his child may be a chattel. He may be white, glorying in the purity of his Anglo Saxon blood; and his child may be ranked with the blackest slaves. Indeed, he may be, and often is, master and father to the same child. He can be father without being a husband, and may sell his child without incurring reproach, if the child be by a woman in whose veins courses one thirty second part of African blood. My father was a white man, or nearly white. It was sometimes whispered that my master was

my father."[4]

This is likely the case here. Due to the lack of records kept on black slaves, we may never know.

His exact birth date and birth year is unknown. One source suggests 1853, another says 1854, but we know he moved to Lexington in 1865 and found employment in the photography business working for John Mullen.[5] That would put him at the age of 11 or 12 at this time, which is not impossible but seems unlikely. The Freedman Bank record of 1870 lists his age as 19 at that time, putting his birth around 1851. That is the more probable year considering his signature is on the record.

In any case, he worked in this business for two years before gaining employment as a brick mason for a construction firm owned by Garrett D. Wilgus. Its of note that Wilgus' firm was one of the largest construction companies in Central Kentucky at this time and Wilgus' home at 327 Wilgus Street has been on the National Registry of Historic Places since 1978. Wilgus street is just off of East Third on Lexington's East End.

Tandy worked his way up to become the foreman of this firm, a position he held until his employers death in 1892. It was then that he alongside partner Albert Byrd, established their own firm, "Tandy and Byrd."

---

4. Douglass, Frederick. "Chapter 3." *My Bondage and My Freedom: Part I - Life as a Slave. Part II - Life as a Freeman*, Miller, Orton & Mulligan, New York: 25 Park Row -- Auburn: 107 Genesee-St., New York, 1855, p. 51.

5. Johnson, William D. (1897). Chapter XXV - Henry A. Tandy. In *Biographical sketches of prominent Negro men and women of Kentucky* (p. 46). Lexington Standard Print.

W. D. Johnson's 1897 publication of prominent black men and women of Kentucky states that:

> "Since that time this has been the leading firm of contractors and builders in Lexington. In every business block, upon every thoroughfare, you see stately buildings and handsome residences built by this firm."[6]

Even further Johnson speaks of how much this firm did for the black community of Lexington by creating employment opportunities stating:

> "Mr. Tandy began his career with only a limited education, attending school at odd times when not engaged in work. He has displayed wonderful tact in business affairs and is truly a successful man. Through his indefatigable efforts a large force of Negro laborers have found steady employment, and thereby obtained comfortable homes for their families. He has done much good for the advancement of the race and helped to open avenues of trade and employment for young men."[7]

Other buildings that the Tandy and Byrd firm built were the annex of the original Good Samaritan Hospital at 333 East Short Street. The same building that Rev. Stevenson and Rev O.L. Murphy were attempting to turn into the Bethesda Industrial College, see the Taylortown chapter. The building that was formerly the

---

6. Ibid,. p. 46

7. Ibid,. p. 46

Ades Dry Goods store, now Portofino's restaurant on Main Street, was also built by Tandy and Byrd.

Tandy purchased his first property from George Kinkead in 1875 and built his home in the Kinkeadtown neighborhood at 421 Illinois Street. Then the address was 19 Price Street. The majority of homes in the community were shotgun styled homes and several were T-plans. Tandy's home however, was the first two story brick structure in the section. He and his wife resided here until they sold the home in 1881 to Margaret Pendleton, who was the wife of Washington Ray.[8]

Tandy would then purchase another home, this one at 642 West Main Street. This home is where he and his family lived until his death in 1918. It still stands today. Tandy was buried in the Greenwood Cemetery and has one of the largest monuments within. Cheapside Park, the former site of Kentucky's largest slave trade, was renamed in 2020 in Tandy's honor, Tandy Park.

Dudley Allen

Another Kinkeadtown resident was Dudley Allen. Born in slavery around 1845, his owner was John Dunn of Lexington. Death certificate indicates that his fathers name was Hosea Allen and his mother was unknown. I have found a death certificate for Hosea Allen that appears to be signed by Dudley Allen dated October 18, 1910. This suggests that his father lived in Gunntown at 333 Corral Street and was married to Kate Smith. It is unknown if this was Dudley's mother, but I am speculat-

---

8. O'Malley, N. (1996). Chapter VI, The Tandy/Ray House Lot. In *Kinkeadtown: Archaeological Investigation of an African-American neighborhood in Lexington, Kentucky* (p. 203)

ing that she was not based on his mother being listed as unknown on his death certificate. The information on the certificate is given by an informant, often the spouse or child of the deceased and they don't always know the particulars to report them, especially when enslavement was involved.

Dudley Allen joined Company M of the 5th United States Colored Calvary at Camp Nelson on August 24, 1864 during the civil war.[9] He was promoted to Quartermaster Sergeant and was second in command. The Quartermaster Sergeant was responsible for the company wagon as well as the horses and various other duties.

Upon freedom, he married Margaret Crittenden. Rev. George Downing, the founder of Asbury M.E. And Gunn Tabernacle, joined the couple into this union 1866.[10]

Allen and his wife Margaret lived in a home they owned located at 416 Kinkead Street. Margaret had purchased this lot on March 29, 1871 from George Kinkead and his wife. It measured 30 by 97 feet.[11]

With funds obtained from the military, Allen was able to purchase himself a farm and a stable of horses. He became a well known horse trainer and owner. In fact, he is the only African American to ever own a horse that won the Kentucky Derby when a horse he trained and owned, Kingman, won the 1891 Derby with the World's Greatest Jockey Isaac Murphy. The two were the

---

9. Historical Data Systems, Inc.; Duxbury, MA 02331; *American Civil War Research Database*

10. "Allen, Dudley," Notable Kentucky African Americans Database, accessed December 11, 2022, https://nkaa.uky.edu/nkaa/items/show/1910.

11. O'Malley, N. (1996). Chapter XI, The Allen House Lot. In *Kinkeadtown: Archaeological Investigation of an African-American neighborhood in Lexington, Kentucky* (p. 267). 372

last African American trainer/jockey duo to win it. The first was trainer and former slave Ansel Williamson and black jockey Oliver Lewis, when they won the first ever Kentucky Derby in 1875, upon a horse named Aristides. Edward Dudley Brown, another black horse trainer who lived on the East End in Gunntown, and black jockey William Walker were another African American duo to win the Kentucky Derby when in 1877, Walker rode the horse Baden-Baden, to victory.[12] Kingmen would win two other notable races in 1891, the Latonia Derby, and the Phoenix Hotel Stakes at the Kentucky Association Race-track, just a couple of blocks away from his Kinkeadtown home. Kingmen finished third in the American derby in Chicago that same year.[13]

Allen wasn't the sole owner of Kingman however. It was a partnership with a white man out of George-town, Ky named Kinzea Stone. They also co-owned a stable named "Jacobins Stable." It is speculated that the name possibly was in honor of the Haitian Revolution-ary and Black Jacobin T'oussaint L'Oventure, who helped lead Haiti to independence from France in 1804. It is also suggested that this alias was used to mask the fact that Kingman was owned by a black man.

"the Jacobin Stable alias was used to
conceal the names of the partners, because Allen

12. Phelps, M. (n.d.). *Notable partnerships: Winning Teams despite Discrimination.* Notable Partnerships: Winning Teams Despite Discrimination. The Chronicle of African Americans in the Horse Industry. Retrieved December 11, 2022, from
https://africanamericanhorsestories.org/explore/stories/notable-partnerships-winning-teams-despite-discrimination

13. Former Noted Trainer Dies. (1911, October 15). *The Lexington Leader,* p. 7.

was a Negro and such business arrangements were frowned on."[14]

Dudley however, makes it clear about his owner-ship of Kingman in a 1891 newspaper article when the following was published on May 1:

> "Dudley Allen, the colored trainer, asks The Leader to publish the statement that he is a half owner of Kingman, and has entire control of the animal. Kingman was purchased as a yearling by Messrs. Stone & Allen in Chica-go for $250."[15]

This was likely due to the fact that all of the pa-pers were reporting on "Kinzea Stone's" horse Kingman and only referring to Allen as the trainer. One can only assume the annoyance this was to him, to be excluded from the conversation about a horse in which he was principal owner, trainer and caretaker.

The Kentucky Derby itself was once dominated by black jockeys and black horse trainers. 13 of the 15 jock-eys in the very first Derby were black men. 15 of the first 28 Derby's were won by black jockeys. Over the years, there was a decline in black men within the Thorough-bred industry. It's safe to say that was by design. Many of these men were formerly enslaved and achieved great

---

14. Phelps, M. (n.d.). *Notable partnerships: Winning Teams despite Discrimination.* Notable Partnerships: Winning Teams Despite Discrimination   The Chronicle of African Americans in the Horse Industry. Retrieved December 11, 2022, from https://africanamericanhorsestories.org/explore/stories/notable-partnerships-winning-teams-despite-discrimination

15. Ownership of Kingman. (1891, May 11). *The Kentucky Leader*, p. 1.

wealth and status in this industry. Something, I'm sure created much jealousy and envy among the many whites within this business. After all, the negro is barely a decade removed from being considered property and $3/5^{ths}$ a man. By 1904, there were very few black trainers remaining in Lexington. Something the newspaper reported on when they wrote:

"One thing most notable here is the seeming passing of the colored trainer. Dudley Allen and Lee Christy have a few horses but the bulk of the racing strings here are controlled by white trainers, and of the 250 horses being handled here, not 25 are in the hands of colored horsemen. A few years ago, the black man was in ascendancy in this line, but each season he has become less numerous, and Allen and Christy are all that are left of the old guard of their color who are still in the thoroughbred business.[16]

Some of the black trainers that trained the best racehorses in the industry included, the aforementioned Edward Dudley Brown, aka "Brown Dick," Lee Christy and Ansel Williamson, Raleigh Colston, Robert(Bob) E. Campbell, Will Perkins, and the trainer of the 1885 Kentucky Derby winner, and grandfather to musician Julia Amanda Perry of Gunntown/Goodloetown, "Abe Perry." Were black trainers pushed out of the business the same way the black jockey was? Prior to the year 2000, the last black jockey to ride in the Kentucky Derby was Jess Conley in 1911. He rode the horse "Colston" owned and

16. Horse Gossip; Passing of Colored Trainers. (1904, January 12). *The Lexington Leader*, p. 3.

trained by Raleigh Colston. Colston finished in third place. There was not another black jockey until the year 2000. That's an eighty-nine year hiatus from a sport once dominated by black men, nearly a century. Jimmy Winkfield was the last black jockey to win a Triple Crown race when he won the Derby in consecutive years in 1901 and 1902. He finished second in 1903.[17] The Triple Crown includes the Preakness Stakes, Belmont Stakes and the Kentucky Derby. In 1900, the New York Times printed the following statement:

> "The public generally accepted the theory that the old time favorites of African blood had outgrown their skill, and really were out of date because of their inability to ride up to form of past years. Racing men know better. As a matter of fact, the Negro jockey is down and out not because he could no longer ride, but because of a quietly formed combination shut him out."[18]

So, what is this quietly formed combination that shut him, the black jockey, out? White Jockey Clubs formed and conspired with white horse owners to remove the negro jockey from the sport.

> "The Negro riders got mounts at first, but they failed to win races. Somehow or other, they met with all sorts of accidents and interferences in their races. The doubting horse owners seem to have

17. Leeds, M., & Rockoff, H. (2020). The Triple Crown. In *Jim Crow in the Saddle: The Expulsion of African American Jockeys from American Racing* (p. 8). National Bureau of Economic Research.

18. "Negro Jockeys Shut Out: Combination of White Riders to bar them From the Turf." New York Times, July 29, 1900, p. 19.

been convinced since the early meetings that if they want to win races they must ride the white jockeys."[19]

And then the dangerous and retaliatory tactics used by white jockeys:

> "Some of his [African - American Jockey Jimmy Lee's] compatriots of color became a trifle cocky in the jockey rooms. The white boys retaliated by ganging up on the black riders on the rails. A black boy would be pocketed, thrust back in the race; or his mount would be bumped out of contention; or a white boy would run alongside, slip a foot under a black boy's stirrup, and toss him out of the saddle. Again, while ostensibly whipping their own horses those white fellows would lash out and cut the nearest Negro rider …They literally ran the black boys off the track."[20]

Again, the last black jockey to ride in the Derby prior to the year 2000, occurred in 1911. These men were shut out from the sport, not just in Kentucky but in the States. Winkfield left the United States altogether and began his career abroad in Russia and France.[21] This was likely the same scenario that forced the black trainer out as well. Maybe not completely as with the jockey but the number of black trainers definitely dwindled to next to none and Dudley Allen, while calling Kinkeadtown

---

19. Ibid., p.19

20. Parmer, Charles B. 1939. For Gold and Glory: The Story of Thoroughbred Racing in America. New York: Carrick and Evans Inc. p. 150

21. Brown, D. (2007, November 21). *Jimmy Winkfield (1882-1974)*. BlackPast.org. https://www.blackpast.org/african-american-history/winkfield-jimmy-1882-1974/

home, certainly made his mark on the horse racing industry and cemented himself forever in the history books.

Rose Street Extension

By the early 1990's, this community existed no more. All of the homes were razed to make way for a new thoroughfare. To ease some of the downtown traffic and congestion, the city of Lexington planned an extension of Rose Street during the mid eighties. This extension would go right through the Kinkeadtown neighborhood. Prior to, Rose Street ended at Main but after all was said and done, extended all the way down to Sixth Street, connecting to Elm Tree Lane. Map of 1912, shows that Elm Tree was a small street between Fifth and Sixth, Kinkeadtown was between Fourth and Fifth and was directly in the "line of fire," preventing this connection.

From Main Street, up to Fourth, that part of Rose Street was formerly Deweese, which we have explained in the Goodloetown chapter, was the black business district of Lexington. At this time, it was nothing more than a side street. Lexington Mayor in the mid eighties, Scotty Baesler, entertained the idea to revitalize Deweese Street to its once former glory. The discussions were to make Deweese a black historical district similar to Bourbon Street in New Orleans.[22] But without funding from the state, this plan never occurred. Nonetheless, the Rose Street extension was completed minus the

22. Deweese project hinges on state aid for Rose Street Extension. (1985, September 30). *Lexington Herald-Leader*, p. 69.

Deweese Revival.

The community was given a voice as to what to name this new extension. Martin Luther King Blvd was a suggestion, while others wanted to keep Rose Street due to it's history in the city of Lexington.[23] At any rate, this part of "Rose Street" became known as Elm Tree Lane, and this is what exists today. Along with this extension, a new low income apartment complex was built along Elm Tree Lane called Rosetown Apartments, on the former site of the Gunntown Missionary Baptist Church.

---

23. Letters to the Editor: A Challenge to Race Relations. (1987, April 29). *Lexington Herald-Leader,* p. 8.

Chapter 18 – Bluegrass Aspendale Housing Project

As the author of this book, I felt it was important that a book of this kind be written not by an outsider, but by someone with a personal connection to many of these neighborhoods. I did not want this to read like an academic text, but more from the standpoint of someone who knew the people, who knew the streets, who knew first-hand what it's like growing up in a low income, predominately black community. This isn't a study, although I used many studies as sources for the purpose of the accurate documentation of history. I intentionally made this text simple, plain, and straight to the point.

This book in various chapters is semi-biographical and included information about several of my family members who lived in these communities. This chapter, the final chapter, will be no different because this is the neighborhood that I was born and raised in.

My mother, Girtha Thompson, or simply "Lois," was born in Barbourville, Kentucky, in Knox County, in the year 1962. As a small child, my mother was playing with a balloon and it went near the water heater. In an attempt to retrieve the balloon, my mother fell and her face was severely burned from the water heater. A scar that she still wears today. The family had frequent trips to Lexington's University of Kentucky hospital because of this and it became a financial burden to make that eighty-eight mile trip as often as they were forced to do. My late Grandmother, Beverly Thompson, packed the family up and a move to the city of Lexington was made. This was in the year 1967. My grandmother was renting a shotgun house on Deweese Street, near the Lyric Theater. From there, sometime in the late 1960's, they moved up the street to the Bluegrass Aspendale Housing Projects. The apartment was located at 238 C McCracken Drive. This is where I was born in 1983. You can say, had my mother never had this accident, her and my father would've never met and this text you are reading now, wouldn't exist because I wouldn't be here. That scar on my mother's face is forever a reminder of my own existence. It's also a reminder that every decision we make in our lives will affect what occurs in the future. My grandmothers decision to move to Lexington for my mothers healthcare made it possible for my parents to meet later in life. This made it possible for me to have children and now I have a child with children of her own, continuing this cycle of life.

My father, Jerome Hayes, also lived in the housing

project with my late paternal grandmother Mary White. Ray was her maiden name. Her father, George Ray came from the Cadentown community and her mother Helen Lyons, hails from Lincoln County, Kentucky. My grandmother was born in Lexington. They lived at 332 East Short Street at the time of her birth in 1932. My father was born in 1954 on a military base in Great Falls, Montana. After my grandparents split, at an unknown date, grandmother moved my father and his siblings to the projects. Likely in the 1960's or 1970's. This is where my parents met.

When I was around a year old, my mother, 22 at the time, got her first apartment down the street at 232 C McCracken Drive. This is where I have my earliest memories. My older brother, Ranoni Thompson was born in 1979 and my little sister Chelica Thompson, was born in 1986. My earliest memory was her birth. I don't have any memories of life before her birth, when it was just me and my brother. I was two, about to turn three in less than a month when she was born. I can recall being at the hospital and putting on a gown. I can remember her being wrinkled and very red. My mother asked would I like to hold her and I was afraid to. I would sit next to my mother while she held her and play with her ears though. I wasn't the baby anymore, of course I will remember this. LOL.

Before I share more of my story, lets discuss how the neighborhood came to be.

Illustration 1: My mother, older brother and that's me in the stroller. This was before my mother got her own place in 1984. This was outside of 238 C McCracken Drive.

Kentucky Association Racetrack

"The projects used to be a race track." I've heard this echoed my entire upbringing in this community, although I never knew the history or even the name of the racetrack. It was just stated often. As I would later learn, the Kentucky Association Racetrack once was located on the land that became the Bluegrass-Aspendale Housing Project. Unbeknownst to most of us in the neighborhood, many of the street names that we walked and played in on a daily basis, were named for men who were members of this Association that began in 1826. By 1872, 65 acres of land was owned by the Association. The entrance to the racetrack was located at the intersection of what today is Fifth and Race Street. Race street was formerly called Lincoln Street. I think it is obvious where the name "Race Street" comes from.

Some of the greatest black jockeys that ever lived, got their start on this racetrack.[1] These formerly enslaved black men cared for and tended to the horses every day of their lives, knew the ends and out of horses, so on and so forth, thus were hired as the groomsmen, trainers and jockeys before and following emancipation. They were indeed the best men for the job.

One such man was arguably the greatest jockey to ever live. That was Isaac Murphy, who won his first race on this track in 1876 at the age of fifteen.[2] Jimmy

1. "Kentucky Association Race Track," *Tour the Historic Bluegrass*, accessed April 26, 2023, https://tourthehistoricbluegrass.com/items/show/37.

2. *Isaac Burns Murphy Historical Marker*. The Historical Marker Database. (2022, January 10). Retrieved April 26, 2023, from https://www.hmdb.org/m.asp?m=119100

Winkfield, whose racing career also began at Kentucky Association in 1898, was the last black jockey to win the Kentucky Derby in 1902. He was the second jockey to win consecutive Kentucky Derbies, winning in 1901 and 1902. Isaac Murphy was the first. Murphy and Winkfield were the only two jockeys to ever accomplish this until another jockey did it seventy years later in 1972 and 1973.[3] Oliver Lewis, another notable black jockey and winner of the first ever Kentucky Derby in 1875, began his racing career at this racetrack. There are countless others not mentioned that began here.

The Phoenix Stakes, which is the oldest stakes race in the country, began on this track in 1831. It ran here until 1930.[4] It was on hiatus for seven years but was revived in 1937 at the new Keeneland Racetrack. The Ashland Oaks was another annual race that began on this track. It started in 1879. Some gaps in it's history but the last run at Kentucky Association was in 1932. It was revived in 1936 under the name the Ashland Stakes. This time, at Keeneland. This race is still run today.

New ownership took over in 1890 after financial troubles plagued the racetrack but closed for a few years in 1898.[5] The new owners suffered the same and it was

---

3. Nyra Press Office (Ed.). (n.d.). *The extraordinary life of Jimmy Winkfield*. NYRA. Retrieved April 26, 2023, from https://www.nyra.com/aqueduct/news/%E2%80%8Bthe-extraordinary-life-of-jimmy-winkfield

4. Moore, N. (2020, August 10). *It's true (we think): The Travers Stakes has to be the oldest...something*. Saratoga Living. Retrieved April 26, 2023, from https://saratogaliving.com/travers-stakes-oldest-something/

5 Brackney, P. (2014). Old Kentucky Association Racetrack. In *Lost Lexington, Kentucky* (p. 78). The History Press.

sold again in 1901, then again in 1903 when it reopened[67]

The racetrack would close for good in 1933 and two years later, it along with it's adjoining facilities were demolished. So, whats next for this sixty-five acre, now barren site?

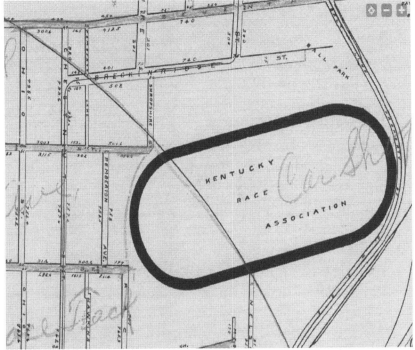

Illustration 2: The racetrack on the 1912 map of Lexington. The street just above the track is Breckinridge Street, which was one of the streets that existed in the projects. The intersection of Fifth and Race, the entrance to the track, is on the southwest side, just below Pemberton Ave. The street you see leading south directly from the track is Nelson Ave. Cut off but right to the left of Nelson is Thomas Street, which when the projects were built, was another street within the community.

---

6. New Owner For Kentucky Track. (1901, March 6). *New York Times.*

7. Race Track Sold. (1903, October 17). *The Spokane Press*, p. 6.

Two Projects, One Black, One White

I do not intend to go into the how and why Housing projects came to be. That's been done in numerous other works such as "The Color of Law: A Forgotten History of How Our Government Segregated America" by Richard Rothstein. Again, this isn't a study or academic text. It is a book written by a layperson from Lexington, who saw the need to write it. Much of the city's black history is being erased, and no one else FROM these communities, has done it. Blurbs were written here and there, articles written here and there, a chapter here and there but not a book like this. So, I took on the challenge.

The major thing I want to emphasize is the history of this specific neighborhood and its formation. Bottom line, in the 1930's, there was a housing crisis in the city of Lexington for it's black and poor citizens. Neighborhoods such as Adamstown, Branch Alley, Chicago Bottoms, and others written about in this book were on the verge of extinction, and "we need to do something with these negros," was the overall sentiment.

Due to the neglectful intent of the city government, Lexington's slums were dubbed some of the worst in the nation in 1937.[8] Much of this land that was once undesirable, now suddenly, the city and it's universities within, are coveting it. Adamstown had to go, the University of Kentucky sought to expand. Chicago Bottoms has to go, we need a new jail. Whats left to do with these people in these communities, who lived where they

---

8. Clarke, M. (2007). Chapter 1 - Voices of Home in Bluegrass Aspendale. In *Voices of Home in Bluegrass-Aspendale: Constructing the ideal* (p. 15). University of Kentucky, Gaines Center for the Humanities.

could afford to live?   No efforts to improve the existing community, let's get rid of it altogether.   Dump them in our new "affordable" housing projects that we are going to come for and destroy in the near future. This new housing project began in 1938. Collectively, we knew it as Bluegrass-Aspendale Housing Project, but it started as two separate projects.   One for whites, the other for blacks.

Bluegrass Park was the area designated for the whites and Aspendale Park was the area for black tenants. Aspendale was named such because it was built on what was a farm called "Aspendale," that was owned by Pryor R. Pemberton.[9] The nearby street between Fifth and Sixth Streets named "Pemberton Street," was also formerly a part of this farm, hence the name. At some point, the areas were mixed up. The article in the foot-note above states this. Originally, Aspendale was for whites and Bluegrass was for blacks. But in any case, the opposite happened. Aspendale was all black and Blue-grass housed the whites. The sections were divided by an eight-foot, barbed wire fence that didn't come down until January 30, 1974.[10] The entrance to Aspendale was at the east end of Fifth Street while the entrance for Bluegrass was at the east end of Sixth Street.

Collectively, these two areas housed a total of 286 families.[11] 144 apartments were in Aspendale and 142

9. Units' Names Are Reversed, White Project is Designated Aspendale and Negro Bluegrass Park.. (1936, April 15). *The Lexington Leader*, p. 1.

10. Kentucky.com. (n.d.). *Fence separating races removed, 1974.* Kentucky   Photo   Archive.   Retrieved   April 26,   2023,   from https://kyphotoarchive.com/2017/02/06/fence-separating-races-removed-1974/

11. Tenants To Move Into Lexington's Federal Housing Projects Within A

were in Bluegrass. If each of these households had at minimal two residents, that would total 572 people. Of course we know most households contained at the very least one child. That brings it to 858 people in close capacity, packed in like sardines in a can. This number of 858, obviously is a rough estimate and not precise, but showing potentially how many people lived in these communities when their doors opened for tenancy in the late 1930's. Most families in those days had more than one child so, the number in actuality was probably much greater than 858 and well over a thousand.

Illustration 3: 1938 aerial view of the two sections. You can see the dividing fence in between them in this photo. The oval shaped street is Bluegrass(whites) and Aspendale is the other(blacks) (Lexington Herald-Leader Jan 2, 1938)

Week. (1938, January 2). *The Lexington Herald*, p. 1.

ONE OF 50 BUILDINGS IN PARKS   —Herald Photo.

The above building is one of the 50 included in the $1,700,000 Blue Grass and Aspendale Parks federal housing project being constructed on the old race track. The project is scheduled to be completed by September 1.

Illustration 4: One of the units prior to opening in 1938 (Lexington Herald Jun 20, 1937)

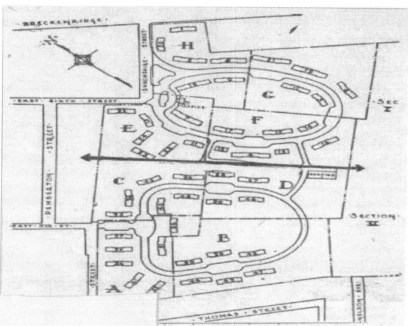

Illustration 5: 1937 sketch of the two Housing Projects (Lexington Herald Jul 18, 1937)

Illustration 6: The old administration building. I remember this building specifically. It was at the east end of Sixth Street where it intersected with Shropshire Ave, before you enter Bluegrass Park. (Lexington Herald Mar 7, 1937)

Fowler Gardens

Bluegrass and Aspendale both were at 100 percent occupancy since the year they opened. So, there was a need for more low income housing. The year 1941 saw the emergence of a new housing project in the area. This one in it's beginning was all white just like Bluegrass Park. The only difference is that Bluegrass and Aspendale were owned by the federal government but leased by the city, while the new Fowler Gardens, was owned by the city. After a sixty year period, Bluegrass and Aspendale would then become the city's property, around the year 1998.[12] However, the Lexington Municipal Housing Committee was able to purchase the projects before the sixty year term, in 1953.[13] The specific details of which I care not to get into in this text.

This new project consisted of about eleven buildings and 86 total units. It also connected to Bluegrass Park. The streets in this new section were McVey and Havely. Fowlers Gardens was named after a man from Virginia named John Fowler. In the early 1800's, he owned land near the housing project and the section that became known as Charles Young Park in Goodloetown. This site was a botanical garden of sorts and almost like a resort for Lexington's white wealthy.[14] The Enslaver Henry Clay bought the land some years later. It was sold several times before coming into the hands of David S. Goodloe, who willed it to his nephew William Goodloe. He then sold this land to the city for the purpose of creating this negro park. Fowler himself, died in 1840. He was buried at the old Episcopal Cemetery that's on

12. First Housing Projects Success. (1940, December 29). *The Lexington Herald*, p. 9.

13. Private Investors Finance New Project Homes. (1954, April 18). *Sunday Herald-Leader*, p. 50.

14. Captain Fowlers Garden Was Favorite. (1932, June 23). *The Lexington Leader*, p. 7.

Third Street.

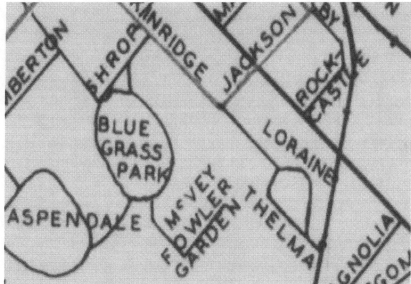

Illustration 7: 1950 map of Lexington. In the middle of the image, you can see Bluegrass, Aspendale and Fowler Garden. You can also see much of the land right next and below it is unoccupied. This land will become home to two other projects that will be discussed on the succeeding pages.

Illustration 8: 1940 Aeriel view of the three projects. Aspendale on the left, Bluegrass to the right and just below the newly built but yet to be occupied Fowler Homes. You can still see remnants of the racetrack at the bottom left. (Lexington Herald-Leader Dec. 29, 1940)

Ward Havely Homes

To keep it simple, in 1953, two more new housing projects opened up. These last two, combined with the previous three, made up collectively what we know as the Bluegrass-Aspendale Housing Project.

I was born in the 1980's, so most of my memories are from the 1990's. We had no knowledge that our neighborhood was originally five separate projects. Didn't really know that three of these sections were originally all white, although I heard mumbles here and there. Used to hear people say, "when blacks moved in, the whites moved out," but I was young so never really gave that much thought. Yet, I can recollect it. These things may have been known by the elders, but certainly not by my generation and I suspect, not by the generation before me. My mother grew up in this neighborhood in the 1970's and I don't recall ever hearing this. Not even in a recent discussion with her when I phoned her specifically for information about the "projects" as we affectionately called them. You could tell however that Aspendale and Bluegrass Park have a different design and they looked older. It was something we noticed but again, we were kids, the history wasn't that important to us at the time. All we knew was this was home and nearly everyone around us, looked like us. Couldn't fathom that the projects were once white. Well, all five sections combined, it was close to 50 percent white and 50 percent black. 514 units were designated black and 598 were white. By the time I was running through the neighborhood, it was probably around 90 plus percent black. There were some white families in the neighborhood, as well as some Hispanics, but the overwhelming majority looked like me.

The street I lived on from birth until around 1991, was McCracken Drive. It was changed that year to Withrow Way. This street was in this newer section that opened up in 1953. This section was called "The Ward Havely Homes" and was originally all white. Ward Havely was named after a Lexington mayor. McCracken Drive bore the name of Ralph McCracken, who was the chairman of the Lexington Municipal Housing Commission.[15] This was an additional 370 units, the largest of the five.

Before the name changes of 1991, the Ward Havely

15. History Linked to Sections Names. (1954, April 18). *Sunday Herald-Leader*, p. 48.

section consisted of the following streets: Breckinridge, Yellman, and McCracken Drive. Yellman bears the name of John Yellman, a former chairman of the Housing Committee.[16] Breckinridge Street, was named for either Robert J. Breckinridge, a politician or his father John C. Breckinridge, a Kentucky Senator.[17] Thelma Street and Loraine Street were an extension of Breckinridge Street on it's east side. These two streets made a circular shape and comprised a little subdivision that was called Sunshine Park. This subdivision was established in the 1920's on land that would be needed for a portion of the 370 new housing units being built. The property owners sold their lots to the Lexington Municipal Housing Commission in 1951.[18] Thelma and Loraine Streets, can be seen on the 1950 map in Illustration 7, three pages back.

Around the year 1992, our mother moved us from what was then Withrow Way up the street to 715 Breckinridge Street. We remained here until 1998. That year we for the first time, moved out of the projects. Spending significant time on this street, I never heard of "Sunshine Park." If I didn't, how many others didn't or don't know as well? Thus the importance of this book.

---

16 Ibid., p. 48

17. Jay, J. (1936, July 17). Four Bits, Getting Names Right. *The Lexington Leader*, p. 1.

18. Project to Replace Some of The Worst Slums. (1951, August 5). *Sunday Herald-Leader*, p. 8.

Illustration 9: This is the entire housing project area. The sections outlined in white are showing where the new projects are being built. The small section at the top is Sunshine Park. The area below was vacant land that will comprise the rest of Ward Havely. At the bottom left is the area that was Thomas Street, This will be discussed on the next page. (Lexington Herald-Leader Aug. 5, 1951)

John Caulder Homes

You may recall seeing the name "John B. Caulder," in various chapters in this book. He was one of Lexington's most prominent black citizens. An early educator at the Jonestown School and the Principal of the Constitution School for over forty years. This is who the John Caulder Homes were named after. Before we discuss more about this brilliant black brother, let's delve into the history of the homes.

This was the fifth and final addition to the Housing Project. It was built simultaneously in 1953, alongside the aforementioned Ward Haverly Homes.   Those were built to the east of the previous three projects.   Caulder Homes were directly south.   This project consisted of 228 units and was exclusively for black residents. It was built on Thomas Street, bordered by Grinstead to the south, Messick to the east and Race Street on the west. The race-track before demolition was just north of Thomas.

Thomas Street was an established street prior to the addition of the Caulder Homes, dating back at least to the 1880's. It was the original home of the black Shiloh Baptist Church and was considered one of Lexington's worst slums. It is believed to be named for Barak G. Thomas.[19] He was a confederate soldier, a slave owner, former sheriff of Lexington and owner of the Dixiana Farm off of Russell Cave Road. It is said that upon his death in 1906,   he left the majority of his estate to his servant Margaret Pryor. In doing so, this made her one of the wealthiest black women in Kentucky at the time, if not the wealthiest.[20] She remained living in his home that was located at 646 West Main Street, next door to the home of builder Henry A. Tandy.   He himself along with business partner Albert Byrd, were at one time the wealthiest black men in Kentucky. She passed just four years later in 1910. For him to leave her that kind of wealth, it's likely that she was not just his servant but his lover as well, a Thomas Jefferson and Sally Hemings type of situation.

It could also possibly be named after Thomas Bradley as well.   I found a deed record from 1881, show-ing Thomas Bradley and James A. Grinstead, selling a lot

19. History Linked to Sections Names. (1954, April 18). *Sunday Herald-Leader*, p. 48.

20. "Pryor, Margaret," Notable Kentucky African Americans Database, accessed April 27, 2023, https://nkaa.uky.edu/nkaa/items/show/1465.

on Thomas Street, then called "Susie C. Fields Addition," to Susie P. Cromwell. Grinstead is the next street over and I have no doubt in my mind that Grinstead Street was named after him. He was a member of the nearby Kentucky Association, so that within itself leaves little doubt. It stands to reason that these two men, owned land collectively in this section. Bradley Street already existed in Chicago Bottoms,   so he could've chosen his first name "Thomas" instead. This is purely speculation. The source that suggested it was Barak G. Thomas, they weren't 100 percent sure. It was widely assumed that it was named for him. Thomas Bradley and his wife owned farmland off of Georgetown Pike, near the Lexington Cemetery.   This is the same Mrs. Bradley that sold some of that land to the Greenwood Company that established the cemetery on Whitney Ave. John Caulder was a founding member.

Messick Street, which intersected with Thomas St. at the east end, was named after businessman and grocer C.T. Messick. Deed records show him selling property on Messick Street, to Isaac and Lucy Murphy on June 6, 1887.   For those born in the 1970's and 80's or those familiar with "Withrow Way" in general, Messick intersects with Third Street,   and runs parallel to Nelson Ave. The entrance to Withrow Way at Third, that we all know, was formerly Messick Street. It intersected with McCracken Drive at the north. Deed records show that Jockey Isaac Murphy had a home on Thomas Street in 1896. It's possible that it was at the intersection of Messick and Thomas. Or Murphy owned several lots in the area.

Whatever the case, Murphy wasn't the only derby winner to call Thomas Street home. James "Soup" Perkins, winner of the 1895 Kentucky Derby, also lived on Thomas Street.

Marrs Alley, or Street, was a small alley in between Thomas Street and Grinstead Street. This was annexed by the Housing Commission in 1952. It doesn't exist on the 1912 map but it shows up on a map from 1923. Sometime within that span, it surfaced. It was named after Lexington Realtor George H. Marrs. In 1912, he secured a permit to begin building cottages on Thomas Street.[21] It's probable that these cottages became Marrs Alley. In 1925, this street was dedicated by the city of Lexington as an official city street.[22]

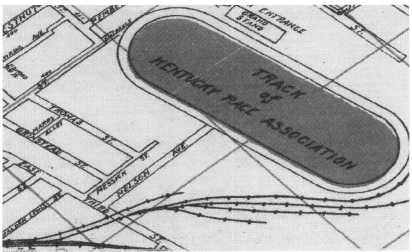

Illustration 10: 1923 Map showing Thomas Street before the Housing projects were built. Thomas street is on the bottom left of the image, just below the racetrack. Messick is to it's right, parallel to Nelson which is running directly from the track, and Marrs "Alley" can be seen in between Thomas and Grinstead.

21. To Build Five Cottages. (1912, October 9). *The Lexington Leader*, p. 10.

22. Board of Commissioners (Official Proceedings), Ordinance No. 2960. (1925, May 30). *The Lexington Leader*, p. 6.

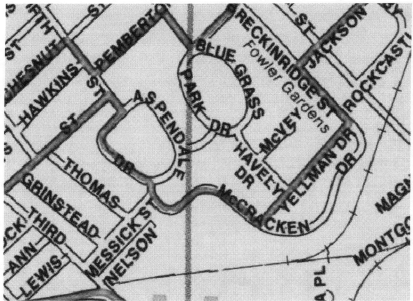

Illustration 11: 1977 map of the same area. You can see that the racetrack is gone and it shows all of the streets that make up the entire housing project. Please note that the angles of this map and the 1923 map are different.

Illustration 12: Thomas Street before the projects.

Illustration 13: The Shiloh Baptist Church on Thomas Street was the only building that was left after the demolition of Thomas Street. The middle photo is Thomas before the John Caulder homes. The top and bottom were after. You can see Shiloh in each image. (Lexington Herald-Leader Apr 18, 1954)

Illustration 14: Aerial view of the entire Bluegrass Aspendale Housing Project. (Lexington Herald Leader Jan 15, 1954)

John Caulder

Since the last Project we discussed was named in honer of this man, it is only right that we dedicate a section to share just who he was. I felt that he deserved his own section a part from the neighborhood. It was already written elsewhere in this book that John B. Caulder was an educator. He began his teaching career at the Jonestown School. After his three to four year stint there, he went on to become the Principal at Constitution Elementary. A position he held for about forty years. Teaching duties aside, he also served as secretary for the Lexington Colored Fair, the secretary for the Lexington Colored Orphanage, founding member and president of the Greenwood Cemetery and Realty Company and the secretary of the Domestic Realty Company. He, I'm sure wore many other hats that may not have been recorded anywhere in history, but if there was any event or meeting that involved the upliftment, education, and improvement of the negro race in Lexington, you would find his name associated with it. He alongside his wife Hattie, lived at 505 East Third Street until his death in 1951 at the age of 73.

Shiloh Baptist Church

Shiloh Baptist Church's roots are with the Main Street Baptist Church and Liberty Baptist Church. About thirty former members of Main Street and six members of Liberty began a worship service together inside a barn on Thomas Street. The year was 1896. Months later they moved their service to a shotgun home on the same street. Then about one year later, the newly formed congregation was able to buy a lot of land and build a new wooden structure.[23] Shiloh Baptist was born.

A Shoemaker by the name of Titus Buckner was their first pastor. He served from 1896 until 1914. Reverend Marshall Moore took over from there.

James Pearsall, the young negro man who met his demise via a "legal" lynching in 1906, his funeral service was held at Shiloh Baptist. After two pastors who were supposed to do the service were a no show, Rev. Buckner stepped up and did it. He used the fate of Pearsall as a warning to the young black men and women of the race. He is quoted in part as saying:

---

23. *Our Church History*. Shiloh Baptist Church. (2019, November 12). Retrieved April 28, 2023, from http://shilohlexington.com/index.php/our-church-history/

"It is an awful death to die on the gallows, but few men meet with this fate unless
they deserve it. Many young men of our race are
not leading the lives that they should and are
continually getting into trouble of some kind,
and through their misconduct they are establishing for themselves a bad reputation, and
through their evil associations are developing
bad characters."[24]

It seems by his words that he believed Pearsall
was guilty as charged. Either that, or he seized the opportunity to speak to young people of our race and give
them something to think about. It could also be a combination of both. The reality is and many newspaper accounts verify this, that in those days, in our communities,
there was indeed a high level of lawlessness that took
place. The same things that plague our communities now,
they existed in the late 1800's and early 20th century. So
Buckner's words weren't without merit. Granted, it is always the loud minority. The majority of our people are
upstanding citizens. I have no knowledge of Pearsall's innocence or guilt. Based on history, I know it doesn't take
"guilt" to convict one of us, especially if a white woman
was brutalized in any way, or even says she was. As i
type this, Carolyn Bryant, Emmitt Till's accuser comes to
mind. She passed away yesterday.(April 27, 2023) Extremely unapologetic when I say "Good Riddance!!"

According to a 1909 lawsuit filed against the
trustees of Shiloh, two lots on Thomas Street were purchased by the church from E.L. Hutchinson and Bishop

---

24. Evil Doers Warned By Pearsalls Fate, Negro Minister Advises The
Young Men Of His Race To Profit By Example. (1906, July 9). *The
Lexington Herald*, p. 8.

Clay on October 21, 1901. The two men claimed that a balance of $264 was remaining to be paid.[25] The judgment from the courts was that the church was to be sold at public auction on June 14th of that year to pay off the debt.[26] In order to acquire the funds and remain in possession of the church, a rally was held by the congregation to obtain the necessary funds.

A new church building was dedicated in 1923. This is the same building that you see in some of the photos a few pages back. With the emergence of the Caulder homes, the congregation saw themselves in the same location but a completely "different neighborhood." Their church building was the only lot on Thomas Street untouched by the bulldozers. The influx of people now living in the neighborhood created a growing membership. That's definitely a good thing for them. The church cannot thrive without membership. And with that, a bigger space was needed. Services continued as normal for another ten years. In 1963, they bought their present church building from the old Felix Memorial Baptist Church for $55,000.[27] This building at 237 East Fifth Street was built in 1923. Personally, I still get an uneasy feeling every time I see this place. It's where I attended my favorite cousins funeral back in August of 2003. May Danielle Lamar Hill rest in peace.

---

25. Suit Filed Against The Shiloh Church. (1909, May 1). *The Lexington Herald*, p. 4.

26. Shiloh Church, Members May Pay $264 Debt, Court Orders It Sold On June 14 At Public Auction, But Congregation Hopes To Save It. (1909, May 4). *The Lexington Leader*, p. 5.

27. Shiloh Baptists Buy Felix Memorial Church Building. (1963, January 13). *Sunday Herald-Leader*, p. 19.

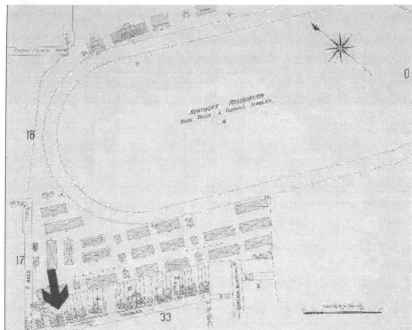

Illustration 15: 1907 Sanborn Fire Insurance Map of the Kentucky Association Racetrack. Just below on the left, is Thomas Street. The arrow is pointing to the location of the barn that their services began out of in 1896.

Photo credits belong to https://www.gardenstogables.com/

Renovations and Reductions

In the early 1990's Bluegrass-Aspendale began taking on a whole new look, the buildings, the streets, the street names, the whole area. There was approximately 7,500 people concentrated in this small area.[28] All but 95 households were black in 1988.[29] As I stated before, we

28. Mayhan, M. (1990, June 3). Chief's Responses Pleases Troubled Area, Respond In Force. *Lexington Herald-Leader,* p. A12.

29. Johns, B. (1989, September 3). Struggle. *Lexington Herald-Leader,* p. B3.

were packed in like sardines in a can.   This can become and did become problematic. I can recall grass barely growing in most of the neighborhood. There were so many buildings and people, that there was not much room for grass at all. We played in dirt. Although this is a personal recollection, it was echoed by the then director of the Lexington Housing Authority (Lexington Municipal Housing Commission), Austin Simms:

> "We deal with children, you've got two eight-unit buildings facing each other, and with a conservative estimate of two children per unit, that's 32 children who play in that space.   When you get 32 children in an area that small, grass doesn't grow."[30]

I can remember we used to go to the administration building on Bluegrass Park, pictured in illustration 6, and get grass seeds. Grass would grow a little bit after- wards but, there were still huge sections of the yard that were nothing but dirt.

This was one of the many factors as to why the Housing Authority and the city wanted to downsize the neighborhood. Crime, but mostly the sale of narcotics, which plagued the neighborhood was another.   This was something I saw everyday, but I didn't think much of it. It was just a way of life for many people in our communi- ty.   An every day thing. Many of my friends indulged in the lifestyle.   I personally stayed away from it but I was always around them and I saw quite a lot. Grinstead

---

30. Nance, K. (1990, February 25). Housing Project Gets A New Look, Bluegrass-Aspendale To Be Renovated. *Lexington Herald-Leader*, p. 1.

Street, even earned the nickname "Crack Alley," a clear reference to the availability of the deadly street drug Crack Cocaine, which was easily accessible in the neighborhood. The whole area of Thomas and Grinstead had that nickname but it originated with Grinstead.

This drug, my own father became addicted to in the 1990's. This was another reason I personally never got involved with the sale of narcotics. I can recall how angry and hurt I felt as a teen with a father addicted to crack. I used to wonder how many of my drug dealing friends sold to my father? I just didn't have the heart to destroy another family in the same way. So I resisted the ever present temptation to make a fast buck by destroying other black families. But these were my friends. I never judged them, just couldn't do it myself.

The Lexington Housing Authority believed that by downsizing the neighborhood, it would lower the crime statistics in the community. Less people, less crime was the viewpoint. Simms explained it this way:

> "We're going to rid public housing of drugs. You do that by reducing these massive numbers of people that are congregated here in such brief square footage, by establishing security patrols, and by creating an atmosphere of community living."[31]

And with that, demolition began. A total of 296 units were razed. Two of these buildings were the building that I lived in when my mother brought me home from the hospital, after my birth. This was 238 C Mc-

---

31. Nance, K. (1990, February 25). New Life For Lexington's Projects: City Tackles Bluegrass-Aspendale Woes. *Lexington Herald-Leader*, p. A12.

Cracken Drive, and 232 C McCracken. The backside of this building was facing the rear of 230 D McCracken, where we lived when they tear down began. My sister and I during this time, sat on our back porch and watched the wrecking ball knock down the building. The whole building wasn't knocked down at once. The second level was razed but the bottom half remained. There was a hole in each wall, that made it possible to run through the whole building, from one end to the other. We were playing in these asbestos filled buildings back then.

After they knocked down each building that they intended to, the community received more of a face lift. The map on illustration 11, shows how all of the streets were connected together. You could travel from Thomas Street, to McCracken, McCracken to Yellman and McVey, etc., all by vehicle. Housing Director Austin Simms also explained that he believed that cutting off the roads in each section, making them all one way in, one way out, could assist with neutralizing the drug trade. He believed that it would "cut down on vehicular loitering," people driving street to street in search of drugs.[32] So, the streets in the community were rerouted and some names changed. Messick Street, Havely, a part of McCracken and a part of McVey became Withrow Way. This street was named after a black former Lexington police captain, Richard Withrow. He played a significant role in the redevelopment of Bluegrass Aspendale. Yellman Drive, the other remaining parts of McCracken and McVey, merged with Breckenridge Street and took on that name. North and South Aspendale became Aspendale, while North and South Bluegrass became Bluegrass Park Drive. Last-

---

32. Ibid

ly, Thomas Street was changed to Arbor Grove Place. Each of the remaining addresses in the community were also renumbered. The apartment lettering such as 232 A, 232 B, etc., were removed. Each one had a different numeral, such as our address that went from 230 D McCracken to 406 Withrow Way.

Not only were the remaining units renumbered, each of them were also renovated. I can remember taking a shower for the very first time. In my early life, we just had a bathtub, there was no showers in any of the apartments. These were installed during this time. Siding was also placed on the top half of each unit, giving them a different look. The old building was brick, top to bottom. And finally, the white aluminum awnings that covered the porches were replaced with more sturdy, triangular shaped, wooden awnings.

Illustration 16: Myself at 230 D McCracken Drive(later 406 Withrow) sometime around 1989, 1990. This is showing what the buildings looked like before renovation. My sister and neighbor in the background.

Illustration 17: Outside of 238 C McCracken Drive. My Grandmother Beverly Thompson, my mother Girtha Thompson(on the right) and My Aunt Camille. late 1960s.

Illustration 18: Outside of the same apartment in 1983. This is me at 6 months old.

Illustration 19: How the projects looked after the renovations. unknown date. Withrow way

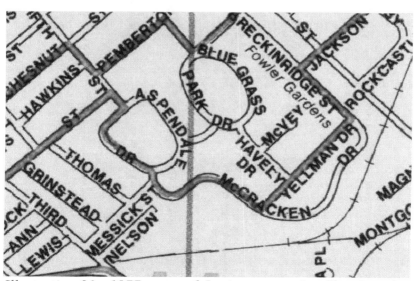

Illustration 21: 1977 map of Lexington again. Showing the streets in the community before the renovations.

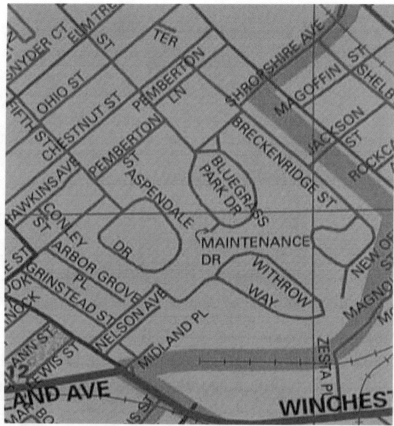

Illustration 18: 1998 Map of Lexington, showing the street changes in the community after the renovations.

Riot of 1994

The 2014 shooting of Mike Brown in Ferguson, Missouri by police officer Darren Wilson, the 2015 shooting of Samuel Dubose in Cincinnati, Ohio, the 2016 shooting of Philando Castile in Minneapolis, and the countless other shootings of unarmed black men by "American race soldiers," aka policemen, across this country, only strengthens the tension that has always existed between the police and the black community. Oftentimes the presence of these officers, who more times than not, do not live in the communities they serve, feels like a military occupation. It is not uncommon for white officers to stereotype and harass ordinary black citizens of these neighborhoods, simply out of racial hatred, self entertainment, and lack of empathy. We have witnessed these executions on camera and nearly every time, the murdering officer goes free, unpunished. Even when an indictment is handed down, they get off either completely or with a light sentence. The Bluegrass Aspendale Housing Project and Lexington, Kentucky, are no strangers to similar events. A young, unarmed black man was killed by the police, just across the street from where I lived at the time, and this is the story.

On Tuesday morning, October 25, 1994, the Lexington Police Department entered a home located at 726 Breckenridge Street, with an arrest warrant for eighteen year old Tony Sullivan. According to the police, Sullivan was a suspect in a shooting that occurred about a week earlier. When the police entered the dwelling, which was his girlfriends residence, Sullivan was hiding in a closet. He came out unarmed, hands in the air. A single shot from Officer Phil Vogel's 9 millimeter Beretta was discharged, hitting him in his forehead. Vogel claims that after Sullivan came out and his hands were raised, the officer attempted to de-cock his Beretta and it accidentally fired. In his own words he describes the mornings events:

> "Mr. Sullivan then raised his hands to shoulder level, and at this time, assuming there was no immediate threat of Mr. Sullivan producing a weapon, I proceeded to make my weapon

safe by lowering the hammer to an uncocked
position.

In the process of making my weapon
safe,   I moved it in an upward position to allow
the hammer to disengage.   While raising my
weapon towards the ceiling, it discharged, striking Mr. Sullivan in the upper left forehead."

Aid was rendered.   He was rushed to the hospital
and pronounced dead at 11:45am.[33]   The shooting was
witnessed by his girlfriend's three year old son, and the
babysitter, who were in the home at this time.

As the news of Sullivan's death spread, around
1 pm, angry youth began gathering in the neighborhood.
Police cruisers were damaged,   shots were reported to be
fired on Withrow Way, near the police roll call station
that had been built in Bluegrass Aspendale during the
renovations of 1990-91.   Rocks and bottles flew in the direction of officers, striking one officer in the head. On
Breckenridge Street, near the scene of the shooting, one
Lexington Herald-Leader photographer was assaulted by
three individuals who punched and kicked her.

About this time,   every street in the neighborhood
had been closed off and officers in riot gear took post in
various sections of the community.   More gunshots were
heard around 2:30pm but no one was hit.

About thirty individuals left the group just a short
while later and proceeded downtown to the government
building, while the rest stayed behind. At the government building,   police chief Larry Walsh explained to the
group what occurred and this infuriated them even fur-

---

33. Gregory, E. (1995, February 3). Witnesses, police files detail events of
october 25. *Lexington Herald-Leader*, pp. 1–8.

ther. They stormed out.   More of the eventful afternoon was reported as follows:

> "Meanwhile, the larger crowd had swelled to 100 and was making it's way down east Third Street. Some chanted 'we want justice.' As a police cruiser moved out of the way, someone smashed it's rear window.
>
> They marched down Rose Street, past the entrance to the jail and into the parking lot behind the district court building on Martin Luther King Boulevard.
>
> About 3:25pm, they met police at the intersection with Barr Street. The youths screamed obscenities and racial slurs at police and pelted them with rocks.
>
> A bystander, Sam Bates, 18, was hit in the head with a rock outside district court....
>
> One man, whose friends were trying to hold him back, lunged at an officer and punched him....police doused the crowd with pepper spray, sending people running down Barr toward North Limestone Street."[34]

Several photographers were hit with bricks, bottles, punches, and kicks. They received minor injuries. One suffered a fractured wrist. About 15 people in total received injuries.

34. Gregory, E. (1994, October 26). Rampage: angry youths marched towards downtown. *Lexington Herald-Leader*, p. 14.

At least 15 injured in unrest

■ Officer William Richmond, hit in the face with a brick at Arbor Grove Place and Race Street about 1 p.m. Tuesday.

■ Officer Gary M. Sennett, hit in the right foot with a cinder block thrown from a crowd at 140 Martin Luther King Boulevard about 5:25 p.m. Tuesday.

■ Betty Conyers, 43, hit in the face with a stick by a group of males at Breckinridge Street and Shropshire Avenue about 2:30 p.m. Tuesday.

■ Wilma Gentry, 40, attacked and punched at 367 East Third Street at noon Tuesday.

■ Hoi Truong, 48, beaten by a crowd and shot in the left arm with a pellet gun after group entered his store at 500 East Seventh Street about 2:30 p.m. Tuesday.

■ Riley Rose, Sam Bates and Jeff Gahafer, all 18, were attacked in their vehicle by a group of males at 140 Martin Luther King about 4 p.m. Tuesday.

■ Rosemary Griffeth, 44, hit in the head by rocks and bottles thrown at her vehicle at Fourth and Race streets about 12:45 p.m. Tuesday.

■ Stewart Bowman, a photographer for The Courier-Journal, was struck on the base of the neck by a bottle about 4:15 p.m. as he followed the crowd.

■ Sam Bates, 18, bystander, hit in the head with a rock outside district court.

■ Greg Eans and James Crisp, student photographers for University of Kentucky newspaper, the Kentucky Kernel. Eans was hit on the wrist with a brick and Crisp was punched in the jaw.

■ Janet Worne, Herald-Leader photographer, punched several times in the head.

■ Eric Gregory, Herald-Leader reporter, hit in the head with rock, sprayed with pepper mace.

SOURCE: LEXINGTON POLICE RECORDS

Illustration 19: A list of the reported injuries during the afternoon of unrest. (Lexington Herald-Leader October 27, 1994)

The children of the neighborhood were at school during these events, oblivious to what was occurring in the community. As the streets were blocked off, the children were bussed to nearby Lexington Traditional Magnet School, and the parents were to pick the children up from there. I, the author of this book, was one of those children.

I was a sixth grader at Morton Middle School at this time. When the bus dropped us off at "LTMS," we weren't told why, just that we had to wait there for our parents. Myself and a friend, Wayne Rowe, decided to walk to the neighborhood. We had no idea what was going on. As we walked down Fourth Street, towards Race, a man approached us and told us to be careful. We looked at each other and proceeded on. This is when we came across a car that had been flipped on it's side. As we walked further, we saw several police vehicles with the windows busted out of them and police in riot gear standing in various places. There was a group of about 20 men, standing near the police station, which was located on Withrow Way. At this time, I did not witness any violence, just the aftermath.

I lived at 715 Breckenridge Street, directly across from where Sullivan was killed. Later that evening, I went to retrieve my backpack that I had left at Alie Waite's home. Her home was just down the street at 408 Withrow Way. She was a friend of my mother and I would often stay there until my mother came home from work. So, that evening on my walk towards her house, across the street from the police station, there were police in riot gear standing outside. One I recall, had a high powered rifle of some sort and he had it pointed in my direction. He kept the gun pointed at me until I was out of his line of sight. Keep in mind, I am eleven years old and less than 100 pounds, a very small kid. This is something I'll never forget. I felt like anybody black, whether a small child or an adult, was a potential threat to some of these individuals.

About fourteen police cruisers and two Urban County Government vehicles were damaged. The total cost of this damage was about $25,000. The police roll call station on Withrow Way also received damages estimated to cost between $1,000 and $5,000[35]

Nothing else occurred on this Tuesday evening following the events of that morning and afternoon. The very next day, bullets were fired at a news crew from Louisville who were on Breckenridge Street. One bullet shattered the back window of their vehicle and pierced the driver seat while another went thru the driver door. They were inside the vehicle but no one was injured.[36]

The majority of the African American population in the city of Lexington, including myself, did not believe the official story that this was accidental. Officer Phil Vogel had twenty-two years on the force and that's just not the kind of mistake someone with that amount of training makes. The police are trained to point their weapon at the torso of a suspect when the need to draw arms arises, yet this young man suffered a bullet to his head. Once he noticed there was no threat, as he stated, had his weapon been aimed at the torso and not the head, he could've easily lowered, uncocked and holstered the gun. There is a small chance that this shooting was accidental. With that being said, Officer Vogel in my opinion was extremely negligent and should've received punishment in some capacity. Instead, he was not indicted. Like all the

35. Gregory, E. (1994, October 29). Damage figures released. *Lexington Herald-Leader*, p. 12.

36. Rios, B., & Campbell, R. H. (1994, October 27). Shooting: FBI joins search for answers. *Lexington Herald-Leader*, p. A15.

others, he received a paid suspension while the police and FBI investigated the shooting. Afterwards, he immediately retired. No indictment came down, but Sullivan's mother did receive a settlement from the city after a wrongful death lawsuit was filed. The terms and amount, I care not to discuss in this book as I feel that's a private matter. No amount can bring Tony back or erase his mother's pain.

I visited his grave site just before writing this, seeking inspiration. I did not know him personally, but I knew his sister. And a relative of mine is also a relative of his. May he rest in peace.

Illustration 20: Photo by me 5/9/2023

Demolition

The early 2000's saw the number of units in the housing projects begin to dwindle even more. In 2000, the older sections of the community were completely razed. These were Bluegrass Park and Aspendale. The number of units were then 389. 2006, the remaining units were razed to make way for a new neighborhood. This neighborhood was a combination of single family homes, townhomes, apartments, as well as an elementary school. This new subdivision became known as "Equestrian View." Streets took on new names, many of them now have horse racing themed names such as: Murphy's Run (Isaac Murphy,) Thoroughbred Way, Mustang Crossing, Grandstand, and Triple Crown Circle.

The projects are no more but I as well as nearly everyone who grew up in the community have very fond memories of the neighborhood. Bluegrass Aspendale lives on through us, in our pictures and in our memories. 1938-2006

Illustration 21: Demolition 2006

Progress To Some, Devastation To Others

Sources:

Chapter 1

1.) Slickaway: Warrentown. (1950, January 15). *Sunday Herald-Leader*, p. 139

2.) Colored Teachers, Close Successful Institute. (1901, September 22). *Lexington Leader*, p. 10.

3.) Colored Notes. (1925, January 18). *The Lexington Herald*, p. 17.

4.) School Property on Paris Pike Sold. (1942, October 23). *The Lexington Herald*, p. 21.

5.) Opposition: Likely to Confront Establishing of Proposed Colored Cemetery near Warrentown. (1906, November 20). *Lexington Leader*, p. 1.

6.) *Our History*. Maddoxtown Baptist Church. (n.d.). Retrieved January 27, 2023, from https://www.fbcm-lex.org/our-history

7.) Coffin, T. P., & Cohen, H. (1974). A Dozen Legendary Figures: The Reverend Peter Vinegar. In *Folklore: From the Working Folk of America* (p. 378). Anchor Books.

8.) Peter Vinegar: Enters The Realm Where De Streets Are Gold and De Lan' Is Filld Wid Milk and Honey. (1905, July 20). *Lexington Leader*, p. 3.

9.) *Our History*. Main Street Baptist Church. (n.d.). Retrieved January 27, 2023, from https://www.mainstreetbaptistchurchlexky.org/about-us/ourhistory

10.) Coffin, T. P., & Cohen, H. (1974). A Dozen Legendary Figures: The Reverend Peter Vinegar. In *Folklore: From the Working Folk of America* (p.378). Anchor Books.

11.) *Our History*. Main Street Baptist Church. (n.d.). Retrieved January 27,2023, from https://www.mainstreetbaptistchurchlexky.org/about-us/ourhistory

12.) First Sunday in July: Peter Vinegar Will Deliver Three Discourses in Gibson Woods. (1895, June 22). *The Leader*, p. 6.

13.) Congregational Notes. (1886, June 27). *The Courier Journal*, p. 11.

14.) Coffin, T. P., & Cohen, H. (1974). A Dozen Legendary Figures: The Reverend Peter Vinegar. In *Folklore: From the Working Folk of America* (p. 379). Anchor Books.

15.) Disturbing Church. (1888, May 7). *The Kentucky Leader*, p. 4.

16.) City and Vicinity: Minor Happenings of the Bluegrass Metropolis. (1896, August 7). *The Daily Leader*, p. 5.

17.) Cowardly Business: A Kentucky Town Attacked in the Night, One of its Inhabitants Mortally Wounded. (1884, September 1). *The Cincinnati Enquirer*, p. 1.

18.) Jimtown, To Have Colored Methodist Church in Which Lot Has Been Purchased. (1908, June 28). *Lexington Leader*, p. 15.

19.) Unusual Customs Part of Settlements Rich Past. (1985, August 11.) *Lexington Herald-Leader*, p. 1.

20.) Cooper, B. (1968, October 24). Tiny Community Founded A Century Ago Gets Water. *The Park City Daily News*, p. 9.

21.)Andrew Patrick, "New Zion," *ExploreKYHistory*, accessed January 28, 2023, https://explorekyhistory.ky.gov/items/show/816.

22.) Peryam, J. (2020, March 13). *New Zion Village celebrates 150 years with music, food, worship*. Georgetown News Graphic. Retrieved January 28, 2023, from https://www.news-graphic.com/news/new-zion-villagecelebrates-150-years-with-music-food-worship/article_5927b0a8-aa37-11e8-a069-9b9e5a0a20fb.html

23.) New Health Camp for Fayette Colored Children Established. (1944, July 30). *The Lexington Herald*, p. 9.

24.) Community is States Oldest Black Settlement. (1997, February 28). *Lexington Herald-Leader*, p. 23.

25.) New Zion Church Is Completed After 30 Years; Organ Installed. (1954, July 1). *The Lexington Herald*, p. 1.

26.) Nice Fortune, Amounting To Over $47,000 Left By Charles M. Garner, Colored, Who Made His Own Way To Success, Despite Discouragement. (1914, May 24). *Lexington Leader*, p. 6.

27.) Public Sale of Farm Lands & City Residence: Monday, February 9, 1914. (1914, February 8). *The Lexington Herald*, p. 22.

28.) Colored Farmers and Business Men's League Holds a Congress at New Zion. (1904, November 23). *Lexington Leader*, p. 5.

29.) Industrial Conference of Best Element of Colored People of Fayette and Scott Counties: Annual Two Days Meeting At New Zion Church An Event More Than Usual Interest and Importance To The Negro Race. (1908, November 15). *Lexington Leader*, p. 2.

Chapter 2

1.) *Our History*. Main Street Baptist Church. (n.d.). Retrieved September 27, 2022, from https://www.mainstreetbaptistchurchlexky.org/about-us/our-history

2.) Davis, Merlene. "Main Street Baptist Church Celebrates 150 Years by Honoring Founding Pastor." *Kentucky*, Lexington Herald Leader, 22 Aug. 2012, https://www.kentucky.com/news/local/community/article44373360.html.

Chapter 3

1.) Smith, G. L., McDaniel, K. C., Hardin, J. A., & Powell, S. (2015). Little Georgetown, African American Community in Fayette County, Ky. In The Kentucky African American Encyclopedia (p. 331). University Press of Kentucky.

2.) Living Next to the Airport. (1971, July 22). Lexington Herald Leader

3.) Smith, G. L., McDaniel, K. C., Hardin, J. A., & Powell, S. (2015). Little Georgetown, African American Community in Fayette County, Ky. In The Kentucky African American Encyclopedia (p. 185). University Press of Kentucky.

4.) Fort Springs. (1901, September 15). The Morning Herald, p. 11.

5.) "Fort Spring (Fayette County, KY)," Notable Kentucky African Americans Database, accessed July 10, 2022, https://nkaa.uky.edu/nkaa/items/show/320.

6.) Edwards, D. (1987, August 28). Blooper Marks Tale of One Day President. Lexington Herald-Leader, p. 29.

7.) Martin, M. (1981, September 8). Buses are Rolling Down Frogtown Lane. Lexington Herald-Leader, p. 4.

8.) Frogtown Has Needed Bridge. (1935, March 24). The Lexington Leader, p. 20.

9.) Frogtown People Held Under Spell of Spirit Power. (1923, September 26). The Lexington Leader, p. 1.

10.) Colored Notes. (1923, October 2). The Lexington Herald, p. 13.

Chapter 4

1.) Defense of the People of Jonestown. (1906, January 16) Lexington Leader, p. 8.

2.) Our History. BETHSAIDA BAPTIST CHURCH. (n.d.). Retrieved April 18, 2023, from https://www.bethsaidalex.org/our-history.html

3.) Smithers, B. Y. (2001). Chapter 1. In The Partial History of Jonestown, Lexington, Kentucky 40517 (p. 3).

4.) Webster, R. D. (2005). The Bethsaida Baptist Church. In The Webster Family Album (p. 76). essay, R.D. Webster.

5.) Smithers, B. Y. (2001). Chapter 1. In The Partial History of Jonestown, Lexington, Kentucky 40517 (p. 6).

6.) Parrish, C. H. (1915). Rev. Isaiah Sailes. In Golden Jubilee of the General Association of Colored Baptists in Kentucky: The story of 50 years' work from 1865-1915 (p. 224). essay, Mayes Printing Co.

7.) Our History. BETHSAIDA BAPTIST CHURCH. (n.d.). Retrieved April 18, 2023, from https://www.bethsaidalex.org/our-history.html

8.) Smithers, B. Y. (2001). In The Partial History of Jonestown, Lexington, Kentucky 40517 (p. 74).

9.) Closing Exercises. (1900, March 25). The Sunday Leader, p. 4.

10.) Jonestown School, New Colored Institution is Dedicated With Interesting Ceremonies. (1917, February 20). The Lexington Leader, p. 5.

11.) Swann, L. P. (2002, February 13). Legislator, educator got start at noted black owned business. Lexington Herald-Leader, p. 59.

12.) "Mammoth Life and Accident Insurance Company," Notable Kentucky African Americans Database, accessed April 19, 2023, https://nkaa.uky.edu/nkaa/items/show/261.

13.) Colored Notes. (1924, July 12). The Lexington Herald, p. 7.

14.) Colored Notes: Colored Republican Civic League. (1915, July 13). Lexington Leader, p. 5.

15.) Stafford, L. (1994, June 15). The Soul of the Community. Lexington Herald-Leader, p. 40

16.) Jonestown and Urban Gainesway. (1971, July 21). The Lexington Leader, p. 4.

17.) "Coletown (Lexington, KY)," Notable Kentucky African Americans Database, accessed April 24, 2023, https://nkaa.uky.edu/nkaa/items/show/315.

18.) Coletown's Future Is Grim. (1971, July 17). The Lexington Leader, p. 5.

19.) $2,000 Company, The Pride of Coletown is The Latest Entry Into Mercantile Field Here. (1913, May 2). The Lexington Leader, p. 14.

20.) Ancient Sanctuaries . (1901, September 1). The Morning Herald, p. 11.

21.) Johnson, A. D. (1987, January 20). Crosses burned, 1 at church door. Lexington Herald Leader, p. 1.

22.) Colored Teachers To Hold Meetings. (1926, September 8). The Lexington Leader, p. 2.

23.) Coletown Pay School. (1910, March 4). The Lexington Leader, p. 4.

24.) Colored News Notes. (1920, October 31). The Lexington Herald, p. 11.

25.) Turley-Adams, A. (1997). Appendix I - Rosenwald Schools in Kentucky. In Rosenwald Schools in Kentucky, 1917-1932 (p. 44). essay, Kentucky Heritage Council.

Chapter 5

1.) Smith, G. L., McDaniel, K. C., Hardin, J. A., & Young-Brown, F. (2015). Cadentown, African American community in Fayette Co. In The Kentucky African American encyclopedia (p. 87). University Press of Kentucky.

2.) National Registry of Historic Places, Cadentown School, Lexington, Fayette, Kentucky

3.) Turley-Adams, A. (2007). Julius Rosenwald (1862-1932). In Rosenwald schools in Kentucky: Exhibit guide (p. 8). Georgetown College.

4.) National Registry of Historic Places, Cadentown School, Lexington, Fayette, Kentucky, p. 1

5.) Johnson, W. D. (1897). John Weldon Johnson. In Biographical Sketches of Prominent Negro Men and Women of Kentucky: With introductory memoir of... the author, and prefatory remarks showing the diff (p. 34). The Standard Print.

6.) Colored School Was Held At The Courthouse Last Night. (1896, June 18). The Morning Herald, p. 2.

7.) Negro Schools Scenes of Riot in the County. (1901, August 21). The Morning Herald, p. 1.

8.) Matthews, P. (2002, November 16). Historic Label Complicates Dispute. Lexington Herald-Leader, p. 27.

9.) Meehan, M. (2001, May 10). UK Archaeologist Consulted. Lexington Herald-Leader, p. 21.

10.) Rogers, F. (2001, August 11). Preserving Fayette's Black Cemeteries. Lexington Herald-Leader, p. 11.

11.) Meehan, M. (2001, May 10). UK Archaeologist Consulted. Lexington Herald-Leader, p. 21.

12.) Beatty, C .M. (1978, November 06). Interview by E. Owens. Black Church in Kentucky Oral History Project. Louie B. Nunn Center for Oral History, University of Kentucky Libraries, Lexington.

13.) Colored Notes. (1937, November 22). The Lexington Leader, p. 12.

14.) Wilkinson, D. (2001, May 20). A Tour of Fayette County's Black Communities. Lexington Herald-Leader, p. 64.

15.) The Power Society: Leads To a Split in a Colored Church at Cadentown, Fayette County. (1894, February 13). The Kentucky Leader, p. 4.

16.) Religious War breaks out in the Cadentown Baptist Church-Fiscal and Police Courts. (1896, June 2). The Lexington Herald, p. 2.

17.) Sister Roxey: Holds Salvation Army Services on Mechanic Street. (1898, August 13). The Daily Leader, p. 3.

18.) Power Band Ordered to Cease Their Midnight Vigils, As A Result of Protest of Citizens. (1910, October 19). Lexington Leader, p. 2.

19.) Unique Deed Filed. (1908, September 13). The Lexington Herald, p. 4.

20.) Colored General Notes. (1908, December 13). Lexington Leader, p. 10.

21.) Rev. George Baltimore, Baptist Pastor, Dies. (1948, November 13). The Indianapolis Star, p. 15.

22. Xiong, N. (1998, July 31). Buyers Pledge to Respect Site. Lexington Herald-Leader, p. 4.

Chapter 6

1.) Ockerman Jr., F. (2021). Recovery and Redefinition. In New history of Lexington, Kentucky (p. 78). HISTORY PRESS US.

2.) Unusual Customs Part of Settlements Rich Past. (1985, August 11). Lexington Herald

Leader, p. 1.

3.) Smith, G. L., McDaniel, K. C., Hardin, J. A., & McDaniel, K. R. (2015). Stevenson, Wille Belle . In The Kentucky African American encyclopedia (p. 480). University Press of Kentucky.

4.) Ibid., p. 480

5.) At Opera House Chandler Exercises are Held. (1909, June 4). Lexington Leader, p. 9.

6.) Dunnigan, A. A. (1982). Willie B. Stevenson. In The Fascinating Story of Black Kentuckians: Their Heritage and Traditions (p. 311). Associated Publishers.

7.) Morris, J. (2015, January 15). Roy W. T ibbs: Founder of Howard University Glee Club. Anacostia Community documentation initiative. Retrieved October 16, 2022, from https://cdi.anacostia.si.edu/2015/01/15/roy-w-tibbs-founder-of-howarduniversity-glee-club/

8.) Colored Notes. (1926, December 29). The Lexington Leader, p. 13.

9.) Colored Notes. (1925, May 13). Lexington Leader, p. 7.

10.) Colored Singers in Fine Concert. (1925, February 3). The Lexington Leader, p. 11.

11.) Colored Notes. (1925, July 6). The Lexington Herald, p. 11.

12.) Colored Notes. (1927, April 11). The Lexington Herald, p. 9.

13.) Wins Musical Honors. (1925, August 30). Lexington Leader, p. 15

14.) Colored Notes. (1931, March 5). The Lexington Leader, p. 16.

15.) Dunnigan, A. A. (1982). Willie B. Stevenson. In The Fascinating Story of Black Kentuckians: Their Heritage and Traditions (p. 311). Associated Publishers.

16.) Colored Notes (1934, August 31). Lexington Herald, p. 16.

17.) Lexington Investment Co. (1899, April 5). The Daily Leader, p. 5.

18.) Colored Notes (1934, August 31). Lexington Herald, p. 16.

19.) Smith, G. L., McDaniel, K. C., Hardin, J. A., & Hudson, J. B. (2015). Simmons College of Kentucky. In The Kentucky African American Encyclopedia (p. 452). University Press of Kentucky.

20.) McIntyre, L. H. (1986). The Sixth Pastor. In One Grain of the Salt: The First African Baptist Church West of the Allegheny Mountains (pp. 43– 44).

21.) Old Hospital Building. (1910, July 14). Lexington Herald Leader, p. 1.

22.) Fire Insurance Co. to Open Offices Here. (1924, September 28). The Lexington Leader, p. 2.

23.) Colored Notes. (1924, September 29). The Lexington Leader, p. 9.

24.) Cochran, L. J. (1925, November 26). Colored Notes. The Lexington Herald, p. 11.

Chapter 7

1.) Ockerman Jr., F. (2021). Recovery and Redefinition. In New history of Lexington, Kentucky (p. 78) HISTORY PRESS US.

2.) Two Communities on Royster Road. (1971, July 30). The Lexington Leader, p. 4.

3.) Fayette's Last One-Room School, Which Opened Thursday, May Be in Its Final Year. (1955, September 2). The Lexington Leader, p. 8.

4.) Commencement. (1894, June 2). The Kentucky Leader, p. 7.

5.) Brown, D. (2007, November 21). Jimmy Winkfield (1882 - 1974) BlackPast.org. https://www.blackpast.org/african-americanhistory/winkfield-jimmy-1882-1974/

6.) Lexington Obituaries and Memorials. (2004, July 9). Lexington Herald Leader, p. 16.

7.) "Pricetown, Nihizertown, and Centerville (Fayette County, KY)," Notable Kentucky African Americans Database, accessed October 16, 2022, https://nkaa.uky.edu/nkaa/items/show/334.

8.) Ockerman Jr., F. (2021). Recovery and Redefinition. In New history of Lexington, Kentucky (p. 78). HISTORY PRESS US.

9.) Mount Calvary's history: Mt. Calvary MBC: Lexington, KY. Mt. Calvary MBC. (n.d.). Retrieved October 16, 2022, from https://www.mtcalvarymbcky.org/mount-calvary-church-history

10.) Fayette's Last One-Room School, Which Opened Thursday, May Be in Its Final Year. (1955, September 2). The Lexington Leader, p. 8.

11.) Ibid., p 8

Chapter 8

1.) Wants Inspection of Houses Kept Up. (1915, January 27). The Lexington Leader, p. 6.

2.) Ibid., p. 6

3.) Phoebe Dobbs. (1898, November 4). The Morning Herald, p. 5.

4.) Two Water Streets. (1952, January 13). Lexington Herald-Leader, p. 51.

5.) Ranck, G. W. (1872). Chapter 6 – Settlement of Lexington. In History of Lexington, Kentucky: Its early annals and recent progress (p. 24).

6.) Ranck, G. W. (1872). Chapter 4 - Discovery and Naming of Lexington. In History of Lexington, Kentucky: Its early annals and recent progress (p. 19).

7.) Can't We have A Union Depot? (1889, February 12). The Kentucky Leader, p. 4.

8.) One Killed and Two Injured in a Shooting. (1914, July 23). The Lexington Herald, p. 4.

9.) Police Raid Cleans Branch Alley Houses. (1914, July 23). Lexington Leader, p. 1.

10.) Ibid.

11. Commissioners Hear Branch Alley Protest Aired. (1914, July 27). Lexington Leader, p. 1.

12.) C. & O. To Clean Up Around Station. (1918, February 20). Lexington Leader, p. 7.

13.) The City's Shame: The Town Branch a Mass of Corruption and Filth. (1888, October 13). The Kentucky Leader, p. 2.

14.) Soper, K. (2015, August 24). Town Branch is the famous creek that runs underneath downtown Lexington Ky. ExploreLexingtonKY.com. Retrieved October 22, 2022, from https://www.explorelexingtonky.com/blog/town-branch-is-the-famouscreek-that-runs-underneath-downtown-lexington-ky/

15.) Smith, G. L., McDaniel, K. C., Hardin, J. A., & McDaniel, K. R (2015). Lytle, Henry Hopkins. In The Kentucky African American encyclopedia (p. 342). University Press of Kentucky.

16.) Seals, W. T. (1955). History of Asbury. In Asbury Methodist Church Anniversary Album 1830-1955 (p. 12). Asbury Methodist Church.

17.) Historic Churches End 88 Year Separation. (1963, June 9). Lexington Herald-Leader, p. 18.

18.) Ibid., p. 18

19.) Reid, D. I. (1935, May 25). Colored Notes. The Lexington Herald, p. 14.

20.) Smith, G. L., McDaniel, K. C., Hardin, J. A., & Farrington, F.D. (2015). Benjamin, Robert Charles O'Hara. In The Kentucky African American encyclopedia (p. 40). University Press of Kentucky.

21.) Thompson, R. (2020). Chapter 2 - R.C.O. Benjamin. In Sankofa Lexington (p. 14). Afrakan World Books n Moor.

22.) Simmons, W. J. (1887). R. C. O. Benjamin, Esq. . In Men of Mark; Eminent, Progressive and Rising (p. 992).

23.) Thompson, R. (2020). Chapter 2 - R. C. O. Benjamin. In Sankofa Lexington (p. 15). Afrakan World Books n Moor.

24.) Simmons, W. J. (1887). R. C. O. Benjamin, Esq. . In Men of Mark; Eminent, Progressive and Rising (p. 993).

25.) An Evansville Colored Orator. (1882, July 15). Evansville Courier and Press, p. 2.

26.) Colored Lawyer in Staunton. (1883, July 24). Staunton Spectator , p. 3.

27.) The Coastline Railroad. (1883, January 11). The Wilmington Morning Star, p. 1.

28.) Lewis, G. A. (1885, December 19). Local and Societal News. The Frankfort Roundabout, p. 1

29.) Personal and Literary. (1888, February 17). The Wichita Daily Beacon, p. 3.

30.) Smith, J. C. (1993). Chapter 5 - The Southern States. In Emancipation: The Making of the Black lawyer, 1844-1944 (p. 272). University of Pennsylvania Press.

31.) News Nuggets. (1887, April 2). Western Appeal , p. 1.

32.) Negros For California: A Project For Wholesale Colonization of Southern Colored People. (1891, August 19). The Wilmington Messenger, p. 4.

33.) Minor Mentions. (1891, August 27). The Wilmington Morning Star, p. 2.

34.) Colored Men For California. (1891, August 13). The Philadelphia Inquirer, p. 4.

35.) Thompson, R. (2020). Chapter 2 - R. C. O. Benjamin. In Sankofa Lexington (p. 15). Afrakan World Books n Moor.

36.) On Behalf of Editor C.C. Moore. (1899, February 18). The Morning Herald, p. 3.

37.) Thompson, R. (2020). Chapter 2 - R. C. O. Benjamin. In Sankofa Lexington (p. 15). Afrakan World Books n Moor.

38.) Benjamin, R. C. O. (1887, October 8). Texas News: Negroes Shot Down in Cold Blood. A Correct Report of the Inhumane Butchery By One Who Visited The Scene. The Washington Bee, p. 1.

39.) An Incendiary Paper: Much Comment in Lexington Over An Article Written By A Negro Editor. (1898, June 1). The Courier-Journal, p. 1.

40.) Thompson, R. (2020). Chapter 2 - R. C. O. Benjamin. In Sankofa Lexington (p. 15). Afrakan World Books n Moor.

41.) The American Liberty Defence League. (1894, October 20). The Washington Bee, p. 2.

42.) Benjamin Killed. (1900, October 3). The Morning Herald, p. 7.

43.) Ibid

44.) Ibid

45.) In Trouble Again: Mike Moynahan Arrested in Charge of Assault and Battery. (1900, November 1). The Daily Leader, p. 1.

46.) Standard Changes Hands. (1901, July 10). The Morning Herald, p. 6.

47.) Smith, G. L., McDaniel, K. C., Hardin, J. A., & Powell, S.L. (2015). Johnson, Laura "Dolly". In The Kentucky African American Encyclopedia (p. 281). University Press of Kentucky.

48.) Ibid,. p. 281

49.) Gratz Park; Rosa Gave The Park Color and Dash. (1955, September 11). The Courier Journal, p. 124.

50.) Amusements. (1910, February 10). Lexington Leader, p. 3.

51.) Negroes Growing With Lexington: Owned Valuable Property. (1920, December 26). The Lexington Herald, p. 34.

52.) Daniel Seales: An Old Time Kentucky Negro, Here on a Pilgrimage. (1898, May 24). The Daily Leader, p. 7.

53.) Dennis Seales. (1863, March 10). Chicago Tribune, p. 2.

54.) The Colored Schools Again. (1887, September 25). The Memphis Daily Avalanche, p. 2.

55. Black King of Finance, Arrival of Daniel Seales, Who Owns Property in Many Cities. (1895, December 6). The San Francisco Call, p. 5.

56.) Wealthy Colored People. (1884, September 4). Daily Nevada State Journal, p. 1.

57.) "Seales, Daniel, Sr.," Notable Kentucky African Americans Database, accessed January 1, 2023, https://nkaa.uky.edu/nkaa/items/show/2516.

Chapter 9

1.) Girl With a Remarkable Memory. (1874, April 21). North British Daily Mail, p. 2.

2.) A Pralltown Negro: Protests that the "What is it" Did Not Terrify His Race. (1894, July 12). The Kentucky Leader, p. 8.

3.) Curious Agreement for Slave Purchase: Executors of Henry Clay Sell Negro to W.W. Bruce of Lexington. (1906, June 3). The Lexington Herald, p. 7.

4.) Thomas, H. A. (1973). Victims of Circumstance: Negroes in a Southern Town, 1865-1880. The Register of the Kentucky Historical Society, 71(3), 258

5.) Unsanitary Conditions. (1914, May 6). Lexington Leader, p. 1.

6.) Heavy Rains Cause Flood. (1908, April 1). Lexington Leader, p. 1.

7.) Church, E. (n.d.). Evergreen Missionary Baptist Church History. Evergreen Missionary Baptist Church. https://www.embchurch.com/content.cfm?id=306.

8.) Smith, G. L., McDaniel, K. C., Hardin, J. A., & Powell, S. (2015). Brucetown, African American community in Lexington, KY. In The Kentucky African American Encyclopedia (p. 72). University Press of Kentucky.

9.) Hellish: High Handed Outrage Committed in Fayette County, About Eleven Miles From Lexington. Two Negroes Hanged to Trees and Another Shot to Death, One a Mere Youth. (1878, January 18). The Courier-Journal, p. 1.

10.) Ibid,. p. 1

11.) The Kentucky Lynchings. (1878, January 19). St, Louis Daily Globe Democrat, p. 5.

12.) The Exemplary Life of Bess Coleman, O.D. Hindsight: Journal of Optometry History, 51(2), 37–50. https://doi.org/10.14434/hindsight.v51i2.30279

13.) "Reid, Daniel Isaiah," Notable Kentucky African Americans Database, accessed September 25, 2022, https://nkaa.uky.edu/nkaa/items/show/2525.

14.) Giles, Y. (2009). Introduction. In Stilled Voices Yet Speak: A History of African American Cemeteries in Lexington and Fayette County, Kentucky: Volume 1, Benevolent Society No. 2 cemetery, Ladies Auxiliary Society Cemetery (p. ix).

15.) Ibid., p. 2

16.) Ibid., p. 95

17.) A Prosperous Society: The Colored People Manage Their Finances to Good Advantage. (1892, February 3). The Kentucky Leader, p. 2.

18.) "Presbyterian Cemetery (Lexington, KY)," Notable Kentucky African Americans Database, accessed January 23, 2023, https://nkaa.uky.edu/nkaa/items/show/2511.

19.) "Murphy, Isaac [Burns]," Notable Kentucky African Americans Database, accessed January 23, 2023, https://nkaa.uky.edu/nkaa/items/show/667.

20.) Isaac Burns Murphy. Kentucky Horse Park. (n.d.). Retrieved January 22, 2023, from https://kyhorsepark.com/equine-theme-park/park-memorials-statues/isaac-burns-murphy/

21.) City May Take Over Old 7th Street Cemetery. (1973, April 18). The Lexington Leader, p. 46.

22.) Martin, M. (1981, May 20). A Cemetery Restored, For Their Labor, Citizens Group Wins Deed To Historic Site. The Lexington Leader, p. 3.

23.) Giles, Y. (2009). Ladies Auxiliary Cemetery. In Stilled Voices Yet Speak: A History of African American Cemeteries in Lexington and Fayette County, Kentucky: Volume 1, Benevolent Society No. 2 cemetery, Ladies Auxiliary Society Cemetery (p. 116)

24.) Thompson, R. (2022). Chapter 16 - Harry, Shadrick, and Prestley. In Drapetomania: Kentucky's Runaways and Rebels, The Good Troublemakers (pp. 193–194). Sankofa Lexington.

25.) Old Slave's Story, He and Others made A Strike For Freedom. The Miami Helmet (Miami, OH), July 29, 1897, p. 4.

26.) "Last Survivor: Old Lexington Darkey Tells An Entertaining Life History." The Messenger (Owensboro, KY), 14 Aug. 1897, p. 2.

Chapter 10

1.) Bolin, J. D. (2000). It Is a New Lexington! In Bossism and reform in a Southern City: Lexington, Kentucky , 1880-1940 (p. 6). University Press of Kentucky

2.) Johnson, K. W. (1968, March 11). Official Proceedings. Lexington Herald Leader, p. 8.

3.) "Taylortown (Lexington, KY), " Notable Kentucky African Americans Database, accessed September 28, 2022, https://nkaa.uky.edu/nkaa/items/show/336.

4.) Association, Northside Neighborhood (n.d.). History. History of Northside Neighborhood Lexington KY. Retrieved September 28, 2022, from https://www.northsidelex.com/history.html

5.) Kellogg, J. (1982). The formation of black residential areas in Lexington, Kentucky, 1865-1887. The Journal of Southern History, 48(1), 21. https://doi.org/10.2307/2207295

6.) "Blue Grass Colored Baseball League, " Notable Kentucky African Americans Database, accessed September 29, 2022, https://nkaa.uky.edu/nkaa/items/show/2627.

7.) "Lexington Hustlers Baseball Team, " Notable Kentucky African Americans Database, accessed September 29, 2022, https://nkaa.uky.edu/nkaa/items/show/164.

8.) Smith, G. L., McDaniel, K. C., Hardin, J. A., & Powell, S. l. (2015). African American

Baseball. In The Kentucky African American Encyclopedia (p. 3). University Press of Kentucky.

9.)Allen, M. (2022, June 15). John Shelby. Society for American Baseball Research. Retrieved September 29, 2022, from https://sabr.org/bioproj/person/john-shelby/

10.) "Presbyterian Cemetery (Lexington, KY)," Notable Kentucky African Americans Database, accessed September 30, 2022, https://nkaa.uky.edu/nkaa/items/show/2511.

11.) Found a Coffin. (1895, August 2). Lexington Herald Leader, p. 8.

12.) Coffin Found in House Excavation. (1910, April 29). Lexington Herald Leader, p. 1.

13.) Still, P. (1995). The Separation. In K. E. R. Pickard (Ed.), The Kidnapped and the Ransomed, The Narrative of Peter and Vina Still after Forty Years of Slavery (p. 63). University of Nebraska Press.

14.) Ibid., pp. 64

15.) The Henry Clay Estate. (n.d.). Aaron Dupuy . Henry Clay - Ashland. Retrieved September 30, 2022, from https://henryclay.org/mansiongrounds/enslaved-people-at-ashland/aaron-dupuy/

16.) Thompson, R. (2020). Charlotte Dupuy. In Sankofa Lexington (pp. 39– 47). Afrakan World Books n Moor.

17.) Sanford T. Roach's biography. he History Makers. (n.d.). Retrieved September 30, 2022, from https://www.thehistorymakers.org/biography/sanford-t-roach-39

18.) Lexington African-American Sports Hall of Fame. (n.d.). Lexington African-American Sports Hall of Fame. Retrieved September 30, 2022, from https://laashof.com/

19.) Hardin, J. A. (1995). Green Pinckney Russell of Kentucky Normal and Industrial Institute for Colored Persons. Journal of Black Studies, 25(5), 610–621. http://www.jstor.org/stable/2784634

20.) St. Peter Claver Parish. Cdlex. (2022, September 23). Retrieved September 30, 2022, from https://cdlex.org/stpeterclaver/

21.) Bethesda Normal School Looks Like a Go. (1906, December 11). Lexington Herald Leader, p. 1.

22.) Old Hospital Building. (1910, July 14). Lexington Herald Leader, p. 1.

23.) New Corporation, Lexington Normal and Industrial College. (1910, September 28). Lexington Herald Leader, p. 10.

24.) The Kaintuckeean. (2015, November 4). The Old Protestant Infirmary grew to become Samaritan Hospital. The Kaintuckeean. Retrieved September 30, 2022, from https://www.thekaintuckeean.com/protestant-infirmary/

25.) Ugly Charge Sworn Out by Woman Against the Power Preacher. (1904, August 25). Lexington Herald Leader, p. 1.

26.) Smith, G. L., McDaniel, K. C., Hardin, J. A., & Powell, S. l. (2015). Britton, Thomas M. "Tommy". In The Kentucky African American Encyclopedia (p. 65) University Press of Kentucky.

27.) Killed Herself: Hattie Britton Kills Herself With A Pistol. (1891, June 1). The Kentucky

Leader, p. 4.

28.) Smith, G. L., McDaniel, K. C., Hardin, J. A., & Nelson, P. D. (2015). Hooks, Julia Britton. In The Kentucky African American Encyclopedia (p. 251). University Press of Kentucky.

29.) Burial of Monk Overtone's Wife Will Be In Lexington. (1905, December 21). The Lexington Leader, p. 1.

30.) Very Creditable: Were The Closing Exercises of the Patterson Street Colored Schools. (1895, June 7). The Leader, p. 6.

31.) Thompson, R. (2020). Chapter 1 – Dr. Mary Britton. In Sankofa Lexington (p. 5). Afrakan World Books n Moor.

32.) A Woman's Appeal To Members of the Kentucky General Assembly. (1892, April 19). The Kentucky Leader, p. 3.

33.) Smith, G. L., McDaniel, K. C., Hardin, J. A., & Sears, R. D. (2015). Britton, Mary Ellen". In The Kentucky African American Encyclopedia (p. 65). University Press of Kentucky

34.) Killed Herself: Hattie Britton Kills Herself With A Pistol. (1891, June 1). The Kentucky Leader, p. 4.

35.) Thompson, R. (2020). Chapter 1 – Dr. Mary Britton. In Sankofa Lexington (p. 7). Afrakan World Books n Moor.

36.) Dunbar, P. L. (1893). To Miss Mary Britton. In Oak and Ivy (pp. 30– 31). Press of United Brethren Publishing House.

Chapter 11

1.) Herr, J. G. (1914, February 1). The Eight Little Towns in Lexington. Lexington Herald Leader, p. 3.

2.) Fatal Craps. (1896, January 20). The Leader, p. 5.

3.) On Seventh Street. (1897, August 1). The Morning Herald, p. 5.

4.) The Trial of George Broadus, the Cutter, is Postponed. (1900, January 8). The Daily Leader, p. 7.

5.) His Brains Blown Out. (1900, November 4). The Morning Herald, p. 1.

6.) The Petition. (1906, June 28). Lexington Leader, p. 4.

7.) Hoover, F. K. (1928, February 23). Lexington Has Had Racing for 140 Years. The Lexington Herald, p. 33.

8.) "African Cemetery No. 2 (Lexington, KY)," Notable Kentucky African Americans Database, accessed July 10, 2022, https://nkaa.uky.edu/nkaa/items/show/1254.

9.) "Greenwood Cemetery / Cove Haven Cemetery," Notable Kentucky African Americans Database, accessed July 10, 2022, https://nkaa.uky.edu/nkaa/items/show/300004510.

10.) Thompson, Rico. "Chapter 1 - Dr. Mary E. Britton." Sankofa Lexington, Afrakan World Books and Moor, 2020, pp. 4–12.

11.) Greenwood Cemetery. (1908, May 2). Lexington Leader, p. 2.

12.) Bond, James, 1863-1929. Facts on the Ed. Harris alias John Henry Jones murder and assault case, ca. February 1926. W. E. B. Du Bois Papers (MS 312). Special Collections and University Archives, University of Massachusetts Amherst Libraries

13.) Thousand State Guardian to Patrol Streets for Trial of Harris; Business to be Temporarily Suspended. (1926, January 31). The Lexington Herald, p. 1.

14.) Ed Harris Buried Within Half Hour After Hanging. (1926, March 5). The Lexington Leader, p. 1.

15.) Ibid,, p. 1

16.) Byars, Lauretta Flynn. "Introduction." Lexington's Colored Orphan Industrial Home: Building for the Future, I. B. Bold Publications, Lexington, KY, 1995, p. 12.

17.) Ibid., p. 16

18.) Ibid., pp. 27-28

19. Thompson, R. "Chapter 8 - Rev. Frederick Braxton." Sankofa Lexington, Afrakan World Books and Moor, Lexington, KY, 2020, p. 64.

20.) Ibid. pp. 32-38

21.) Ibid. pp. 48-54

22.) "Howard School / Normal Institute / Chandler Normal School / Webster Hall (Lexington, KY)," Notable Kentucky African Americans Database, accessed July 13, 2022, https://nkaa.uky.edu/nkaa/items/show/2153.

23.) Colored Schools. (1910, April 10). Lexington Leader, p. 24.

24.) "Forest Hill School (Lexington, KY)," Notable Kentucky African Americans Database, accessed September 25, 2022, https://nkaa.uky.edu/nkaa/items/show/2515.

25.) School System is Praised. (1910, October 14). The Lexington Herald, p. 3.

26.) "Laura Carroll Colored Branch Library, Lexington, KY (Fayette County), " Notable Kentucky African Americans Database, accessed September 25, 2022, https://nkaa.uky.edu/nkaa/items/show/2836.

27.) Perrin, W. H. (1882). Chapter X, The Colored People of Lexington, Their Religious Advantages, Colored Churches, Educational Facilities, Secret and Benevolent Organizations, Fairs, ETC. In History of Fayette County, Kentucky (p. 472). Southern Historical Press.

28.) Quinn Chapel A. M. E. Church. (1999, April 10). Lexington Herald Leader, p. 34.

29.) Staten, C. (2014, June 30). William Paul Quinn (1788 - 1873). BlackPast.org. https://www.blackpast.org/african-american-history/quinnwilliam-paul-1788-1873/

30.) New Quinn Chapel; Being Built By A. M. E. Church In Attractive Location and Assistance is Greatly Needed. (1913, January 17). Lexington Leader, p. 4.

31.) Thompson, R. "Chapter 6 – Luther Porter Jackson ." Sankofa Lexington, Afrakan World Books and Moor, Lexington, KY, 2020, p. 49.

32.) Jones, M. B. (n.d.). Luther Porter Jackson. Retrieved January 24, 2023, from https://qa.vsu.edu/files/docs/student-activities/studenthandbook.pdf

33.) Pruitt, S. (2017, February 2). The Man Behind Black History Month. History.com. Retrieved January 24, 2023, from https://www.history.com/news/the-man-behind-black-history-month

34.) Thompson, R. "Chapter 6 – Luther Porter Jackson." Sankofa Lexington, Afrakan World Books and Moor, Lexington, KY, 2020, p. 50.

35.) Ibid,. p. 51

36.) Ibid,. p. 51

37.) Ibid,. p. 52

Chapter 12

1.) Riley and His Henchman Morgan Rap Their Lifetime Friends Over The Shoulders of Charlie Frame. (1905, November 15). Lexington Leader, p. 5.

2.) Territory to be Annexed. (1906, March 13). The Lexington Herald, p. 10.

3.) Commissioner McCorkle Hopes To Secure Lights For Peach Orchard. (1913, October 2). Lexington Leader, p. 12.

4.) Schools of The County Open Tuesday. The Assignment of Teachers. (1901, September 3). The Morning Herald, p. 6.

5.) "King Solomon--By Someone Who Knew Him Well." Lexington Leader, 30 Aug. 1908, p. 7

6.) Thompson, R. "Chapter 9 – Aunt Charlotte." Sankofa Lexington, Afrakan World Books and Moor, 2020, pp. 68-72.

7.) "Colored Libraries in the Charlotte Court and Aspendale Housing Projects, Lexington, KY (Fayette County)," Notable Kentucky African American Database https://nkaa.uky.edu/nkaa/items/show/2829.

8.) Smith, G. L., McDaniel, K. C., Hardin, J. A., & Adams, L. (2015). Dirt Bowl. In The Kentucky African American Encyclopedia (1st ed., p. 144). essay, University Press of Kentucky.

9.) Johnson, M. (1975, August 13). Dirt Bowl Offers Basketball at it's Best. Lexington Herald Leader, p. 13.

10.) Fitzmaurice, D. G. (1978, June 18). College Scouts Scramble For Dirt Bowl Seats. Lexington Herald Leader, p. 34.

11.) In a 1922 Lexington Herald Leader it states that Bell was an officer for several years and not the ten weeks various other sources are reporting. It is likely suggesting that this was a role he was elected to annually for the summer months. Leader, L. H. (1922, June 17). To Push Work on West Sixth. Lexington Herald Leader, p. 8.

12.) This same newspaper article refers to her as Jennie Christie. Ibid., p. 8

13.) Jones, C. (n.d.). Lexington Police Dept. recognizing first black police officers who served in the city. https://www.wkyt.com. Retrieved September 27, 2022, from https://www.wkyt.com/2021/02/24/lexington-police-deptrecognizing-first-black-police-officers-who-served-in-the-city/

14.) "Colored Notes." The Lexington Herald, 12 Sept. 1925, p. 6.

15.) "Roosevelt Said." The Lexington Leader, 25 May 1926, p. 15.

Chapter 13

1.) Jones, R. F. (n.d.). The Development of Pralltown, 1868. In History of the Pralltown Community, Lexington, Kentucky (p. 1).

2.) Jones, R. F. (n.d.). Further Development of Pralltown, 1876-1940s. In History of the Pralltown Community, Lexington, Kentucky (p. 4).

3.) Jones, R. F. (n.d.). The Seven Early Lot Owners in 1868. In History of the Pralltown Community, Lexington, Kentucky (p. 3).

4.) KETVideos . "Pralltown | Kentucky Life | KET." YouTube, YouTube, 9 Oct. 2019, www.youtube.com/watch?v=iiNtOdVayCA.

5.) Prall Street Church. (1926, August 19). The Lexington Leader, p. 8

6.) Prall Street Church of Christ. New Birth CC. (n.d.). Retrieved January 16, 2023, from https://www.newbirthchurchofchrist.com/histroy

7.) Frank Lucas Interviewed By Korey Rowe. (2015). YouTube. Retrieved January 16, 2023, from https://www.youtube.com/watchv=q8mYqmzz1_o&t=751s.

8.) Press, Associated. "'Sweet' Lou Johnson, Who Hit Winning Homer for Los Angeles Dodgers in '65 World Series, Dies." ESPN, ESPN Internet Ventures, 2 Oct. 2020, www.espn.com/mlb/story/_/id/30025247/sweet- -lou-johnson-hit-winning-homer-los-angeles-dodgers-65-world-series-dies.

9.) "Givens, Reuben and Ruth Newby Givens Roper," Notable Kentucky African Americans Database, accessed May 29, 2021, https://nkaa.uky.edu/nkaa/items/show/1655.

10.) Board of Health, City of Lexington, Kentucky, Report of Housing Survey of the City of Lexington (Lexington, Ky: City of Lexington 1924), 10

11.) Jones, R. F. (n.d.). Further Development of Pralltown, 1876-1940s. In History of the Pralltown Community, Lexington, Kentucky (p. 5).

12.) Becker, L. (1998, July 2). Pralltown plan allows two year leases of homes before buying. Lexington Herald-Leader, p. 4.

13.) Appler, Douglas R., and Julie Riesenweber. "Urban Renewal through the Lens of Unsuccessful Projects: The Pralltown Neighborhood of Lexington, Kentucky." Journal of Planning History 19.3 (2020): 164-186.

14.) Becker, L. (1998, August 30). Fighting for a Living History. Lexington Herald-Leader, p. 21.

15.) Heston, V. (1974, February 17). Pralltowns Attributes Unequal to Challenge of Environment. Lexington Herald-Leader, p. 5.

Chapter 14

1.) Bad Condition on Adams Street. (1914, July 12). Lexington Herald Leader, p. 5.

2.) Aims at Colored Part of Winslow and Adamstown. (1914, August 2). Lexington Herald Leader, p. 7.

3.) Ibid., pp.7

4.) Ibid., pp.7

5.) Ibid., pp.7

6.) Vacating Order to be Carried Out. (1914, September 5). Lexington Herald Leader, p. 3.

7.) Slum Districts Are Inspected. (1934, September 14). Lexington Herald Leader , p. 2.

8.) New Auditorium Still in Lead in Poll of Lexington's Needs. (1947, March 25). Lexington Herald Leader, p. 8.

Chapter 15

1.) The Davis Bottom History Preservation Project: William Willard Davis . (n.d.). Retrieved February 12, 2023, from https://arch.as.uky.edu/sites/default/files/6%20William%20Willard%20Davis%20Biography.pdf

2.) Resolution No. 377, Naming Certain Unnamed Alleys in The City of Lexington. (1927, December 17). The Lexington Herald, p. 9.

3.) Kentucky Faces Tradition Of Offensive Road Names. (1996, November 11). The New York Times, p. 13.

4.) Dollins, H. M. (2011). In East End and Davis Bottom: A study of the demographic and landscape changes of two neighborhoods in Lexington, Kentucky (p. 59).

5.) Fourth Street Floats, Results of Heavy Rain. (1907, January 18). The Lexington Leader, p. 1.

6.) Colored Notes. (1922, September 6). The Lexington Herald, p. 13.

7.) Dollins, H. M. (2011). In East End and Davis Bottom: A study of the demographic and landscape changes of two neighborhoods in Lexington, Kentucky (pp. 61-62).

8.) Wilkinson, D. Y. (1989). A Directory of Afro-American Businesses in Lexington in 1939. Dept. of Sociology, University of Kentucky.

9.) Carver community center. Kentucky Archaeological Survey. (2020, April 15). Retrieved March 17, 2023, from https://www.kentuckyarchaeologicalsurvey.org/carver-community-center/

10.) Fahey, P. (1972, November 5). A Bit of History Dies With Closing of The Schools. Lexington Herald-Leader, p. 5.

11.) Ibid,. p. 5

12.) Name Suggested For New Patterson School. (1934, January 31). The Lexington Leader, p. 1

13.) Public Schools Will Open Soon, New Buildings are Ready. (1935, August 25). The Lexington Herald, p. 2.

14.) Giles, Yvonne. 2011 Interview, "The Davis Bottom History Preservation Project," KAS/KHC.

15.) Ibid

16.) Thompson, R. (2020). Chapter 4 - Isaac Scott Hathaway. In Sankofa Lexington (p. 33). Afrakan World Books n Moor, LLC.

17.) Ibid., p. 33

18.) Ibid., p. 34

19.) Otfinoski, S. (2011). Hathaway, Isaac Scott, The Dean of Negro Ceramists(ca. 1874-1967), ceramist, sculptor, illustrator, educator. In African Americans in the visual arts (p. 93). Facts on File

20.) Isaac Scott Hathaway: Artist and Teacher. (1958). Negro History Bulletin, 21(4), p. 79 http://www.jstor.org/stable/44213169

21.) Perry, R. L. (n.d.). Isaac Hathaway, Sculptor. The University of North Carolina at Chapel Hill. Retrieved from https://dc.lib.unc.edu/cgibin/showfile.exe?CISOROOT=/03709&CISOPTR=896&filename=869.pdf

22.) Register, Heather. "Hathaway, Isaac Scott." Encyclopedia of Arkansas, 29 July 2011, https://encyclopediaofarkansas.net/entries/isaac-scotthathaway-5973/.

23.) Ibid.

24.) Sculpting a better Auburn: Isaac Scott Hathaway. Auburn Alumni Association. (2021, June 24). Retrieved from https://www.alumni.auburn.edu/isaac-scott-hathaway-sculpting-a-betterauburn/

25.) Marriage Licenses. (1915, October 25). The Evening Star, p. 8.

26.) Dollins, H. M. (2011). In East End and Davis Bottom: A study of the demographic and landscape changes of two neighborhoods in Lexington, Kentucky (pp. 69).

27.) Protest Filed Against Davis Bottom Dump. (1950, July 19). The Lexington Herald, p. 2.

28.) Woestendiek, J. (1980, December 19). Valley of Neglect. The Lexington Leader, p. 58.

29.) Gatz, C. (1975, November 21). Lawsuit Filed... The Lexington Herald, p. 10.

30.) Ranck, G. W. (1872). Chapter 1 - Ancient Lexington. In History of Lexington, Kentucky: Its early annals and recent progress (p. 2).

31.) Pleasant Green Missionary Baptist Church - About Us. Pleasant Green Missionary Baptist Church . (n.d.). Retrieved March 21, 2023, from http://www.hpgmbc.com/about-us/

32.) Perrin, W. H. (1882). Chapter X. The Colored People of Lexington-- Their Religious Advantages—Colored Churches—Educational Facilities-- Secret and Benevolent Organizations—Fairs, Etc. In History of Fayette County, Kentucky (p. 470). Southern Historical Press.

33.) Ibid., p. 471

34.) McIntyre, L. H. (1986). Dispositions. In One grain of the salt: The first African baptist church west of the Allegheny Mountains (p. 80). essay, L.H. McIntyre.

35.) Pleasant Green Missionary Baptist Church - About Us. Pleasant Green Missionary Baptist Church . (n.d.). Retrieved March 21, 2023, from http://www.hpgmbc.com/about-us/

36.) Perrin, W. H. (1882). Chapter X. The Colored People of Lexington-- Their Religious Advantages—Colored Churches--Educational Facilities-- Secret and Benevolent Organizations--Fairs, Etc. In History of Fayette County, Kentucky (p. 471). Southern Historical Press.

37.) H. Quills Paper, Fayette County Circuit Court Case File #760. Division of Archives and records Management, Commonwealth of Kentucky.

38.) McIntyre, L. H. (1986). The First Co-Pastor, London Ferrill. In One grain of the salt: The first African baptist church west of the Allegheny Mountains (p. 12). L.H. McIntyre.

39.) Burdette, D. (2000, August 30). Pleasant Green: Church Took Whole New Direction. Lexington Herald-Leader, p. 49.

40.) McIntyre, L. H. (1986). Preface. In One grain of the salt: The first African baptist church west of the Allegheny Mountains (p. x). L.H. McIntyre.

41.) Historic Pleasant Green Baptist Church. Kentucky Women in the Civil Rights Era Site Wide Activity RSS. (n.d.). Retrieved March 25, 2023, from http://www.kywcrh.org/voices/churches/historic-pleasant-green-baptist-church

42.) Quarles Gives His Side. (1898, March 3). The Daily Leader, p. 2.

43.) Simmons, W. J. (1887). CXXVI. Rev. George Washington Dupee. In Men of Mark; Eminent, Progressive and Rising by William J. Simmons (p. 847)

44.) Ibid., p. 854

45.) Pleasant Green Missionary Baptist Church - About Us. Pleasant Green Missionary Baptist Church . (n.d.). Retrieved March 21, 2023, from http://www.hpgmbc.com/about-us/

46.) Simmons, W. J. (1887). CXXVI. Rev. George Washington Dupee. In Men of Mark; Eminent, Progressive and Rising by William J. Simmons (p. 847).

47.) History. Washington Street Baptist Church. (n.d.). Retrieved March 29, 2023, from https://washingtonstreetbaptist.org/index.php/history/

48.) VisitLEX. (2021, February 24). Free Black Entrepreneurs - A Neighborhood for Free Black Entrepreneurs. VisitLEX. Retrieved April 7, 2023, from https://www.visitlex.com/guides/post/free-black-entrepreneursa-neighborhood-for-free-black-entrepreneurs/

49.) Ibid

50.) Davis, M. (2011, September 25). Walking Tour Spotlights Black History. Lexington Herald Leader, p. T14.

51.) Ibid

52.) Ibid

53.) Ku, M. (2002, February 23). South Hill Neighborhood District. Lexington Herald-Leader,

p. 25.

54.) Mastin, B. L. (1993, October 17). Cottage Was Built To Be A Buffer. Lexington Herald-Leader, p. 73.

55.) Lexington Inventor Robert Gray Procures a Patent on New Pump Apparatus. (1903, May 11). The Lexington Leader, p. 6.

56.) Picture Theater For Negroes Soon To Open. (1913, September 11). The Lexington Herald, p. 8.

57.) Police Court, Couple That Wouldn't Work in Double Harness. (1905, November 2). The Lexington Leader, p. 2.

58.) Davis, M. (2006, June 25). Neighborhoods Reunion Will Have Activities For All Ages. Lexington Herald-Leader, p. 19.

59.) Campen, T. V. (1999, January 16). Antioch Baptist Church. Lexington Herald-Leader, p. 30.

Chapter 16

1.) "Goodlowtown, Goodloetown, or Goodloe (Lexington, KY)," Notable Kentucky African Americans Database, accessed September 27, 2020, https://nkaa.uky.edu/nkaa/items/show/322.

2.) A Sad Ending: The Corner Store at East Third and Race Streets, Lexington, Kentucky. (2017, October 11). Retrieved September 27, 2020, from http://www.gardenstogables.com/a-sad-ending-the-corner-store-at-eastthird-and-race-streets-lexington-kentucky

3.) "Turner, Roxy," Notable Kentucky African Americans Database, accessed September 27, 2020, http://nkaa.uky.edu/nkaa/items/show/2815.

4.) Roxy: Head of a Strange Kentucky Sect is an Ebony Priestess (1900, December 23). St. Louis Dispatch, p. 43.

5.) Roxey Turner: Founder of the Famous Power Church is Dead. (1901, February 26). Lexington Leader, p. 8.

6.) Roxy: Head of a Strange Kentucky Sect is an Ebony Priestess. (1900, December 23). St. Louis Dispatch, p. 43.

7.) The Seven Powers. (1896, October 24). The Inquirer(Lancaster, PA), p. 3.

8.) Ibid,. p. 3

9.) Bronze Christ Weds. (1912, June 20). The Lexington Herald, p. 16.

10.) Clayborn Martin. (1903, June 24). Lexington Leader, p. 4.

11.) Sent to Asylum. (1904, November 11). Lexington Leader, p. 1.

12.) Sang At Station: Street Preachers Placed Under Arrest. (1901, September 13). The Cincinnati Post, p. 6.

13.) Wears Shoes First Time in 25 Years. (1905, December 12). Evening World Herald(Omaha, NE), p. 12.

14.) Seven Year Penance. (1907, January 30). Lexington Leader, p. 10.

15.) Reid, D. I. (1937, July 26). Colored Notes. The Lexington Herald, p. 2.

16.) Parrish, C. H. (1915). History of Main Street Baptist Church, Lexington, Ky. In Golden Jubilee of the General Association of Colored Baptists in Kentucky ; the story of 50 Years' work from 1865-1915, including many photos and sketches, comp. from unpublished manuscripts and other sources (p. 245). Mayes Printing Co.

17.) "Greater Liberty Baptist Church," Tour the Historic Bluegrass, accessed December 31, 2022, https://tourthehistoricbluegrass.com/items/show/27.

18.) Negroes Growing With Lexington: Susan Jane Washington. (1920, December 26). The Lexington Herald, p. 34.

19.) The National Archives in Washington, DC; Washington, DC; Records of the Field Offices For the State of Kentucky, Bureau of Refugees, Freedmen, and Abandoned Lands, 1865-1872; NARA Series Number: M1904; NARA Reel Number: 52; NARA Record Group Number: 105; NARA Record Group Name: Records of the Bureau of Refugees, Freedmen, and Abandoned Lands, 1861 - 1880; Collection Title: United States Freedmen's Bureau, Records of the Superintendent of Education and of the Division of Education 1865-1872

20.) Negroes Growing With Lexington: Susan Jane Washington. (1920, December 26). The Lexington Herald, p. 34.

21.) Year: 1870; Census Place: Versailles, Woodford, Kentucky; Roll: M593_504; Page: 524B

22.) Year: 1880; Census Place: Lexington, Fayette, Kentucky; Roll: 413; Page: 338A; Enumeration District: 066

23.) Ancestry.com. U.S., City Directories, 1822-1995 [database online]. Lehi, UT, USA: Ancestry.com Operations, Inc., 2011.

24.) Year: 1910; Census Place: Lexington Ward 6, Fayette, Kentucky; Roll: T624_474; Page: 9B; Enumeration District: 0033; FHL microfilm: 1374487

25.) Chandler Normal Reopens Sept. 29. (1921, September 18). The Lexington Leader, p. 26.

26.) Colored Notes: Colored Industrial School. (1907, February 19). Lexington Leader, p. 2.

27.) Industry Will Be Practiced At School. (1907, August 31). The Lexington Leader, p. 8

28.) "Young, Charles D.," Notable Kentucky African Americans Database, accessed October 26, 2022, https://nkaa.uky.edu/nkaa/items/show/897.

29.) Davis, M. (2022, May 12). Discover Lexington's east end history on a walking tour wasn't bad. TP Mechanical. Retrieved July 7, 2022, from https://tpmechanical.com/2013/04/30/discover-lexingtons-east-end-historyon-a-walking-tour/

30.) Wilkinson, D. Y. (1989). Restaurants and Lunchrooms. In A directory of afro-american businesses in Lexington in 1939 (pp. 9–11). Dept. of Sociology, University of Kentucky.

31.) Waller, G. A. (1995). Another Audience. In Main street amusements: Movies and commercial entertainment in a Southern City, 1896-1930 (pp. 170–179). Smithsonian Institution Press.

32.) Ibid, pp. 241

33.) "Early African American Theaters in Lexington, KY," Notable Kentucky African Americans Database, accessed October 26, 2022, https://nkaa.uky.edu/nkaa/items/show/41.

34.) Jay, J. (1940, April 30). Four Bits. The Lexington Leader, p. 1.

35.) Sutherland, C. (2013, January 23). Julia Amanda Perry (1924- 1979). BlackPast.org. https://www.blackpast.org/african-american-history/perry-julia-amanda-1924-1979/

36.) About Us. John Simon Guggenheim Memorial Foundation. (2022, April 6). Retrieved October 26, 2022, from https://www.gf.org/about-us/

37.) Southern, E. (2006). Singers, Instrumentalists, and Composers. In The music of Black Americans: A history (p. 551). W. W. Norton & Company.

38.) July 6 The Date (1906, June 4). Lexington Leader, p. 1.

39.) Pendergast, P. (2017). Findings and Observation. In The Life and Lynching of James Pearsall (p. 5)

40.) Vital Statistics. (1906, January 19). Lexington Leader, p. 6.

41.) Law Extracts Extreme Penalty for the Awful Crime of James Pearsall. (1906, July 6). The Lexington Herald, p. 9.

42.) Law Extracts Extreme Penalty for the Awful Crime of James Pearsall. (1906, July 6). The Lexington Herald, p. 9.

43.) Dies on the Gallows for His Awful Crime. (1906, July 7). The Lexington Herald, p. 4

Chapter 17

1.) O'Malley, N. (1996). Chapter 2, Kinkeadtown in Historical Context. In Kinkeadtown: Archaeological Investigation of an African-American neighborhood in Lexington, Kentucky (p. 13).

2.) Ibid., p. 25

3.) Henry Tandy. The Blue Grass Trust for Historic Preservation. (n.d.). Retrieved December 4, 2022, from https://www.bluegrasstrust.org/henrytandy

4.) Douglass, Frederick. "Chapter 3." My Bondage and My Freedom: Part I - Life as a Slave. Part II - Life as a Freeman, Miller, Orton & Mulligan, New York: 25 Park Row -- Auburn: 107 Genesee-St., New York, 1855, p. 51.

5.) Johnson, William D. (1897). Chapter XXV - Henry A. Tandy. In Biographical sketches of prominent Negro men and women of Kentucky (p. 46). Lexington Standard Print.

6.) Ibid,. p. 46

7.) Ibid,. p. 46

8.) O'Malley, N. (1996). Chapter VI, The Tandy/Ray House Lot. In Kinkeadtown: Archaeological Investigation of an African-American neighborhood in Lexington, Kentucky (p. 203).

9.) Historical Data Systems, Inc.; Duxbury, MA 02331; American Civil War Research Database

10.) "Allen, Dudley," Notable Kentucky African Americans Database, accessed December 11, 2022, https://nkaa.uky.edu/nkaa/items/show/1910.

11.) O'Malley, N. (1996). Chapter XI, The Allen House Lot. In Kinkeadtown: Archaeological Investigation of an African-American neighborhood in Lexington, Kentucky (p. 267).

12.) Phelps, M. (n.d.). Notable partnerships: Winning Teams despite Discrimination. Notable Partnerships: Winning Teams Despite Discrimination. The Chronicle of African Americans in the Horse Industry. Retrieved December 11, 2022, from https://africanamericanhorsestories.org/explore/stories/notable-partnershipswinning-teams-despite-discrimination

13.) Former Noted Trainer Dies. (1911, October 15). The Lexington Leader, p. 7.

14.) Phelps, M. (n.d.). Notable partnerships: Winning Teams despite Discrimination. Notable Partnerships: Winning Teams Despite Discrimination The Chronicle of African Americans in the Horse Industry. Retrieved December 11, 2022, from https://africanamericanhorsestories.org/explore/stories/notable-partnershipswinning-teams-despite-discrimination

15.) Ownership of Kingman. (1891, May 11). The Kentucky Leader, p. 1.

16.) Horse Gossip; Passing of Colored Trainers. (1904, January 12). The Lexington Leader, p. 3.

17.) Leeds, M., & Rockoff, H. (2020). The Triple Crown. In Jim Crow in the Saddle: The Expulsion of African American Jockeys from American Racing (p. 8). National Bureau of Economic Research.

18.) "Negro Jockeys Shut Out: Combination of White Riders to bar them From the Turf." New York Times, July 29, 1900, p. 19.

19.) Ibid., p.19

20.) Parmer, Charles B. 1939. For Gold and Glory: The Story of Thoroughbred Racing in America. New York: Carrick and Evans Inc. p. 150

21.) Brown, D. (2007, November 21). Jimmy Winkfield (1882-1974). BlackPast.org. https://www.blackpast.org/african-americanhistory/winkfield-jimmy-1882-1974/

22.) Deweese project hinges on state aid for Rose Street Extension. (1985, September 30). Lexington Herald-Leader, p. 69.

23.) Letters to the Editor: A Challenge to Race Relations. (1987, April 29). Lexington Herald-Leader, p. 8.

Chapter 18

1.) "Kentucky Association Race Track," Tour the Historic Bluegrass, accessed April 26, 2023, https://tourthehistoricbluegrass.com/items/show/37.

2.) Isaac Burns Murphy Historical Marker. The Historical Marker Database. (2022, January 10). Retrieved April 26, 2023, from https://www.hmdb.org/m.asp?m=119100 \

3.) Nyra Press Office (Ed.). (n.d.). The extraordinary life of Jimmy Winkfield. NYRA. Retrieved April 26, 2023, from https://www.nyra.com/aqueduct/news/%E2%80%8Bthe-extraordinary-lifeof-jimmy-winkfield

4.) Moore, N. (2020, August 10). It's true (we think): The Travers Stakes has to be the oldest...something. Saratoga Living. Retrieved April 26, 2023, from https://saratogaliving.com/travers-stakes-oldest-something/

5.) Brackney, P. (2014). Old Kentucky Association Racetrack. In Lost Lexington, Kentucky (p. 78). The History Press.

6.) New Owner For Kentucky Track. (1901, March 6). New York Times.

7.) Race Track Sold. (1903, October 17). The Spokane Press, p. 6.

8.) Clarke, M. (2007). Chapter 1 - Voices of Home in Bluegrass Aspendale. In Voices of Home in Bluegrass-Aspendale: Constructing the ideal (p. 15). University of Kentucky, Gaines Center for the Humanities.

9.) Units' Names Are Reversed, White Project is Designated Aspendale and Negro Bluegrass Park.. (1936, April 15). The Lexington Leader, p. 1.

10.) Kentucky.com. (n.d.). Fence separating races removed, 1974. Kentucky Photo Archive. Retrieved April 26, 2023, from https://kyphotoarchive.com/2017/02/06/fence-separating-races-removed1974/

11.) Tenants To Move Into Lexington's Federal Housing Projects Within A Week. (1938, January 2). The Lexington Herald, p. 1.

12.) First Housing Projects Success. (1940, December 29). The Lexington Herald, p. 9.

13.) Private Investors Finance New Project Homes. (1954, April 18). Sunday Herald-Leader, p. 50.

14.) Captain Fowlers Garden Was Favorite. (1932, June 23). The Lexington Leader, p. 7.

15.) History Linked to Sections Names. (1954, April 18). Sunday Herald Leader, p. 48.

16.) Ibid., p. 48

17.) Jay, J. (1936, July 17). Four Bits, Getting Names Right. The Lexington Leader, p. 1.

18.) Project to Replace Some of The Worst Slums. (1951, August 5). Sunday Herald-Leader, p. 8.

19.) History Linked to Sections Names. (1954, April 18). Sunday HeraldLeader, p. 48.

20.) "Pryor, Margaret," Notable Kentucky African Americans Database, accessed April 27, 2023, https://nkaa.uky.edu/nkaa/items/show/1465.

21.) To Build Five Cottages. (1912, October 9). The Lexington Leader, p. 10.

22.) Board of Commissioners (Official Proceedings), Ordinance No. 2960. (1925, May 30). The Lexington Leader, p. 6.

23.) Our Church History. Shiloh Baptist Church. (2019, November 12). Retrieved April 28, 2023, from http://shilohlexington.com/index.php/ourchurch-history/

24.) Evil Doers Warned By Pearsalls Fate, Negro Minister Advises The Young Men Of His Race To Profit By Example. (1906, July 9). The Lexington Herald, p. 8.

25.) Suit Filed Against The Shiloh Church. (1909, May 1). The Lexington Herald, p. 4.

26.) Shiloh Church, Members May Pay $264 Debt, Court Orders It Sold On June 14 At Public Auction, But Congregation Hopes To Save It. (1909, May 4). The Lexington Leader, p. 5.

27.) Shiloh Baptists Buy Felix Memorial Church Building. (1963, January 13). Sunday Herald-Leader, p. 19.

28.) Mayhan, M. (1990, June 3). Chief's Responses Pleases Troubled Area, Respond In Force. Lexington Herald-Leader, p. A12.

29.) Johns, B. (1989, September 3). Struggle. Lexington Herald-Leader, p. B3.

30.) Nance, K. (1990, February 25). Housing Project Gets A New Look, Bluegrass-Aspendale To Be Renovated. Lexington Herald-Leader, p. 1.

31.) Nance, K. (1990, February 25) . New Life For Lexington's Projects: City Tackles Bluegrass-Aspendale Woes. Lexington Herald-Leader, p. A12.

32.) Ibid

33.) Gregory, E. (1995, February 3). Witnesses, police files detail events of October 25. Lexington Herald-Leader, pp. 1–8.

34.) Gregory, E. (1994, October 26). Rampage: angry youths marched towards downtown. Lexington Herald-Leader, p. 14

35.) Gregory, E. (1994, October 29). Damage figures released. Lexington Herald-Leader, p. 12.

36.) Rios, B., & Campbell, R. H. (1994, October 27). Shooting: FBI joins search for answers. Lexington Herald-Leader, p. A15.

44364942R00248